ESCAPE THROUGH CHINA

Escape Through China

by

David Bosanquet

ROBERT HALE · LONDON

ISBN 0 7090 1288 8

Robert Hale Limited
Clerkenwell House
Clerkenwell Green
London EC1R 0HT

Distributed in Canada by McClelland & Stewart Limited
25 Hollinger Road, Toronto, M4B 3G2

The author wishes to
thank the Imperial War Museum
and the Hong Kong Government Office
for their kind permission
to reproduce photographs

Photoset in Times Roman by
Kelly Typesetting Limited
Bradford-on-Avon, Wiltshire
Printed in Great Britain by
Redwood Burn Limited
Trowbridge, Wiltshire
Bound by W.B.C. Bookbinders Limited

To Hazel, my wife, but for whom there might never have been a story to tell.
To Melanie, my daughter, but for whom the story might never have been published.

Foreword

After a lapse of nearly forty years, I would not want anyone to think that this book has been written from memory.

All details of the events leading up to the attack of the Japanese upon Hong Kong, the fighting, as far as I saw it, the prisoner of war camps and the escape itself were written in one form or another while I was attached to the British Embassy in Chungking during 1942.

Much was rewritten during the long sea voyage from Bombay to New York, using the notes which I had recorded daily after first making contact with the Chinese guerillas.

Those sad and painful times which people spend in war often bring out many kinds of strength. Great courage grows in many unnoticed crevices. And the human spirit is such that no matter what its education, background or nationality, it can force itself above the degrading and apparently impossible, to win its own battle.

However, you cannot have a hero without a villain, and villains are perhaps merely flawed heroes. Such are many of the people in this book.

The misery and horror caused by the few often came to represent the whole race. The mere memory of one man's evil hand stamped the seal of terror on the uniforms of all his brothers. Not all conquering Japanese behaved as did Colonel Tokunaga, nor did all British prisoners behave as the exemplary Colonel Newnham. But the contrast is interesting for it lays bare human dignity in suffering. It is a subject of great fascination to me and one of the reasons that this book has been written.

It is a simple story, it is true, a story of adventure, tension and stress under appalling conditions. But I hope it also asks a few questions. Why does despair feed on some men and let others remain free? Why do some of one's fellow prisoners steal, lie, cheat and inform on each other? Why do some men break and others grow with suffering?

The story of Captain M. A. Ansari, 7th Rajputs, says it all, perhaps. Ansari was at point of court martial for his 'disgraceful behaviour' prior to going into action. Captured in battle, he was starved and tortured to seduce him from his British loyalty. He held firm, even at the time when he was beheaded.

The story of Tokunaga also makes the point. Tokunaga was one of the more cruel, unfeeling men among the Japanese 'victors'. Sentenced to death at the war's end, he was reprieved. However, he eventually turned up as abbot of a monastery.

The contrasts of human behaviour in war cannot be categorized. They can only be singled out as examples of what can happen when men's minds are either inspired or twisted. This book has both, on both sides. I have tried to portray people as I saw them. In the light of Providence they may all look different. Who is to judge? Who throws the first stone?

David Bosanquet
Horsham,
Sussex

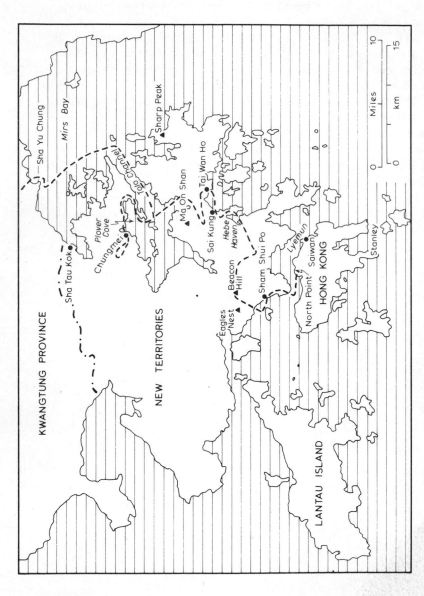

Escape route taken by the author and his three companions through the
New Territories of Hong Kong, 11–22 April 1942

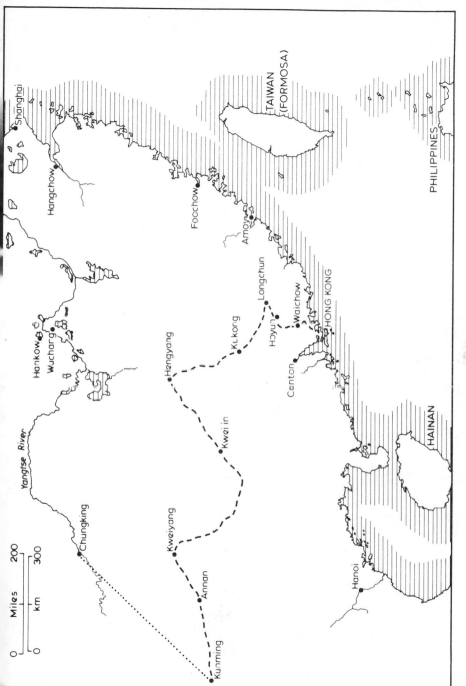

The author's escape route through China to Chunking, 11 April–18 June 1942

Chapter 1

As we approached the fishing village of Shau Ki Wan, near the entrance to Hong Kong's harbour at Lyemun, the column of prisoners stretched for well over a mile.

The Japanese guard just ahead of me held up his hand. The prisoners came to a shuffling halt. We were weighed down by the remains of our possessions, a motley lot, with kitbags, old suitcases and cardboard boxes. We were extremely tired, disillusioned and numbed by events.

We had been beaten ignominiously. It had happened so fast. It left us utterly deflated. Our world had collapsed. Many of us, me included, were racked with strange new doubts, apprehensive of what the future held—if there was to be one. The bottom had fallen out of everything we knew.

The Japanese guards, one a sergeant, a giant of his race at well over six feet, and his monkey-like officer companion, were marching through the ranks.

I began to wonder how many of us were to survive what lay ahead. Providence had plucked me and these others from certain massacre at the end of a lightning campaign in which the highly trained Japanese overran the colony of Hong Kong, bayoneting prisoners to death, raping nurses and, as they did so, dragging the very essence of our way of life from us. Would Providence come again to help us through the unknown, uncertain future? Had I known what actually did lie ahead, I might have doubted it, for I was, with my close friends Duggie and John, to survive an almost incredible series of events. They covered many months, hundreds of miles of walking and conditions which I could not then believe possible to survive. On second thoughts, nothing *but* Providence could have seen us through it.

We were in full view of Sai Wan Hill; the tips of the old 1918 ack-ack guns we had manned still pointed heavenwards over the walls of the gun pits. What horrors that gun site held for me! I had come to Hong Kong a games-loving, peaceful young man. I was now twenty-seven, and I had been thrown into the war as a gunner-sergeant in the Hong Kong Volunteer Defence Corps.

Better not to think about it all now, I remember saying to myself. Better to concentrate on the next thing ahead and to live from moment to moment.

The next thing ahead at that point was to start marching again. During my reverie the column had already begun to move listlessly forward. I had to keep up with the man in front. The spur to do it was the thought of a Japanese rifle butt in the stomach. But a greater spur was the simple drive to get with my belongings to whatever the next destination might be.

Thinking back, the fear of the future, rather than the fear of our present plight, was what filled our hearts. And yet, as I marched on, I could feel around me the solid determination among most of us that, in spite of all hardship and degradation, we would not succumb. I know I suddenly began to feel this inside. It was a feeling soon to be put to the test through the most exacting period of my life.

Up ahead a man stumbled, exhausted. The Japanese sergeant ordered a corporal to beat him on the head with his rifle butt. Then the sergeant kicked him in the stomach.

As my part of the column reached him, I saw a face I recognized, yet did not know. Whoever it was, he was not yet quite dead.

At that moment we knew, if any of us did not know already, that we were in the hands of the cruellest, most arrogant creatures that any man could encounter. Only later did I learn the way in which these most treacherous men were brainwashed into their sub-human thinking. What better could be expected when the moral training to which they were subjected taught them:

'To serve the Emperor with single-hearted loyalty is the super-lative treasure of the Japanese subject, by reason of which he rises superior to all foreign people.'

'International treaties cannot be depended upon, nor can the promise of peace.'

'Should wormlike foreign reptiles dare to insult the dignity of the Emperor or pollute his virtuous name, the spirits of heaven and earth cannot refrain from meting out punishment, nor can his subjects withhold their indignation and ire. They will never rest until they have avenged the insult.'

And only later still did I learn that the same bestial conquerors of some foreign soil were often in their own country polite, peaceful and artistic men.

12

Chapter 2

February in Kent can be bitterly cold. In the winter of 1936 I was in my last year at Wye Agricultural College, which is part of the University of London. I was running to a lecture, watching my breath crystallize in the air. At the college entrance the porter stopped me. There was an important telephone call for me from London. A great friend had offered me a chance of a job with the large and prestigious eastern trading firm of Jardine's.

Even I, whose thoughts at that time were almost totally pre-occupied with rugger, cricket and a handful of charming young girls, had heard of Jardine's. Before going to Wye, I'd been to Lancing, a well-known English public school where games were stressed perhaps to the detriment of academic studies—not an unusual situation in English public schools at the time. But the thought of working for Jardine's was like saying the Bank of England was offering me a job. And besides, in 1936 England was still in one of the worst depressions in its history. Any worthwhile job was hard to come by. Jardine's! I considered myself a very lucky young man. China had been the trading centre of the Jardine empire for over a hundred years.

As I drove up to London in my newly acquired second-hand MG sports car, my pride and joy which I'd saved long to buy, I mulled over the thought of possibly working in China. My ideas of it centred round the escapades of ruthless warlords, wise but Machiavellian mandarins and stories of the great British merchant adventurers who traded there. Now, here I was, having gone to Wye College expecting to end up in some agricultural work, seriously considering a life trading in the country of 'ten thousand dragons'.

The full name of Jardine's was Jardine Matheson. In London the company was simply called Matheson's.

When I arrived at their offices, I was in for one of those sudden surprises which were to characterize my life for the next seven years. I wasn't offered a job in China. I was asked if I was interested in going to East Africa. They were apparently expanding their operations on that continent. So much, I thought, for all my clever imaginings about life among junks and sampans on the Yangtse.

Even at this young age I was very aware of the part Providence played in my life, and jumped at the offer, thankful to get a job though it initially only paid £100 a year. (At the rate of exchange of that time this was a total of about $400 US a year.) It was a meagre sum, but I could make do. I was lucky to have a job.

I went back to Wye excited about many things. And the first chance I had I told a very special girl of mine, Hazel Richardson. She was excited for me. I knew her family owned one of the larger construction engineering companies in India and she knew the sort of life she and I might expect if and when we were ever to marry.

I worked in the City of London for Matheson's during the next two years, training in various departments. And I was just getting bored with being a mere trainee when I was called to Jim Bovill's office.

It was Jim, as a director of Matheson's, who had offered me the job in the beginning. He had known me since I was a boy. He said, 'I've just had word Jardine's have a job for you in Hong Kong.'

In the summer of 1938 the world was on the brink of war. Everyone could feel it coming and yet there was still a tendency to think that, as far as we were concerned, it would be averted and there would be 'business as usual'. On the other hand, in China, war was in full spate; the Japanese already controlled much of the North and were committing atrocities so appalling that we tried to shut them from our minds. There was bitter fighting in and around Shanghai, and the fall of Canton in the South was imminent. Was this the climate in which to embark upon a career in China? Small wonder that Jim asked me, 'Do you want to take it?'

Without hesitation I replied, 'Jim, if you think it is the right thing to do, of course I'll take it.'

'I do,' he said gravely. 'Indeed, I am glad you have reacted so positively because the whole history of the firm is bound up in the Far East. Africa will always remain a side-show.' A smile came over his face as he added, 'It's a feather in your cap.'

I knew he was right. What I didn't know was the scope of the adventure on which I was embarking.

I left England in the first week of October 1938. In order to have an extra week at home, I flew in an Air France aircraft to Marseilles to pick up my ship. My departure from Croydon should have been a moment of great excitement for me. Yet the gilt was taken off the gingerbread because it meant leaving Hazel, my family and lovely

England. I knew as I waved my last farewells that it could be five years before I saw any of them again, for that was the term of a Jardine contract in those days.

Physically I was very fit. I still played rugger, squash and cricket regularly. Life without games would have been unthinkable. I had a shock of fair hair and green eyes and was what might have been described as a typical young Englishman or, as seen through Chinese eyes, a replica of the traditional 'Red-haired Foreign Devil'.

Mentally I had learned to work in an office and enjoyed doing so. It was what I wanted to do.

The ship—the RMS *Canton*—and I had one thing in common. It was my first time journeying away from the land of my birth. It was the ship's maiden voyage also. It took us both three weeks to reach Hong Kong, going via Suez.

Shortly after leaving Singapore, we ran into a typhoon in the South China Sea. The ship rolled and tossed as great waves smashed against her bows as she headed into the wind. It was my first experience of such a storm. It was exciting and invigorating although many were only too thankful as we passed through it to calm waters in sufficient time for all to enjoy the final approach to Hong Kong.

The ship sailed majestically towards the narrow entrance to the harbour at Lyemun. To port lay the Island itself, with the hills coming down to the sea, but there were many promontories, on some of which were attractive houses set well apart, their white walls shining in the sun, their red or green tiled roofs setting the seal on spacious comfort. The coastline was jagged, interspersed with sparklingly sandy beaches on which the deep-blue water gently lapped, or, where there was no land protection, the waves rolled in. To starboard was a long peninsula, the mainland, barren of houses but still a part of the Colony.

Through Lyemun the ship entered the magnificent land-locked waters of the natural harbour and immediately passed the fishing village of Shau Ki Wan, teeming with junks and sampans anchored together cheek by jowl and teeming with water-folk. Some were busy drying fish, others doing chores aboard their vessel, their permanent home, while others simply squatted in the stern to watch the world go by. Many of the women and some of the older children had younger members of the family strapped to their backs while they worked.

Ahead lay the wharf at which the ship was to berth in Kowloon, the focal point on the mainland. Behind the peninsula on which much of the town was built rose a range of hills as a wall seemingly to protect it against anything which lay beyond the rest of the territory leased to Britain, and China itself. It was these hills, *Kao Lung*, meaning Nine Dragons, from which Kowloon derived its name, and yet the central feature of them, a large rocky outcrop, was called Lion Rock! Of course, both lions and dragons figure constantly in Chinese effigies.

At the same time, as we steamed slowly up the harbour, I could see the city of Victoria, directly opposite Kowloon, sprawling in a narrow strip behind the Island's waterfront as if it had been set by some giant hand, beneath a massive peak which dominated the harbour. Victoria Peak, or colloquially the Peak, was dotted with houses and large buildings to its mid-level. Above, there was nothing until the top, where I saw more houses and the track of a vehicular railway running directly up to them. 'Was that the only means of reaching them?' I thought to myself as I leaned over the rail of the boat deck and absorbed the beauty of this place which I was to come to love so much. I was to learn the same evening that it was not.

We finally docked and Roger Grieve, the man whose place I was taking while he spent some leave in England, met me. Grieve was a shortish, clean-shaven man and well tanned by the ninety-degree Hong Kong summer. He took me across the harbour to Jardine's offices in Pedder Street. It was an old-style colonial building with a verandah running all around, great high ceilings and fans. Most of the staff worked in open-plan offices. The directors worked in a wing on the first floor, known as the Private Office. I was taken round the offices and introduced not only to my fellow countrymen but also to some of the Chinese, many of whom still wore long silk gowns to their ankles or short, high-necked silk shirts with black silk trousers. People of many races worked in Jardine's in those days, and among them were the Portuguese, their families originally coming from the nearby Portuguese colony of Macao.

Roger took me to meet the *Taipan* (the head man), D. F. Landale, who had taken over from J. J. Paterson who was away on leave, and then D. L. Newbigging, who over the next three years helped me greatly both in and out of the office. Newbigging was known by nearly everyone as 'Buggins'.

My desk was in the Book Office, which I gathered was the accounts department. The chief accountant was a splendid, solid Scot, Mr Murdock, to us juniors, but 'Murdie' behind his back.

16

Within days of my arrival he called me into his office and said, 'Do you realize you are a very privileged young man? Starting on the cash desk? Do you know what that means?'

I shook my head obediently, like a schoolboy standing before him.

'It means, young man, you are in a well-honoured tradition. You've a lot to live up to. Mr Landale started on the cash desk. So did Mr Newbigging and Mr Paterson.'

Murdock delivered these remarks as if he were referring to divinities. He went on to say, 'Those men are all directors of the company.' He paused for emphasis. 'So it is up to you, isn't it?'

'Yes, sir.'

At the end of the day Geoffrey Gompertz, who worked in the Insurance Department, came to take me to the Jardine Mess. It was then that I discovered that this was one of the houses on the Peak. It was a magnificent drive and at each turn I saw a different breathtaking panorama of Hong Kong, which I thought must surely be one of the finest places of natural beauty in the world. At last we took a hairpin bend and were soon at the mess. It looked south-west towards Dumbell Island some nine miles away. We left the car in the car park, forty feet below the mess, and walked up a path flanked by a bank of large blue hydrangeas.

The mess was a spacious bungalow, typical of the East. It had a closed verandah on the southern side beyond the sitting-room and dining-room. Six of us shared the mess: two had to share a room.

As we looked out at the glorious view from the verandah, Geoffrey Gompertz (who was mess president) said, 'Quite a hill, isn't it?'

'Yes, very steep in places,' I replied.

'You'll need a car. Get a small one. The roads here are about as wide as your hat.'

Having just ground up a hill with gradients of 1 in 4 or 5 in his Vauxhall 14, I made a mental note *not* to take his advice and very soon bought one of the more powerful cars in Hong Kong, a 1934 Canadian Ford V8 drop-head coupé two-seater, which sped me up and down the Peak with ease and comfort.

Within a few weeks I fell happily into life in Hong Kong. It was very pleasant and yet there was a lot to learn. People were very friendly and within a month I was a member of various clubs which enabled me to play rugger, cricket, squash and golf. Unfortunately, both rugger and cricket were played during the fine winter season, and it was difficult to play both games. The first time I was asked to play in a two-day weekend cricket match, I'd already promised to play rugger so I asked Alec Pearce, the captain of the eleven, who was keen for me to play, whether I could possibly do both.

'What time is your rugger?' he asked.

'Four-thirty.'

'We start at two,' he said. 'So you can play until four, then push off and play rugger. And if we are fielding, I'll get someone to substitute for you. It's eleven-thirty start on Sunday.' I did just that on several weekends.

Early in 1940 Buggins walked into the Book Office late one evening. I stood up. He was dapper, slightly balding, always immaculate and very charming.

'David,' he said, 'you are being transferred to the Shipping Department in Shanghai.'

My heart sank. I'd just found my feet in Hong Kong. I looked at him and he returned my look with a smile. 'Thank you, sir, for giving me a little warning.' Damn it, I thought, I'll have to sell my car.

I knew I couldn't take it with me. But I was determined not to sell it until the last minute, because it would seriously interfere with my social life. Not that I was one of those who constantly frequented the 'Gripps', as the Hong Kong Hotel was known, or any real night life in the Colony. On an income which was now £400 a year ($1,600), which seemed riches to me when I left England, nights on the town had to be strictly rationed.

About that time J. J. Paterson, the chairman of Jardine's, returned from leave. 'J.J.', as he was affectionately known, was a great character, the life and soul of the party when he could be persuaded to stay in Hong Kong instead of leaving for his home in Fanling, near the Chinese border. J.J. was also a member of the Colony's Executive Council. When I was taken in to meet him, one of the first things he asked me was whether I'd joined the Volunteer Defence Force.

'Yes, sir,' I said. 'I've joined the Troop, but they are going to take away our ponies and give us machine guns instead.'

'Running up and down the hills in the New Territories with those things will make a man of you,' he laughed.

'I'm sure it would, sir, but a volunteer ack-ack battery is being formed and I've been given a transfer with promotion to sergeant. But that's all by the way now I'm going to Shanghai,' I said.

J.J. made no comment and did not even ask how I liked the idea of the move.

Not long after this Buggins asked to see me, just days before I was due to go to Shanghai. 'Oh David,' he said, 'have you sold your car?' I couldn't think why he should be in the least concerned whether I had or not but I answered, 'Well, sir, as a matter of fact I haven't.'

'Aren't you leaving it a bit late?'

'I was leaving it to the last minute. I know someone who wants it.'

Then with a broad smile he said, 'Well, don't sell it. You're not being transferred to Shanghai.' How marvellous, I thought. 'The *Taipan* supports the Order-in-Council not to transfer anyone of military age out of the Colony. We're putting you in the Import Department instead.'

The Import Department? Oh, hell. That was really bad news. Peter Morrison was head of Imports. And I'd had a flaming row with him about some papers. If any person in Jardine's was after my blood, it was Morrison.

The next evening I was working late when I became conscious of someone standing by my desk. I looked up. It was Morrison. I hadn't seen him come in.

'I hear you are coming to me in the Import Department, Bosanquet?' he said in his dour voice.

'Yes,' I said.

'How do you like the idea?'

I looked at him a little quizzically before saying, 'I like the idea very much.'

'Good,' he smiled. 'Then come on, David. Let's go to the Cricket Club and have a drink.'

I nearly fell off my chair and began to tidy up my papers. As we walked out of the office, he took my arm for a moment, 'We'll bury the hatchet.'

It was the spirit of Jardine's, a great firm to work for, but I was very glad I wasn't going on to Shanghai.

Chapter 3

The operator spoke into her mouthpiece, 'Good morning. Jardine's.'

'May I speak to Mr Bosanquet, please?'

'Oh, good *morning*, Mr Pearce. I'll put you through with pleasure.' Maggie Williams, the firm's telephone operator, was renowned for the uncanny way in which she could recognize a voice. Everyone in Hong Kong knew Maggie and she knew everyone although few saw her. It was just as well. She was no beauty, and it might have spoiled the image of Jardine's golden-voiced switchboard lady who was always so obliging.

John Pearce suggested lunch at the Gloucester. He and I had become friends soon after I had arrived. We played golf together on most Sundays when there was no cricket, and afterwards I invariably had supper with the family.

The Pearces were long established in Hong Kong. John's father owned an import–export business while Alec, his elder brother, a fine cricketer who had played for Kent, worked with a firm of exchange brokers.

Until the middle of 1940 John had worked in his father's company, but when regular war-time commissions were offered to a selected few in the Volunteer Force, both John and Alec accepted. They were posted to the 5th AA Regiment Royal Artillery which had its headquarters at Lyemun Barracks.

I was offered a similar commission but was asked not to accept by J. J. Paterson, who told me in his usual direct manner, 'David, you've got a job to do in the firm. You can get all the training needed by remaining in the Volunteer Defence Force. In this way you'll be doing two jobs and will be far greater use to the Colony.' There was little to be said against such an argument, so I remained a sergeant in the Volunteers.

The Gloucester Hotel was immediately opposite Jardine's offices, and from the restaurant on the top floor there was a magnificent view of the rush and bustle of the harbour across to Kowloon and the range of hills in the background.

John now had two pips on his shoulder. The second was new since

I'd last seen him. I congratulated him and on his command of the troop stationed at West Bay on the Stanley Peninsula side of the Island.

John was tall with dark crinkly hair, thin and usually a rather languid individual. We sat at a table, ordered a gimlet and studied the menu as if we had never seen it before, although we both knew exactly what we were going to order. Lobster thermidor. The boy took the order.

'What's new, John?' I asked.

'Not much,' he replied. 'The damn Japs are still trying to provoke us. There's been a submarine off Stanley well within our waters and a cruiser steaming back and forth near Dumbell Island.'

This was by no means the first time the Japanese had been close in to the Island.

'God! I wish the Coast Defence boys could tickle them up,' I said. 'But I know they can't.'

'Like hell they can't. We're far too vulnerable,' he said.

'I shouldn't think the powers that be would want to put our defences to the test unless they have to.'

We changed the subject. 'You're coming to our cocktail party in the mess next Saturday, aren't you?' I nodded.

'Let's go on afterwards and dance in the Gripps.'

'Yes, let's do that, but we had better grab a couple of girls before they all get booked up. Who's going?'

'Everyone,' said John. 'The Governor, the General and all the top brass.'

'I mean which girls?' I said.

Many families had already left the Colony, and girls were scarce.

'Try Joan Armstrong,' said John.

'Joan! Joan will be going with Alec.'

He shook his head. Joan had been the preserve of Alec Pearce, John's brother, for so long that none of us thought of asking her to do anything without Alec.

'If that's really so, of course I'll ask her. I am sorry if they are breaking up. Will Duggie come?'

'No. I asked him. He can't.'

Lieutenant Douglas Clague had been commissioned as a gunner in England and had been posted to Hong Kong in 1940. Duggie was fair, solidly built and also a keen games player. We three were constantly doing things together and had become the best of friends.

Joan, who worked in Jardine's Insurance Department, said she would love to come after the cocktail party. Although I did not know her particularly well, I was glad she sounded enthusiastic. She was tall with a charming open face. I liked her and thought that Saturday evening might turn into quite a party. It did, but not in the way I had imagined.

The weather at that time of the year in Hong Kong is about as perfect as it can be anywhere in the world. There is no rain, no excess humidity, just a comfortably warm sun shining in a clear blue sky day after day.

Saturday, the 6th of December 1941, was just such a day. On the Peak, rather more than a thousand feet above sea-level, it was beautifully fresh. My Chinese boy opened the front door at the mess and handed me my rugger clothes packed in a Hong Kong basket—these wicker baskets were made locally and used by everyone. I was not coming back for lunch after the office. before playing for the Club against the Army.

Driving down the Peak still fascinated me. There was a different view at every turn in the road. First, elegant houses which themselves had spectacular panoramas whichever way they faced. Then a clear view across the hillside covered in close scrub to Deep Water and Repulse Bays with their white sandy beaches. Beyond and far out to sea the mass of small islands which looked as though each one of them had been delicately placed on an azure-tinted mirror. They set the seal on what must have been one of the most beautiful sights in the world. All the time the car was fast losing height until suddenly at Magazine Gap the harbour in all its beauty came into sight.

By December 1941 I had been in the Far East for three years. I was now temporarily in charge of Imports as Morrison was away in Singapore. I was enjoying it and as I left the office at lunch time on that Saturday, I was quite unaware that everything in Hong Kong was to be horribly changed by the following Monday.

Life felt very good. That evening I lay in a hot bath with the window open wide and watched the shadows creep across Mount Kellet and a fiery red sun sink into the sea. Only one thing could have made it better, or so I thought, as indeed I had thought many many times during the previous three years. If only I was going to jump out of the bath, dress and take my own girl, Hazel, to the Gunners' cocktail party and to dance afterwards, but she was ten thousand miles away in poor old battered England. Twenty-four hours later, as I looked for the last time at her photograph on my mantelpiece, I had a very different thought. I was thankful she was in England.

I picked up Joan from her mother's flat and we drove to the Gunner Officers' Mess at Lyemun, which was some distance from the top of the Peak.

John was right: almost the whole of Hong Kong was there. Men in mess kit or dinner jackets and the ladies in evening gowns. It was very colourful. We had a wonderful evening and, later on, by the time John and I, and our two girls, arrived at the Gripps, we were all on top of the world.

We had just finished dinner. Jimmy Lyon, who was a senior member of our Shipping Department, came over to our table and said, 'Sorry to barge in on your party but, David, please come with me!' There was an edge in his voice. I got up and moved away.

'Buggins wants you in the Private Office immediately. It has something to do with a key which you have.'

'A key?'

'I don't know what key, but you'd better hurry. It's a flap!'

I dashed over to the office to find Buggins and Arthur Piercy pacing up and down.

Arthur Piercy had arrived from Shanghai a few days before and, because he was a senior import manager, had asked me to keep all his documents in the safe in my office.

Buggins said, 'David, the latest reports on the situation are not good. I have just given orders for all our ships to leave as quickly as possible. Arthur is being sent to India to set up an office there in case of trouble. He leaves in the *Yu Sang*, which will sail within the next two hours. You have Arthur's power-of-attorney and passport in your safe. Have you got the key on you? It's urgent.'

'No. It's in my room at the mess,' I said.

'Then go and get it, and drive like hell.'

Arthur said, 'Bring everything to my room in the Gloucester, please David.'

I fled. Never had the 4½ miles seemed so far and yet my wonderful old Ford V8 made nothing of the 1 in 4 gradient up to Magazine Gap. Returning down the Peak, it was much more exacting to keep the car on the road at the speed I was travelling.

I dashed into the office, up four flights of the spiral staircase (the lift was not working), extracted Arthur's documents from the safe and raced across the street to his hotel room. I banged on the door. There was no reply. Still breathless I found a sleepy room-boy.

'Master in room 316 have got?' I asked.

'No, Master have go.'

23

'When?'

'Littee time, ten minute, maybe.'

I left him and as I charged down to the foyer, I thought, Arthur will hold the launch. I can't just abandon Joan like this without a word of explanation. I must go back to the Gripps next door and tell them.

At the table I found none of the gaiety that I'd left. I told them what I had to do.

John immediately said, 'I ought to get back to my troop.'

'I'm sure you're right, John, but could you possibly take the girls home first?'

'I'm not going home,' said Joan. 'I'll come with you, David. I'd love to say goodbye to Arthur.'

I looked at her, 'OK if you really mean that, but we must run.'

We left the others and I made Joan hitch up her long evening dress as we ran to Queen's Pier. Joan stumbled in her high heels. There was no launch in sight, not even a *walla walla* (motorboat).

'Look, Joan, this is dreadful. I'm going to take you home.'

'No you're not,' she said. 'It'll waste time. You'll miss the ship. I'm staying with you,' and she added with a giggle, 'it's a long time since I did anything mad.'

'You really mean that, don't you?'

'Of course I do.'

I thought to myself, I bet you do. Staid old Alec would have seen to it that you did nothing mad. I felt she read my thoughts.

'Bless you,' I said, squeezing her arm, 'you're in for the fun of it. I hope it turns out to be just fun but I think the situation is dicey.'

We waited. No *walla walla* came near us. We could see some across the harbour at Kowloon. In a desperate gamble we took the last ferry across. As we landed, one *walla walla* was still waiting. I dashed for it only to be beaten by a short head. A Chinese had appeared as if from nowhere, but I refused to get off. I left Joan on the jetty to prevent the boatman casting off while I tried to explain the importance of our mission.

The Chinese wouldn't budge and there was nothing for it but to drop him off first and take the *walla walla* on afterwards. I got Joan aboard and believe it or not we went straight back where we had come from. The Chinese smiled as he stepped ashore. He had got what he wanted but, at least, we still had the *walla walla*.

It was now after three o'clock in the morning, and I expected to see the *Yu Sang* sailing down the harbour towards Lyemun Pass. It was quite cold wallowing about the harbour at that time. We huddled together, praying that we would still see the ship at anchor and trying not to take in too much of the sick-making diesel fumes. At last we saw her. 'Joan, we've made it. Look, the companion ladder is still down. There are lights on it.'

I told the boatman to wait for us. We clambered up the companion ladder to be greeted by an astonished second officer who cocked his head on one side like a dog and raised an eyebrow at Joan. Before he could ask us what we were doing, I said, 'It's all right. That's not her going-away dress! Is Mr Piercy aboard? It is most important that I see him.'

We found Arthur in the saloon. He was delighted to see us.

'You did not give me much of a chance to get to the top of the Peak and down again. I broke all records to get to you. What happened?' I handed him his precious papers.

Apparently the launch would not wait. It had been given top-priority instructions to get everyone aboard as fast as possible. As they said, it was better to go without papers than run the risk of being left in Hong Kong. We told him our story as we all walked to the top of the companion ladder together. Then Joan looked over the rail.

'David,' she said, 'there is no *walla walla*.'

My God, there was none! There was no sign of a boat anywhere.

'Joan, that may be your going-away dress after all.' We all laughed rather half-heartedly.

'Come and have a drink,' said Arthur. 'Something is sure to come alongside before we sail. It is pointless to stand here in the cold.'

We gave instructions that we were to be called the moment anything appeared. The Chinese bosun was told to hail any launch or *walla walla* which might pass nearby.

Back in the lounge with Arthur and a few drinks, we waited. And we waited. I kept darting out to check with the bosun. We went on waiting. It seemed like hours. Just when we were about to find the captain and tell him our problem, the bosun told us a *walla walla* was coming alongside.

'Get down that ladder and hold it, for God's sake,' I said. We said goodbye to Arthur hurriedly and hoped that he would get through to India without any trouble. Once in the *walla walla*, we waved to him until it rounded the bow of the ship. Then we huddled together for warmth again, both of us deep in thought at the sudden serious-ness in the air.

What if the ship had sailed with us on board, I thought, and war had come to Hong Kong? Would everyone think that I had engineered it? What, I wondered, were Joan's thoughts? But would the ship even get there? It did not. The Master ran for Manila next morning. There, the *Yu Sang* was sunk and Arthur Piercy was imprisoned for the rest of the war. He survived dreadful privations, but he was able to return to Jardine's after the war for a short time.

As I drove Joan up the Peak and took her home, dawn was breaking.

I kissed her. 'Joan, you are marvellous. It was a bit madder than you had bargained for, wasn't it?' She looked up at me, smiled and went into her flat. I never saw her again, although she did survive Japanese internment.

There was no point in going to bed. I had to play golf at Fanling. Teeing-off time was nine. I had to allow an hour and half to get there. I decided I had time for a bath and was just out of it when the telephone rang. It was Buggins.

'David, I'm sorry to ring you so early but I can't play golf today. I have to be here in case the situation really blows up. Gerry will take my place, but can you take everyone out?'

'Not in my old Ford,' I said. 'It's only got two seats.'

'Then swap cars. You take mine.'

'Fine. I'll be with you in half an hour.'

'I take it Arthur got away all right?'

I told him the story.

'Well done,' he said.

We changed cars and I set off to pick up my passengers. We crossed the harbour in the car ferry, and I was glad to see no sign of the *Yu Sang*.

At the end of the morning round, when I'd played my second shot to the 18th green, I remember thinking how good a couple of gins would be before lunch and wondering why there was so much activity outside the clubhouse. Many people were leaving hurriedly, which seemed very odd, but we putted out and told our caddies to be ready at 2.30 p.m. We walked off the green to the clubhouse. On the door was a large notice which read: 'ALL VOLUNTEERS MOBILIZED. REPORT TO HEADQUARTERS BY 16.30 HOURS.'

'Why in the name of hell do they have to choose a Sunday to start a scare?' I said. 'I'm having a drink anyway.'

'They knew that we would all be playing golf,' said my partner.

He was right, especially as we had been playing golf within little more than two miles of the border and the Japanese.

Sergeant David Bosanquet, 5th AA Battery, Hong Kong

Volunteer Defence Corps, did not report for duty until 18.30 hours. It did not matter. Headquarters was a seething mass of men reporting and there was not enough transport to convey all units to their positions. The battery was not able to man the gun site at Sai Wan until midnight. To get everyone there we had to use private cars.

Sai Wan was immediately above Lyemun, and it was almost impossible to believe the change in the last twenty-four hours. Here was I, my car groaning under an overload of men and equipment, driving up the same road I had driven lovely Joan only the previous night. Could it really be war?

By then, I was almost beyond caring. I had not slept since Friday. It was now Monday morning. I was becoming less and less use to anyone, which my CO, Lolly Goldman, realized, and he thoughtfully ordered my section to stand down. It was a perfect night and I set up my camp bed in the open behind a little-used hut, well away from the hubbub. I was sound asleep in seconds.

I came to with the sun beating down and Bombardier George Chow shaking me. I sat up. 'You hid yourself pretty well, didn't you? The CO thought you would like to know that we have been at war for the last two hours and that perhaps you would grace him with your presence,' he said with a broad grin.

'Come on, get up. We're taking over No. 1 gun in ten minutes.' No sooner had we done so than the Japanese bombed Hong Kong's only airfield, at Kaitak. We now knew the worst . . . or did we?

Chapter 4

Later on I discovered the reason why it had been so difficult for us to find a *walla walla*. The first news of a serious deterioration in the situation had come about midnight.

It was announced to the public largely through the use of stages on dance floors in the hotels. At the Peninsula Hotel in Kowloon, for instance, the orchestra was apparently playing 'The Best Things in Life Are Free' when it was interrupted by a man waving a megaphone. He asked that all men connected with any of the American Steamships Line vessels report immediately aboard.

That evening too after the rugger match against the Army in which I played, there were several large parties at the Hong Kong Hotel, which was packed, and after I left with Joan, rumours began to circulate. They sobered everyone, and the parties broke up.

There was another party in the Jockey Club bar, where gimlets and scotch were quaffed until around 1 a.m., when the place began hurriedly to empty of ladies in pretty dresses and men in white evening jackets.

The Canadian troops were also out on the town when the news started to break. The Winnipeg Grenadiers and the Royal Rifles of Canada had arrived in late November. They were to be the first Canadian troops to see action in the war. Although many of them had been in the army only a few weeks, they were deemed by their authorities to be ready to fight. In the meantime, understandably, they were living it up that Saturday. Several of the senior officers were at a party with some British nurses. Major Lyndon, Captain Bush and Colonel Hennessy and all staff officers were called away suddenly. The Commissioner of Police was also at a party with some Canadians, and when he heard the rumour he gave a characteristic shrug and decided that no Japanese was going to break up *his* party. But he did leave and caught the last ferry from Kowloon to the Island. In fact, Hong Kong was behaving as it normally would on a Saturday evening.

Next morning the 1st Battalion Middlesex Regiment was on Church Parade at St John's Cathedral. The parade was awash with talk of the impending Japanese attack. Later, in the cathedral,

Major-General Maltby, the general officer commanding in Hong Kong, sat in the front pew. The service had not yet reached the prayer for peace when an orderly went forward to the General and whispered to him. He left quickly, followed by his staff officers.

He was told that the Japanese were mustering at the border near Sum Chun and that forward troop movements had been seen also at Am Tau. Both these places were little more than twenty miles from the cathedral.

The Defence Council was hurriedly called at Government House. At 11 a.m. on that Sunday all troops were placed on standby.

The Royal Rifles and the Winnipeg Grenadiers moved into their positions along the hills from Victoria Peak to Mount Collinson, forming a line—impossibly difficult to defend without further support.

In the New Territories, the Royal Scots, Punjabis and Rajputs (two seasoned Indian Army regiments) went to their battle stations in prepared positions from Shingmun Redoubt through to the north-east side of Devil's Peak. Thus they formed a sort of horse-shoe, protecting the western, northern and eastern approaches to the Colony. But there was no depth to these defences. There were insufficient men. The focal point was undoubtedly Shingmun Redoubt, which was a shallow valley caught between two large hills and afforded great advantage to any attacker.

The Hong Kong Civil Defence units were also mobilized. On the face of it the Colony had aroused itself and realized that we were on the brink of war.

At 4.45 a.m. on the morning of Monday the 8th of December, a special wireless intelligence unit monitored a broadcast from Tokyo warning all Japanese nationals overseas that war with the US and Britain was imminent.

The whole of the armed forces in the Colony were alerted. The engineers were ordered to blow the bridges in the New Territories. At 8 a.m. air-raid warnings sounded all over the Island. The Japanese bombed Kaitak airport. They already knew our ack-ack gun positions. Within a few minutes the only aircraft we had there were destroyed.

The Japanese shelled the barracks where the Canadians had been stationed. The chaplain was saying Mass but, as luck would have it, most of the troops were by then in their positions. The first two casualties were Canadians at the Mass, Sergeant Routledge and Signalman Fairley. They were the first Canadians to be wounded in the war.

Then the BBC broke into a dance-music programme to announce the attack on Pearl Harbor. America was in the war. So were we in Hong Kong.

About twenty miles to the north in Kwangtung Province, Lieutenant-General Sakai and his staff were preparing for the main onslaught.

Colonel Doi Teihichi of the Imperial Japanese Regiment 228 and his staff were studying their final plans. Their first objective was the Shingmun Redoubt.

By the early afternoon of the 9th of December, he had advanced to such a position that he could observe our men on the line from Gin Drinkers' Bay. By 23.00 hours one of his battalions was attacking the line, clearing the barbed wire and making a breakthrough for the rest of his regiment. The first to go were the Royal Scots. They held out for eight hours only. Colonel Doi had severely breached the western end of our defence horseshoe.

The Japanese now started on the Punjabis and the Rajputs. They came in sampans, dressed as Chinese coolies. Later the Japanese 230 Regiment, a tough unit, all fighting fit and imbued with an utter contempt for the British and all other nations, attacked in great strength along the main front.

The Japanese came with such rapidity and with such determination that the defenders were totally unaware they were there until they were on them, sometimes even already behind them. By that evening of the 10th of December, the British forces had to fall back to a weak, unprepared line running from Shamshuipo Camp (later to be our prison) around Kowloon itself. One Canadian company of the Winnipeg Grenadiers took part in the action. And by midday the next day the place was so overrun, disorganized and confused that General Maltby ordered the withdrawal of all troops in the New Territories to the Island with the exception of some of the Rajputs. That afternoon the cable lines linking Hong Kong with the world were cut. We were on our own unless the Chinese attacked the enemy in the rear. This they could not be persuaded to do.

Chapter 5

A shout came from the aircraft-spotter standing just above our command post. He pointed towards the Pearl River delta. 'Action,' shouted the officer commanding. 'Action,' repeated the number one of each gun.

'Height-finder, give me a bearing!'

'Bearing two one zero, height nineteen thousand, sir,' came the reply. The predictor locked onto the bearing, and the guns swung automatically as it did so. A tinge of excitement surged through the gun crews. Not a sound could be heard except the intermittent call from the predictor, 'Out of range!'

The flight of twenty-seven aircraft passed over, wings glistening in the early morning sun.

This was the first time that any of us in the Volunteers had seen modern bombers flying in formation. The call 'out of range' was most disappointing. Although the formation had passed almost directly overhead, it had remained beyond the reach of the old three-inch guns.

During that week we scanned the skies continually, but no other aircraft came near us. There was no need for them. The Colony's defences were so weak and confused that the Japanese did virtually as they pleased.

At Lyemun the Island was separated from the mainland by only 300 yards of water. On both sides of it the ground rose steeply, with our battery positioned on top of the hill above Sai Wan, and the enemy immediately opposite on Devil's Peak. He could observe every movement in our gun emplacement. When he did, we would be sitting ducks for the Japanese gunners. Weekend amateurs in the front line facing crack professional troops.

As I saw it, two things could happen. Neither pleasant. The first was that we had obviously been marked as a target for the Japanese guns across the harbour and that they were going to try to blow the position to smithereens, even though our guns could not be depressed sufficiently to engage a ground target. The second was that the Japs would soon attempt a landing, probably in the harbour, and if successful come in among us, forcing us to fight hand-to-hand.

The day after all our troops had withdrawn from the mainland I was on duty with A. C. I. Bowker ('Aci' we all called him), who was our second-in-command. We were raking Devil's Peak with our field glasses for any sign of the observation post we were so sure would soon be established. And, for no apparent reason, he said, 'David, have you thought what it might be like to be in a Japanese concentration camp?'

'No, can't say I have,' I replied.

'Well, you should start. We'll end up there very shortly unless . . .'

'Unless what?' I interrupted him.

'Good God, I don't have to spell it out, do I?'

'No, Aci, you don't,' and I looked at him. 'Are you wondering which may be the least evil . . . to be blown off the face of the map . . . to be engulfed in the first wave of the Japanese attack . . . or to rot in a prison camp?'

He did not answer. We were caught like rats in a trap. And we both knew it. Aci survived the fighting but died a year later in camp.

That same evening we listened to the BBC from London and heard the announcer tell the world that the British Forces in Hong Kong had retired to their island fortress.

' "Island fortress" my fanny!' I said, looking at Aci. A wry smile spread across his face.

Although we saw no aircraft which we could engage during the next days, the shelling started and to minimize the risk of casualties only air sentries were posted above ground. Fortunately the living-quarters had been dug into the hillside below the gun pits, which afforded good protection against everything but really heavy-calibre shells.

During a sharp burst of shelling there was an alert. We manned the guns and instruments with only skeleton crews. There had been so many false alarms.

A near miss showered us with earth and stones, damaging both instruments, and Lolly Goldman ordered all those manning them to get below as there was nothing they could do. I moved to the command post to give him a hand, leaving number one gun in charge of another sergeant. Two more shells in quick succession landed in the position.

'Thank God you sent all but the gun crew below,' I said to Lolly. 'We'd have lost the lot, me included.'

'Where are these bloody aircraft?' he said. 'Can't see a sign of them, can you?'

I had no time to answer for another shell burst alongside the command post. We were half-buried but unhurt.

'Jesus,' said Lolly, 'you and I would be playing our harps if they'd been using big 'uns.' I gave him a half-hearted smile.

'Order the gun crew below, David. This is too unhealthy. Tell 'em to move at intervals in pairs. We'll go last.' I shouted the order, and the men began darting down the iron stairway in twos to the comparative safety of the quarters below. When it seemed that the last pair had left, I ducked into what was left of the command post. 'OK, Lolly, let's go.' As I said it, there was another crump.

We dashed for the iron stairway but stopped dead in our tracks. The shell had hit the half-open metal gates of the gun pit. Beneath the twisted metal was the mutilated body of the sergeant who had taken over from me. Beside him lay a bombardier, horribly wounded.

We called for help and, as we performed the gruesome task of carrying them both below, I thought, but for the hand of Providence this would have been me. That evening my section was sent to West Bay on the other side of the Island for a forty-eight-hour rest period. There we were billeted with John Pearce's troop. It was good to see him. We had not met since our party in the Gripps. The other section was sent out when we returned and as they left, I had a premonition that they were going to have by far the better deal. They did.

On the second day after we were back at the gun site, the 19th December, the Japs stepped up the intensity of their shelling, and HQ recognized that our position had become untenable—at least in the role as ack-ack gunners. We were told that transport would be sent at 22.30 hours to remove one gun and that we were to withdraw with it. By then we had pin-pointed the observation post on Devil's Peak to which the enemy had added a mortar section which was relentlessly dropping mortars into a coast-defence battery below us. By depressing the guns to the lowest point to clear the gun pits, we could just engage the post. Lolly tried in vain to get permission to fire. It was refused. We were ack-ack gunners. It wasn't our job! We were furious at the seemingly stupid attitude.

Hours later an officer from a nearby howitzer battery appeared on a motor bike. Our fury had not abated.

'I have been sent to confirm that there is an enemy mortar position across the water,' he said in an irritatingly casual manner, waving an arm in the general direction of Devil's Peak.

'There is,' said Lolly Goldman coldly. 'Sergeant Bosanquet will show you,' and he turned away in disgust. I took him up the stairway. He took one look.

'The little bastards are there all right.'

'That's what we have been saying for half the day,' I replied testily, following Lolly's example to rub in our hurt feelings that we had not been allowed to attack.

'Never mind,' he said, sensing our frustration. 'We'll soon fix 'em.' He used our land-line. From the third salvo there was a sheet of flame from Devil's Peak.

'Got 'em,' he said with a smile. 'Does that make you feel better?'

'Yes, of course, but why in hell's name couldn't it have been done before?'

'Indeed,' he replied. 'Why not? I'll come again if you have anything to offer.' He went on his way.

As the sun set, sentries were posted and I stood and watched a large rubber factory that had been burning for some time. It threw light on the inland approach to the gun site, and I remember thinking that it would help in getting the gun out. To seaward, the hill was in deep shadow.

I returned to the living-quarters. The stale air made the atmosphere heavy. Everyone felt drowsy. Lolly Goldman, a bombardier and three men remained on duty. Everyone else lay on their palliasses half-dressed, resting. No one would be on duty until 22.00 hours.

Later a man got up, put his boots on and went out through the only exit to get some fresh air, so he said. Sleepily I looked at my watch. There was no hurry to rouse myself. I had not stirred when the door burst open. It was the man who had gone out for fresh air.

'The Japs are in the gun pits,' he shouted.

'Christ,' I said, 'they must have killed all the sentries,' No one answered. Lolly and those with him were at the door in seconds.

'Everyone out,' he shouted. 'Follow me, quick.'

And he was gone. Agonizing moments passed before we had gathered our equipment. Just as we were ready, a hand-grenade came hurtling through the door. There was a blinding flash, a deafening explosion. The blast threw me to the floor. I picked myself up very shaken but unhurt. The grenade killed no one though some were wounded and blinded. The rest of us did what we could for them, but if anyone was to survive, we had to get out before another grenade was thrown.

'Everyone out who can move,' I shouted. 'The rest of you lie doggo. They may think we've all gone. We'll get help to you somehow.' I didn't feel very confident that we would, even if some of us did manage to regain contact with our own forces.

A bombardier seconded to our battery from the regular army, at first, would not hear of leaving the wounded to the mercy of the enemy but eventually agreed. I told the men to go singly, dash over the gun road and seek what cover they could on the hillside. We would then make an orderly retreat.

The bombardier went first, followed by several others. They did not follow instructions but moved down the gun road to their death.

Pushing several men through the door with me, I dashed across the road and flung myself onto the hillside. Two followed. Then another. There was not much cover. We wormed our way down the roof of our ammunition shelter and waited for others to join us. None did.

'We must keep together,' I whispered. 'Jump off the roof and follow straight down the hill to the Island Road.' I jumped. The drop was much more than I expected. I missed my footing and, as I fell, instinctively tucked my knees up to my chin and allowed myself to roll over and over. My fall was stopped by a barbed-wire apron fence. I tore myself loose, not feeling the barbs as they bit into my flesh, and dropped to the ground on the far side. I waited and listened. I thought I heard a movement above me but no one came. I waited until I dared wait no longer. I turned and fought my way down through the thick scrub until somehow I hit the road.

'Halt, who goes there?' I knew the voice.

'Friend, for Christ's sake. Bomp, where are you? I have . . .'

'Get off the bloody road,' he said. 'The Japs are everywhere.' I ducked into a ditch. Lieutenant Bompas with two Sepoys emerged from the undergrowth and joined me. I told him what had happened and he told me that the Japanese had cut through what little infantry defence there was in the Lyemun Sector and that no organized defence remained to the seaward side of the Island Road.

'From what you've told me,' he said, 'they will be threatening the howitzer position at any moment. Let's get there quick!' On the way we ran into some Canadians who seemed not to know where they were or where they ought to be. Bompas immediately took command. He led the bewildered Canadians and bedraggled me to the defence of the howitzer position. When we got there, we found utter confusion, but I was able to use the field telephone and report to Gunner HQ what had happened to my battery.

As I emerged from beneath the camouflage netting, the battery commander shouted, 'Hey you.' I looked around. 'Yes you, Sergeant. What the bloody hell are you doing in my position? And who the hell do you think you are using my land-line? I don't know you.' I looked at him, seething inwardly at this totally unnecessary approach.

'Perhaps not,' I said, deliberately omitting 'sir'. 'Mr Bompas will tell you who I am, if we can find him. I left him trying to organize some defence of your position,' I said pointedly, 'while I reported that the Volunteer battery position above you has been overrun, with few survivors. I am one of them, and the Japanese are advancing down towards this position.' By this time we were glaring at each other face to face. He relaxed slightly, obviously aware of my contempt at his behaviour.

'There is some of your mob further up Island Road. You'd better join 'em.' I needed no second bidding and left him to his problems, thinking I would have stayed with Bomp through thick and thin, but not that perisher.

We were, of course, under great strain.

Eventually I found No. 2 Section, which had been on its way to relieve us, and with them Lolly Goldman. He was very upset that so few had followed him out.

'You didn't give us time, Lolly,' I said as he plied me with questions.

'Surely you realized we were only half-dressed and couldn't follow you except barefoot and without arms?'

'I know now,' he said dolefully. 'At that moment I just knew we had to get out and quick.'

'You were right. If only the attack had been ten minutes later, many more of us would have been ready to follow you,' I said. 'Even after the bloody little Nip crawled along beneath the wall and threw in the grenade among us, many others could have got through with me, if they'd followed instructions.' I hoped this would make him feel better.

For the rest of the night we were deployed to prevent the enemy crossing Island Road. Remarkably there was no attack upon it. I could only surmise that the Japanese were regrouping and that even they were surprised at our puny effort to defend the Lyemun area which allowed them to achieve so strong a foothold in all too short a time. Perhaps more surprising was how, at dawn, we were ordered to withdraw and were taken again to the gun site at West Bay. After a few words with John, I was able to wash and change into a fresh uniform I had previously left there.

Late that day, since the Japanese were all over the Island, John's troop was ordered to withdraw into the fort at the end of the Stanley Peninsula. It was accomplished in an orderly fashion.

Now we could withdraw no further, for the sea was at our backs. We had to stand and fight or raise the white flag of surrender.

On the morning of Christmas Eve the Japanese delivered a sharp frontal attack and drove what remained of East Force into the village of Stanley less than a mile from the perimeter of the fort.

Every available man was sent forward in a vain attempt to stem the tide. Our battery was lucky in being ordered to take up a position just in front of the perimeter. Not so 1st Battery, which consisted mainly of the more elderly members of the Volunteer Force, who were quite unsuited to be engaged in an infantry battle. The result was tragic. Of fifty-four men only seventeen survived the fighting during the night.

We all knew that this was the crunch and that the Japanese would delight in our slaughter as that Christmas Day drew out, hour by long hour. But the expected final attack never came. They did not overrun the fort or the positions immediately before it. The Governor, as Commander-in-Chief, had surrendered. He did so at three o'clock in the afternoon, but we knew nothing of it until 7 p.m. that evening.

For all of us it was a reprieve. For some only temporary, for others a reprieve to test them to the limit of human endurance—for the very few, like John and myself—a new lease on life.

Chapter 6

Those not on duty in Stanley Fort began to gather on the parade ground. Small knots of men, each speculating upon what the future held. Every so often men would pass from one group to another, hoping to glean the latest information. To all senior NCOs word was passed that there was beer in the sergeants' mess, and any who took advantage of it were greeted on the threshold with, 'Come in. Don't leave a drop for the little bastards. A sober Jap is bad enough.'

As supplies began to run out, the party dissolved. Men drifted away, content that they at least had survived the fighting whatever the morrow might bring.

For three days we saw no move on the part of the Japanese. The garrison was left strangely alone. The sun shone in a cloudless sky. A calm sea, a beautiful Mediterranean blue, lapped gently against the rocks of Bluff Head; all seemed serene and peaceful as some stood idly gazing at the group of uninhabited islands on the horizon. How could carnage, lust and greed be perpetuated in such surroundings? The dreamer needed only to turn his head, however, and the answer lay before him: a shell hole, a bomb crater and partially destroyed buildings. He should perhaps have remembered that we, the British, had grabbed the Island through war exactly one hundred years previously in order to force trade upon the vast Chinese Empire.

Now the men from the land of the Rising Sun had grabbed this beautiful island at the point of the sword, not with intent to use it as a trading post but as a first move to smash all trace of British, European and American influence within the sphere of Asia and then to subjugate not only China but all Asian races to the dominance of Japan.

As if to prove it, a small Japanese detachment came marching into the barracks to give us our first view at close quarters of victorious Japanese soldiery.

Undoubtedly one day the myth of their professed superiority would be exploded but, in the meantime, we were totally in their hands and even then could not help wondering how many would survive to see the day. What would they do with us? Keep us in Stanley? Hardly: the conditions would be too comfortable. Press-ganged to work in China or shipped to Japan to be exhibited to the people as the first fruits of the world-conquering Imperial Army?

We might be made to do anything or be sent anywhere, so why speculate? We would know soon enough; better by far to make the most of every hour in which we were left alone. However, for some, there was work to be done, since orders were issued to all units that side arms and all equipment were to be stacked on the parade ground. With those orders came implicit instructions that under no circumstances was any equipment to be destroyed. Sadly, the order was closely observed and there was no demolition, no spiking of guns, indeed no destruction of any sort. Apparently the Japanese threatened drastic consequences unless their orders were carried out to the letter, but nowhere else in the Colony was it so rigorously observed. Among the garrison there was strong criticism that no demolition had been ordered the moment news of the surrender was received and before contact was made by the enemy commander.

There was particular resentment, and rightly so, that men were ordered to carry six-inch shells from the position at Bluff Head to the road, to make their removal that much easier for the enemy. The fear of reprisals had started.

From some of the others in Stanley at that time we heard news of what happened after the Japanese broke through our original defences.

In Kowloon apparently dead bodies lay rotting in the sun, sewage seeped into the putrid street air and, as there was no refrigeration in the godowns (warehouses), the goods were also rotting.

The walls and door of the shops were torn down and both Chinese and Japanese were looting.

At the Bowen Road Hospital the Japanese broke in and shot anyone who moved, including the wounded patients. They took the nurses aside and raped them. One nurse at least survived by pretending to be dead.

At Eucliffe Castle, a large house at Repulse Bay built by a Chinese multi-millionaire, men of the Royal Rifles were taken prisoner. Their hands were tied and they were prodded with bayonets to the edge of the cliff. Those who jumped were smashed on the rocks a hundred feet below; those who did not were shot in the back. Later over fifty bodies were found.

On the evening of the 29th, orders were received for all units to parade at 8 a.m. Each man could bring only what he could carry. No one seemed to know how long the march might be. But everyone knew that it was twelve miles to the outskirts of town.

Those in our battery were lucky. We had managed to keep most of our kit. Most others had little but the clothes on their backs and they gladly accepted anything offered. The battery could have given a lot but it 'befriended' a section which had been withdrawn from the fighting in Stanley village, on Christmas Eve. The men arrived tired, as we went on duty. By the time we returned, the men had moved out, having rifled our kitbags.

I was detailed as right marker for the Volunteers. Festooned like Christmas trees, their last remaining and infinitely precious worldly belongings hanging from shoulders or strapped to waists, the markers took their stations, and the remainder of the parade was called and formed up on them. There was a long wait before the Japanese guards arrived to take command. This, we were to learn, was a typical psychological manœuvre.

The first halt was called as the column reached Stanley village. There was no sign of what had happened to the nearby dead. None were visible from the road. It seemed the Japs themselves cleared the evidence of the ghastly orgy they had wrought in St Stephen's College where Dr Black and his assistant had been shot dead, bravely trying to prevent the wounded being bayoneted as they lay helpless on palliasses. We later learned that others were herded into small rooms to be butchered later, one by one, to satisfy some inexplicable bloodlust. Here too the nurses, sexually assaulted before being brutally despatched, had added their blood to the terrible scene. Perhaps the poor unfortunate Chinese living in the village had been forced to clear the evidence. Few of us then knew that a padre, who had witnessed these terrible and inexcusable deeds, was alive and that one day he would help to bring retribution upon the heads of some who were responsible.

While the column rested, two Japanese soldiers appeared from a house carrying buckets and, instead of crossing the road where there was a gap between one unit and the next, they deliberately barged through the ranks, knocking down men as they did so. On its own, this was a tiny incident but it confirmed that a prisoner of war was beneath contempt in the eyes of the Japanese. The few Chinese who were going about their own business stopped to watch but their impassive faces gave no sign of what they thought.

Indeed, what did they think? Was it contempt that an Asiatic race had so easily humbled so many Europeans who had long dominated the indigenous population, or was there a trace of pity? Was there a sense that they had been let down, for these simple folk could not have known that the British were fighting for their very lives halfway across the world. Probably they had no thoughts at all on the matter. It was enough that their new masters were known to be ruthless and cruel and that life could be maintained only by subservience. It was certain, as time proved, that there were few who did not hold a deep-set loathing of the Japanese, and even those who did collaborate did so mainly because, from time immemorial, opportunism had ruled their conduct.

The long column dragged its weary way with good heart, past Tytam Reservoir, up over the hill and down again to Shau Ki Wan, past the gun road to Lyemun Barracks. As it did so, I could not keep my eyes off the battery position at the top of Sai Wan, haunted by the thought of what might have happened to the wounded and all those who had failed to take the route which had enabled me to regain contact with our own forces. We halted at Sai Wan, and every other man was glad of the brief rest. But I was glad when Sai Wan was out of sight again.

Our first destination was the refugee camp at North Point. The camp, never salubrious, had been within the sector of the original landing operations and had suffered accordingly. The huts which had been partially damaged could be patched up, using the remains of those totally destroyed, but the primary task was the immediate removal of the incredible filth. The area had been used by the Japanese as a horse hospital. Blood-stained pads, dung and putrefying carcasses had to be cleaned away.

There were Canadians, Indians, regular British troops and about three hundred Volunteers, in all some eighteen hundred men crammed together in this hellhole.

The huts were originally designed to hold no more than fifty Chinese refugees, and the space allocated for each of the fifty had not been generous. For every prisoner to have a roof over his head, it was necessary for as many as 175 men to share a hut. There were two-tier wooden bunks in many of them and, had this not been so, it would have been impossible for everyone to lie down at the same time. The bunks were pushed together in pairs, and in this way seven could sleep in the floor space otherwise occupied by three— two on the top bunk, three below and two on the floor. Often the nights were too cold for those on the concrete floor to sleep for long. They were forced to get up and exercise to restore circulation. I was on the floor. But I scrounged three wooden boards. Comparative luxury!

Initially, water was strictly rationed as every drop had to be brought into the camp by water-cart. Work was permitted on the damaged main, and it was not too long before it was restored, bringing great relief to everyone.

The few latrines were totally inadequate for even half the number of men which the camp now held. There was not space for more. The use of the sea wall was our alternative, a relief but a very public relief. Soon dysentery swept through the camp. The distress of the disease stifled any sense of squeamishness about using a communal wall.

Some joked about the sight it presented, viewed from the harbour. But soon it was no joke at all. Men would almost crawl to the sea wall, weakened by constant visits, tie themselves to a post or to the wire to prevent falling over the edge, and squat in agony, then, still in agony, creep back to their hut as best they could, only to be forced to make the same expedition over again before they had barely recovered from the last exertion.

There were swarms of flies everywhere. Cleansing of the entire camp produced little effect on their numbers because just outside the perimeter was a refuse dump and the Japanese would neither deal with this menace themselves nor allow us to do so.

We almost breathed flies. They settled on every mouthful of food. Men who had nothing better to do spent the day swatting flies, and at night, when they swarmed on the rafters in the roofs of the huts, parties would climb up, squash thick black layers of them and scrape the mess into buckets, but all efforts made not the slightest difference. They were buzzing in their myriads the next day, and the thick black layers were there again in every hut, as soon as it began to get dark. January is a cool month in Hong Kong, and unless the Japanese were to permit drastic action to be taken against this truly fearful menace, the consequences of what might happen during the humid summer did not bear contemplation.

At North Point there was at least little interference from the Japanese. There were few acts of violence. Rations from nearby food dumps were collected regularly, under guard, by parties detailed for the job, and although the quantity and quality were considered quite inadequate, it was discovered later that the feeding of those early days was luxury itself compared with the Japanese idea of a maintenance diet for prisoners at Shamshuipo Camp to which we were later moved.

I was included in one of the food details. It made a change to get out of the camp, the flies and the crowds for an hour or two. On the return journey the lorry was stopped by a Japanese officer who indicated by signs that he wanted a fir tree cut down and taken back to the camp. It was wanted for the guards' New Year celebrations but later it was put to a far more sinister use. Any Chinese in the vicinity who committed no greater crime than failing to bow to a Japanese while he passed on the other side of the road would be seized and tied to this tree just outside the guard-room where the poor wretch would be left without food or water to be scorched by the sun during the day and almost frozen stiff at night since it was a favourite trick to throw a bucket of water over the prisoner at sundown.

A semblance of order in North Point was achieved remarkably quickly thanks to good and firm direction by our own officers. Parties kept the camp clean as far as it was possible; others were detailed to the cookhouse. Language classes were organized in which the Volunteers figured prominently, since in their ranks were Dutch, French, Russians and Chinese who spoke Mandarin and Cantonese dialects. All these activities did much to prevent boredom as each man settled down to eke out an existence as best he could.

About a week after we were marched into North Point, two of us were sitting on my so-called bed swatting flies. We were having a competition to see who could kill the most flies at a given time. With nothing better to do, it was as good a way of passing time as anything.

The door at the far end opened and a voice shouted, 'Is Sergeant Bosanquet there?' I got up and walked to the door to find Lolly Goldman outside.

'David,' he said, 'the Japanese have given instructions that a series of burial parties are to be sent out tomorrow, and not surprisingly the 5th Battery has been allocated the Sai Wan area. I would like you to go—I hope you don't mind.'

'Is that an order or a request, Lolly?' We both laughed. 'Of course I mind. And of course I will go although it is the last thing I want to do.'

'I feel the same,' he said. 'See you at the guard-room at 9.30 tomorrow.'

I went back to swatting flies before going off to the cookhouse to collect the evening meal. What would we find tomorrow?

At the guard-room the various burial parties were loaded into four lorries, each to cover a different sector of the Island. Our lorry set off in the direction of Lyemun, and at the gun road we were ordered to de-bus. The guard pointed in the general direction of the old fort and knocked on the cab of the lorry, which promptly disappeared up the Island Road with two or three other parties, leaving us unescorted. We were amazed.

There seemed to be no one about, but it was generally agreed that we had better go on up to the fort just in case any Japs were there who might be expecting us. There seemed little point in running the risk of arousing their anger unless it was possible to put this free time to good purpose. At that stage few gave escape a single thought although it was never far from my mind. We made our way up the gun road, and the nearer we got to the fort the more we prayed that our mission would develop into no more than a pleasant outing. It was pleasing to see that our own shelling had had considerable effect. The two principal magazines below the fort had been hit with devastating results; rubble and remnants of unexploded anti-aircraft shells littered a wide area, and while there were no bodies, we hoped that some of the enemy had been in the vicinity when it happened.

But our sudden elation soon vanished. Our party rounded the last corner of the gun road before the final approach to the fort and we came upon the first body in an advanced state of decay. We moved on silently in single file, past others which lay distorted, decomposing, until we reached the entrance to the living-quarters in which the section had been trapped.

There we stopped, each looking from one to the other, each reluctant to enter for fear of what we were almost certain to find.

At length we plucked up courage and went in. The quarters had been ransacked but there were no bodies. We hoped some of the Chinese gunners, at least, might have got away by stealing down to the small fishing village in Sai Wan Bay. We climbed the iron steps to the gun pits. There, as expected, were the bodies of the sentries.

It was a grizzly scene, but neither these nor the bodies on the road accounted for all the men, and just as we were beginning to believe that some of the Chinese had managed to get away undetected, one of the party who had moved off on his own shouted and beckoned the rest to join him. We did so and looked over the wall to where he was pointing. Below was a heap of thirteen twisted remains.

Oh God! What were we to do? A party of six with just one pick and two spades couldn't tackle the appalling task of burying so many. This galvanized us into action. It seemed to take our minds

44

off the horror which lay around us.

Having found a part of the hillside which appeared reasonably free of boulders, we marked out an area and began to dig a communal grave. We were making very poor headway when a Japanese officer appeared, as if from nowhere, with a gang of Chinese coolies. He at once took charge and to our amazement made signs that we should sit on the ground while the coolies were ordered to dig.

It was quite remarkable to us that a Japanese officer existed who was prepared to treat prisoners of war this way and even more remarkable that he should happen on our little party and treat us rather better than the gang he had with him.

However, true to type, at regular intervals he ordered us to dig while the coolies sat and watched. Each time the change was made, the coolies would get up muttering under their breath that they were road-menders not grave-diggers! We were neither, but we were prisoners.

The grave was far from complete by the time we had to leave to meet the returning transport at the junction of the gun road with Island Road. We gestured we had to leave, and our sign language was understood. We made our way down the hill, thankful to be away from Sai Wan, thankful that we had not been forced to move any corpse for we had little more than our bare hands with which to do so. It was obvious that a return visit would have to be made but at least it should then be possible to be better equipped to fulfil the gruesome task.

The other parties had had a very much better day. There had been no grave-digging. As one of the parties scoured the hills, they had found a wounded man who had managed to keep himself alive for over two weeks. He was barely conscious when they stumbled upon him in a gully. They carried him for a considerable distance to the road, and the Japanese allowed him to be taken immediately to the Military Hospital in Bowen Road, where it was thought he would survive.

When the time came for another party to be sent to Sai Wan, the worst of the job had already been done. The road, the gun pits and the terrible heap of the thirteen bodies had been cleared but there were still others—those who had started off after me—to be accounted for. Eventually they were found further down the hillside, and their remains were given the best burial possible. And yet there were two Chinese never found because, wonderful to relate, they did get away.

Chapter 7

Someone had smuggled a portable wireless set into the camp, so the triumphant progress of the enemy in Malaya and the Philippines was known to some of us, and it became increasingly obvious after little more than three weeks that the Hong Kong garrison faced years of captivity.

Now there began some talk of escape. Not much. The problems seemed enormous. It would not have been difficult to get out of the camp but there were hundreds of Japs all round the North Point area, and we knew that even if the Chinese wanted to help, they would be too frightened. And we felt we had no means of getting from the Island to the mainland without them. Little did I know that escape from our present prison was easy compared to trying to get out of Shamshuipo.

At the end of January orders were received for us to move to Shamshuipo. It had been an army camp on the edge of Kowloon. It was on the mainland. All other military prisoners had been sent there after the capitulation. It had been reported that rations there were barely enough to keep a man alive. But, I thought, just to get away from the flies would be a great relief in itself and, as I said to John Pearce whom I saw frequently, 'The Japs are being kind enough to give us a lift across the harbour, which could be a move in the right direction.'

'Yes,' said John rather dubiously. He was not fully in tune with what was passing through my mind. In any case, the order to move did not, at that moment, include him.

The very next day the various units were marched to a nearby pier and embarked on a ferry. We crossed the harbour, and all the familiar sights of Hong Kong's waterfront were there. The Peak behind it was, as usual, magnificent in the early morning sun. But instead of dominating a scene of hustle and bustle with ships moored, junks in full sail criss-crossing up and down the harbour and motorized sampans darting hither and thither, the Peak seemed to frown upon the deathly stillness and desolation spread beneath it. The ferry passed close to a number of sunken ships, and it was difficult to keep my heart from sinking with them. I thought of what our life had been only weeks ago. We passed very close to one of Jardine's ships, the *Ming Sang*, the mast of which was clear of the water, the company house flag still fluttering in the breeze. What an awful waste. She had been a good little ship. From our position in the ferry it looked certain that we were to be landed at Kowloon pier and not at a pier close to Shamshuipo itself. This meant that we probably faced a humiliating long march through the streets of Kowloon, humping our last remaining and most precious belongings. However, lorries came and, instead of humiliation, we were to be transported to Shamshuipo.

While we were dumping our kit into the lorries, I stood by for a second and I suddenly realized that this was the exact spot where we held the *walla walla* that night with Joan. Now all that was thousands of light-years away.

'*Anata!*' someone was shouting in my ear. '*Ikemasu! Ingirisu uma!*'

I didn't understand a word of it, but I got the meaning from the rifle aimed at my groin as the Japanese *gunso* let his eye flick towards the lorry. I climbed aboard.

That first night in Shamshuipo was a nightmare. I had almost everything I possessed stolen. When you have almost nothing, it is very precious. Your last remaining luxuries, a spare pair of pants, socks, a bar of chocolate and cigarettes, are better than money. It cast me into depths of despair. It was that act that sparked in me the first seeds of the need to get out.

The camp was once the headquarters of one of the infantry battalions. It consisted of a large block of flats—officers' married-quarters facing the harbour. Behind it was a parade ground larger than two football pitches. There were two other parade grounds, and even when the Japanese wired off one, there was still plenty of room to exercise. The remainder of the area was taken up by concrete huts, and there was space for everyone to lie down under cover. When all units had been brought to Shamshuipo, there were some 4,500 men in the camp.

I was fortunate in sharing a small hut with three other Volunteer NCOs, and because we were less crowded in the hut, we invited two others, whose quarters were cramped, to use ours during the day.

When we took over the hut, it was no more than a shell, three gaping holes where the windows had been ripped out and two others where doors had been. Bill Dudman, who had been quartermaster to our battery, was largely responsible for getting the hut. He was a great fixer and an even better scrounger. All of us were quickly organized to scour the camp for anything which might be useful: rusty bent nails, odd bits of tin, an old iron bed leg were all put to use or carefully preserved in case they should come in handy.

Soon we had doors and windows made from pieces of corrugated iron battered flat; unwanted exits were even 'bricked' in. A sheet of asbestos on brick piers was our table. For seats we had two bricks placed on top of each other in the shape of a T. This form of seating became the acme of discomfort as I grew thin on the rations and the bones of my behind lost their normal fleshy padding. But they were adequate.

A meal lasted a few minutes, and there were not many of them during each day.

Unlike prisoners in camps in Europe, the officers were not separated from the men. General Maltby had made this request immediately after the capitulation because it was thought that the presence of officers in the camp might help to limit ill-treatment. The Japanese granted this request initially, but after four or five months they had a change of heart. Whether our activities influenced this, we never knew. The move was made after our 'departure'. Nonetheless, a few were allowed to remain to administer what then became a camp for other ranks.

Once we had completed our settling-in process, there was precious little for the average man to do except the usual chores, and the lack of facilities made it extremely difficult for the officers to maintain morale. The day would start with a muster at 8 a.m. These parades in themselves were both mentally and physically undermining because more often than not the Japanese would deliberately delay the count an hour or more. It was a soul-destroying performance, repeated all over again in the evening. After the parade there were the huts and the camp itself to be kept clean, and it was remarkable how difficult it seemed to get everyone to realize the vital importance of this work if any of us were to survive. Precious clothes had to be washed and repaired, if you were lucky enough to have anything with which to repair them. As time went by, it was quite amusing to see the result of some people's inept handiwork.

The Japanese demanded working parties most days, but with so many men in the camp there was generally no need to go. I did go once. I thought that we were to be sent to clear the road leading from the town over the Kowloon Hills into the New Territories. I thought it might be possible to glean some information about an escape route, but it proved a waste of time. We were sent to Kaitak airfield.

The language and other classes which had been started in North Point were continued but were hampered by an almost total lack of paper. After some weeks a few books were smuggled in by both Portuguese and Chinese women who had men in the camp. But it was almost impossible to get any of them. Some games equipment also came in. This was welcomed initially but it was soon realized that, if games were encouraged, those who played them would soon be barefoot.

A good deal later a piano was brought into Shamshuipo for church services by the padres, and a few enterprising people put it to other use by arranging musical evenings. These were well attended and gave us all a lift.

The Japanese war mentality was never conditioned to think we might try to escape. We were beneath anything living in their contemptuous thinking. We should never have allowed ourselves to be captured. We knew very well what to expect if caught escaping. We had seen their treatment of 'unruly' prisoners. Yet nothing better than a slow starvation diet, a living death, could be expected. Also any prisoner at any time could be subjected to humiliation and degradation for no apparent reason. Because of this attitude, most prisoners gave the guards the widest possible berth at all times. Sometimes that was impossible, in which case it was sensible to sink one's pride and bow as was regulation and law and also a precaution against a rifle butt in the teeth or being kicked in the groin.

The morale in the camp was low. The discipline of some units was poor, and all too often a dog-eat-dog attitude prevailed.

The Japanese officer commanding the camp, Lieutenant Wada, was a typical Japanese military 'climber'. He was the little 'yes' man of the commander of all the Hong Kong POW camps, Colonel Tokunaga. This 'gentleman' was thickset, fat and larger than some Japs. His favourite hobby was to stand his own men on parade and have a *gunso* (sergeant) step forward and cut off one man's head as an example. The atrocities he committed have all been documented. He was a ruthless butcher who ironically was even duped by his own mistress. He lived with a Chinese who was a fifth-column girl, and she sent parcels of food from Tokunaga's table into the POW camps. After the war Tokunaga was sentenced to death for his butchery.

Shamshuipo Camp at the time I was there was actually run by a Japanese *gunso* whom we nicknamed George. George was fully six feet tall, probably from Hokkaido. He delighted in making free play with his regulation-issue short sword, slashing anything in sight. But he was not a bad man. There was one real stinker. He was known as 'Slap Happy' and was born in Kamloops, British Columbia. His real name was Kinawa Inouye and he spoke with a strong BC accent.

From a military point of view, George ran the camp. To reel off a list of the horrors under these men would be to drive the nail home too hard. It is enough to say that conditions were considered many times worse than those suffered in most European POW camps. They were on a par with some Nazi concentration camps.

When all the military units were inside Shamshuipo, many of my friends were brought together for the first time since the fall of Hong Kong. I remember when, for instance, Remedios da Silva, who had been chief clerk in Jardine's Accounts Department, and with whom I'd worked closely, came up to me.

'Mr B., I am pleased to see you. I have only just found out that you are in camp.'

'Good to see you too, Silva. How is Victor Nunes?'

'Oh, he's fine really. We all are. Our wives are sending us food parcels. That's why I came looking for you. You must be famished. Come and have something to eat.'

In spite of my protestations, I was made to follow him.

'Don't be stupid,' he said, forcing a piece of pie into my hand. 'You have no one outside to help you.'

In his hut I met again all the members of Jardine's Portuguese staff who had served with the Volunteers and been taken prisoner. Among them was Victor Nunes.

'My God,' he said as he shook me warmly by the hand. 'We thought you had been killed at Sai Wan.'

Victor Nunes and his wife, who was still free in Hong Kong, being a neutral Portuguese subject, were to be of great help later. I could rely on them both completely. As it happened, I'd been able to help them before the war.

I had been in Shamshuipo only two days when I heard that all the remaining units which had been left in North Point had just arrived. This was good news for it meant that John Pearce and I were once again behind the same barbed wire.

Now that all the units were concentrated in Shamshuipo, many friends were reunited for the first time since the Japanese attack. This was so as far as Douglas Clague, John and myself were concerned. Neither John nor I had seen Duggie since the surrender, and if we all had to be prisoners, the fact that we were all together did something to lift the depression of those early days.

On the eastern side of the camp only the width of a street separated the first row of Chinese tenement houses from the perimeter fence, and it was here that the wives and girlfriends came in the hope of catching a glimpse of, or even exchanging a shouted word with, the local men in the camp. It was surprising to me how many women came. The Hong Kong Volunteer Defence Corps was made up of Chinese, Portuguese and Eurasians as well as British. Added to this, many of our troops had their own Chinese girl-friends, and it was wonderful how loyal some of these girls proved to be. After all, there was no need for them to run the risk of being beaten up by a Japanese for a boyfriend who was no longer able to be with them. Food and money were very short outside. The trouble was that not all these men were worthy of such attention. Some even complained that their girlfriends had not brought what they wanted.

Sometimes the Japanese would allow no communication and would drive the women away for no apparent reason. The prison guards patrolled the whole road, and it was always impossible to tell how they would react. Once I saw the same guard walk over to the place where the women waited, slap some in the face with a leather belt and the next minute pick up a small child, carry him across the road, walk up and down the wire until he found the father, and allow the father and child to talk to each other for quite some time. Then tenderly he led the child back to the mother.

At other times, when the guards were being particularly bloody-minded, we would create a diversion so that someone could dash across the road to the wire, make brief contact, dash back again as quickly as possible and disappear up one of the alleyways between the Chinese tenement houses which bordered the camp.

In this way Victor Nunes got my shoes out of the camp to his wife, who had them repaired. The shoes were vital to my future plans. Victor threw them over the wire into the middle of the road and let them lie there while the guards' attention was distracted. The shoes were safely picked up. Some three weeks later Victor Nunes received them back in a parcel, carefully repaired.

In Shamshuipo food was a regular topic of conversation. Those who complained at the continued appearance in the North Point camp of bully beef hash and dry army biscuits were soon longing for such delicacies. Day after day we had nothing to eat but rice. A bowl in the morning and another at night. Occasionally a few sacks containing some kind of green vegetable were delivered with the rice, from which the cooks brewed some sort of soup. At odd intervals we received a few spoonfuls of soya beans or dates but such luxuries were very rare. This diet was barely enough to keep body and soul together but we ate it and prayed it would do just that.

As day after monotonous day passed, the diet made us weaker and weaker. The morale, never good, made it difficult to get some to realize that to keep themselves clean was essential to survival. The stuffing had gone out of them. On top of this the possibility of torture was always round the corner.

I was told that one of the Jap sergeants had taken one prisoner who had refused to bow properly and had him hung by his feet for several hours. I didn't see this myself.

However, for Duggie, John and me this was not a prime worry. We became more and more concerned that because of the lack of food we might not be able to survive long imprisonment in the camp. We felt we had to get out.

The first problem—so we thought originally—was not how to get out of the camp but what we faced as soon as we were out. How far would we have to travel into China before we could be reasonably sure of being clear of the Japs? What would the reaction of the Chinese be? Would they help? Would they feed us? Or would they turn us in for the inevitable reward which would be offered for our capture?

Chungking on the upper reaches of the Yangtse was the wartime capital of China, and our own people would be there. But Chungking was nearly a thousand miles north-west, and the task of getting there looked overwhelming unless we could be sure of some help as soon as we crossed the border into China proper.

If we could contact Chinese forces, we might have a chance. On the other hand, the longer we waited the less capable we were likely to be of completing an attempt. Also none of us spoke Chinese. As a child, John had had a Chinese *amah* but he had forgotten all his Cantonese dialect, he said. So we put him on a refresher course. I had already asked George Chow, a Canadian Chinese who had been with me in the 5th Ack-Ack, to come but he told us he wanted to go alone, because he had a fiancée in Kowloon. He planned to take her to neighbouring Macao, which was still under the Portuguese flag, and from there to slip into China.

That being the case, I asked him when he got out if he would contact Jardine's *compradore*, a charming man called Henry Lo. (A *compradore* was a senior Chinese manager.) I knew Henry would have to be completely assured that any approach from George Chow was genuine. It would be madness for him to run the risk of dealing with someone who could turn out to be in league with the enemy. So I initialled the inside of George's trousers as a sign that he came from the camp. Henry had seen my initials so often that I knew he wouldn't fail to recognize them.

At the time the idea seemed a good one, because if Henry could be persuaded to come to Shamshuipo, there might be a chance of a shouted word across the street when the sentries were otherwise occupied, or at least some information about outside conditions, and the attitude of the Chinese towards us, might be passed by pre-arranged signals, so a whole series of them were devised.

On the day George Chow 'left us', it all worked so easily that watching it made us very envious. There were a lot of visitors on the other side of the street. George came to the fence with a few of his friends. He wore a singlet and a pair of khaki shorts, which was very common garb for any Chinese. Then a diversion was staged. When the two patrolling sentries were furthest apart, George slipped under the wire, which had already been loosened. He dashed across the street and disappeared before our eyes in between the tenement houses. He was then a 'harmless' civilian.

Each day John and I took a turn at that particular part of the fence, looking for Henry to appear with some signal.

Meanwhile, security was tightening at the camp. The Japanese began to watch all the possible exit points which we were planning to use. Some they closed off. Many more sentries were posted in the camp. Patrols were more frequent. Lights were erected at seventy yard intervals, and besides these, the perimeter fence carried electrified wire.

As these developments grew, we began to wonder if we should wait for any possible outside information. If we could not get out, the information would be useless.

Almost three weeks after George got away, Henry Lo appeared. It was a thrill to see him but he signalled that he could do nothing. He made it obvious that he was too carefully watched but he had delivered a parcel to the guard-house. When we got it, there was food and a knitted sweater in it. It was a blow but the parcel was most welcome and of real value to our plans. Later we understood what a grave risk Henry had taken in coming all the way from his home on the Island under the eyes of the Japanese.

Chapter 8

Shamshuipo Barracks had been built on land reclaimed from the harbour. The town of Kowloon was immediately to the east. To the north beyond the perimeter fence lay a strip of ground some sixty yards wide which was used as vegetable gardens, and beyond these the fringe of Kowloon ran westwards on either side of the main coast road to the New Territories via Lai Chi Kok. At the north-west end of the strip of land a small retaining wall ran back to the perimeter fence to protect the land against the sea which lapped against half of its length at high tide. The Japanese used the last house on the seaward side of the main coast road as living-quarters for the guards. The bay itself was a large junk-anchorage. In bad weather it could be full of sea-going junks using it as a typhoon shelter. But usually there would be no more than fifty or sixty which would run in during the evening to drop anchor close to the very muddy beach. The beach was close to the coast road, built on a small embankment.

Therefore, from the north-west to the south-west corner of the camp, the perimeter wire ran along the top of a retaining wall which faced Lai Chi Kok across the bay, while the last side of the camp faced the harbour proper with the island of Hong Kong itself some three miles away at this point.

At one stage the north-west corner seemed the most promising spot from which to make a break. There was a deep open culvert which took storm water into the sea at a point where it was possible to get onto the beach. The sea wall of the vegetable garden could be our cover to reach the road embankment. It would be risky to try to cross the road so near to the house occupied by the Japanese, so we studied their movements most carefully. The sentries off duty lazed about in front of it. Any movement or anyone approaching came from the Kowloon side and *not* Lai Chi Kok.

We began to make definite plans to use this culvert only a day or two before Henry Lo gave us the 'no go' signal. However, the Japanese suddenly installed a light which shone directly down the culvert and increased the sentry coverage of that particular area. This was not only a blow, it was suspicious. Was anyone tipping

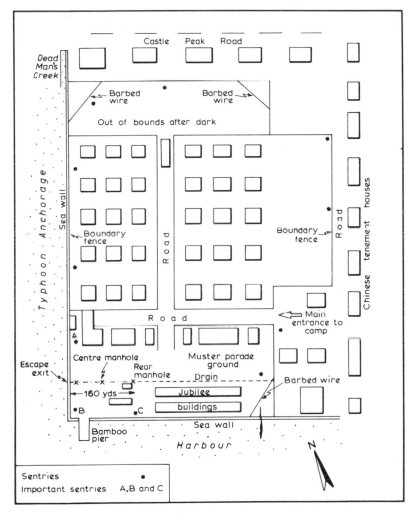

Sketch of Shamshuipo Camp (not to scale), showing the typhoon drain and the manholes used in the escape underground to the waters of the typhoon anchorage

them off? Now the only possible way—so we thought—was into the sea. Either from the south into the harbour with a long swim round and across the mouth of the typhoon anchorage to Lai Chi Kok, or alternatively into the bay itself, with the object of landing on a section of the beach where there were not too many juunks and where we could cross the coast road and start our climb to the top of the Kowloon Hills.

So we switched our attention to the sea wall and were even more determined to go. In fact the tension and excitement of the planning had become a sort of mania to me, and I could think of little else. Always at the back of my mind I wondered whether all the new preventative measures meant the Japanese were becoming more alive to the possibility of escapes.

Day after day we exercised up and down the south and west sides of the camp, looking for any weakness. Each evening we meticulously studied and noted the movements of the sentries. We all knew that the classic way of escape was to tunnel under the wire, but even if we had anything with which to dig, we also knew that the end of any such tunnel must hit the sea wall and we had no means to break through a couple of feet of solid stone. But the more we thought about it and the more we observed the sentries, it seemed the only thing to do.

'Surely someone must have some tools,' said John. 'Let's make some careful enquiries at different cookhouses; that's the most likely place to find them.' He was quite right.

There was a disused, partly destroyed building only fifteen feet from the retaining wall. It was next door to the so-called hospital, which was actually a long hut where the sick were put so that they wouldn't die in their own quarters.

The thought of digging from there began to excite us. We would be working almost under the nose of one of the sentries. But the disposal of earth from the tunnel could easily be disguised among the heaps of rubble which cluttered the area.

However, before going ahead with this plan it was proper procedure for Duggie to tell his Commanding Officer. We thought we'd let him decide if General Maltby should be told. The CO's immediate reaction was most favourable, and the three of us went to bed feeling we were almost on our way.

Little did we know of the problems attached to digging a tunnel, even one no more than fifteen to twenty feet long. However, it was not those problems which were immediately to confront us. Next day Duggie burst into my hut.

56

'David, come and take some exercise.'

I was rather surprised at the urgency in his voice. Outside the hut he said, 'We've been forbidden to go ahead with our plan. The CO has just told me that the disused hut is in the area which Maltby has designated as a hospital. We would be breaking the Hague Convention if we were to escape from it. Reprisals would be certain. And, what is more, if we go on with the scheme, the General says steps will be taken to see that we are unable to complete the tunnel.'

'My God!' I said. 'Since when have the little bastards paid attention to any convention but their own? Don't tell me that it will make the slightest difference where we get out. If there are to be reprisals, there will be reprisals.'

'I know,' said Duggie, 'but what's the use? If that is the attitude, we've just got to make quite certain that it remains a closely guarded secret from all the top brass.'

'OK, Duggie,' I said. 'Where's John?' We went off to find him and to continue our search for an alternative exit point.

'Duggie,' I said, 'I'm even more determined. This makes no difference.'

'I agree,' he replied. 'But it's a bloody nuisance having to contend with our chaps as well as with the Japs.'

That afternoon I was sitting outside our hut rather dejectedly thinking what the hell we were going to do when I saw J. J. Paterson coming in my direction. The old man was continually round the camp encouraging all Jardine staff members who were prisoners like himself. He had been CO of the old gentlemen's brigade—the Home Guard of Hong Kong—which had had a very unpleasant time trying to defend the power station on the Island. J.J. had had a miraculous escape there which he delighted in recounting on every possible occasion.

As I got up to greet him, he said, 'Come on, David, let's walk round the camp.' We had not gone very far when he said, 'I hear that you are thinking about an escape.'

'Yes, sir. How the hell did you find out?'

'Very simple,' said J.J. with a broad grin. 'I mess with the General, and I was there when the Gunner Colonel came to report that Clague, Pearce and Bosanquet were thinking of digging a tunnel. Rather naturally I pricked up my ears when I heard your name and thought I ought to come and find out a little more about it, especially when the General wanted to know who this Sergeant Bosanquet might be.'

'Well,' I said, 'there is little to tell since the General has put a real damper on the whole scheme. Quite frankly, sir, the three of us take a very dim view. If we are prepared to take the risk of some very unpleasant consequences if we fail, I would have thought it was not up to our own people to put a spoke in our wheel.'

He laughed and said, 'Don't forget he has the responsibility of trying to bring every man through what could be a long, difficult and painful period of internment. Rather naturally, he is desperately worried about reprisals.'

'I understand that, but . . .'

'But what?' J.J. interjected.

'But all POWs should try to escape if they think they have got a chance.'

'And do you really think you have a chance? You've got a helluva long way to go once you get out.'

'The three of us are prepared to take that risk providing we find the means of getting out,' I said.

He stopped walking and looked directly at me. 'Good for you,' he said. 'If I was ten years younger, I would bloody well ask to come with you. Instead I will help you in any way I can.'

'Thank you, sir. I shall take you at your word and let you know what develops.'

By this time we were outside the senior officers' quarters and he left me. I dashed off to the opposite end of the block of flats where I knew I would find the others, to tell them of the conversation. If it was going to be necessary to fight our own authorities for some kind of recognition of our escape, we could have no better ally than J.J., since the only reason that he was invited to mess with the General was the respect in which he had been held by all sections of the Hong Kong community before the war.

Nothing much happened during the next few days. We did the usual chores of that depressing existence. Each morning and evening we had muster parades at which the Japanese usually kept us all standing for several hours. These parades had become less punishing to me mentally. I geared my mind only to see the Kowloon Hills to the north and I figured, schemed and imagined which way we'd get over them to freedom.

From the Lai Chi Kok anchorage, where we hoped to land one day, the ground started to rise almost immediately after the coast road, and standing on the parade ground I would imagine picking my way up the lower levels among the terraced vegetable plots to the scrub on the rocky outcrop below the cuttings in the hillside, which had been made for the road leading from Kowloon directly to the border with China. Above the road, the ground rose more steeply. The same scrub persisted. With the naked eye no path of any kind was visible. It was going to be a very testing climb after a long swim and weeks of very little food. Nonetheless, the anticipation of being on the top of those hills was something I'd savoured ever since becoming a prisoner. Yet, for it to become a reality, we had first to get out.

Then our luck changed. Quite by chance, Duggie happened to be walking on a waste piece of land which lay between the western end of the main parade ground and the southern sea wall. As he mooched about on it for no particular reason, he spotted a manhole cover, which none of us had seen before. John and I were immediately summoned because quite obviously it was a drain of some importance. It was partially covered by weeds! It had to be examined. To do so could be a real problem because it was in full view of at least two sentries and anyone who happened to be on the parade ground. There was no cover of any sort for a hundred yards in every direction.

Which way did the drain under it run, east to west or north to south? It could be either. There were no seemingly obvious corresponding manhole covers on the parade ground but, since all the open culverts ran east to west, we started to walk on a likely line towards the officers' quarters, and sure enough we found another beside the gunner officers' cookhouse. Assuming that the two were connected, the drain would discharge into the typhoon anchorage.

'Pray God it's not a sewer,' said Duggie.

'Pray God that it is big enough to take a man,' I said.

We could hardly wait to find out, but we had to do it without arousing any suspicion in what we were doing. If we could find out without the sentries noticing, we'd have made a great start.

Our activities would attract far less attention from sentries or fellow prisoners in broad daylight than attempting to find out when it was dark. We started that way. The manhole was so close to the cookhouse that the sentry at the south-west corner of the officers' quarters was no more than thirty yards away. 'If he happens to notice us, we'll make him think that we were dealing with a blocked drain,' said John with a grin.

'David, have you still got the boiler suit that you used to wear on the gun sites?' asked Duggie.

'Yes.'

'Good! Please go and put it on, and I will have the cover loosened by the time you get back. It looks as if it hasn't been lifted for years and may take a bit of shifting. These damn things are quite heavy.'

I went off and was back in ten minutes to find that they had eased the iron cover and were armed with two window hooks with which they were able to lift it. There was no one in the cookhouse and, having chosen the moment when the sentry moved out of sight behind the building, they whipped off the cover and I was down through the opening and out of sight underground in a second. Above I could see a circle of light from where the cover had been. It was about two feet across. I found myself in a surprisingly large inspection chamber with a built-up section on each side of the half drain through which a trickle of water was running. Thank God it was only water! However, there was a far, far greater reason to thank Him because the large drain led away towards the sea. It couldn't be better. I could see daylight at the end of it which seemed miles away. A clear hole indicated that the drain was the same diameter all the way to the sea wall. Lying flat on my stomach, I worked my shoulders into the drain and dragged my body along it by pulling on my elbows and drawing up one leg at a time. I moved along for a few yards just to test if it could actually be done and then backed into the inspection chamber. Crouching so my head remained below ground level, I whispered, 'Duggie, can I come up?'

'Hold it.' A few moments later, 'Now!'

I stood straight and my head and shoulders were above ground—I got my arms through the manhole and began to lever myself out, when I was caught by the scruff of the neck and pulled clear.

'Get into the officers' quarters in Jubilee Buildings. Quick! John, go with David.' We did not question this command. I was breathless as we left. John said, 'Come on, David, what's the verdict?'

'Let's wait for Duggie,' I said. But he knew by my tone that a possible way out had been found.

As soon as Duggie appeared, I related in detail what I had done and seen. It would be an arduous drag, but nothing could subdue our exuberance. It was almost too good to be true. Planning could start in earnest. We went out to look at the manhole cover again. No-one could see that it had been tampered with because Duggie had replaced the weeds that grew around it. We were ecstatic.

Within days of our discovery I had a talk with J.J. I told him that we had found a way of getting out and even though I was bursting to tell him every detail, I stifled the urge. At that stage the drain had to be an absolute secret to the three of us. J.J. never asked. Instead we talked about possible outside routes, and the likely reaction of the

Chinese when they saw us, as indeed they were bound to do at some stage. I then broached the subject of receiving official recognition of the escape, for it was something which we badly wanted. He promised to see what could be done but the particular moment was not propitious since the General had been working hard on the Japanese to get an improvement in our rations; in fact he had heard that Colonel Tokunaga was likely to visit the camp at any time, and he knew what the General's reaction would be if the word 'escape' was so much as mentioned.

Sure enough Tokunaga did come. His visit had nothing at all to do with food. We spent three hours waiting for him, and he ordered a harangue to be delivered to all units in his presence about escaping. For one ugly moment I thought everyone was to be asked for their parole not to escape, and I knew full well that all those around me would give it rather than irritate the Japanese. What to do? Refuse then and there or withdraw one's parole later? In either case, it would draw attention to myself, which was the last thing we wanted. I wondered what the others had done. The Volunteers were the last in line and got the full benefit of every inaccuracy and embellishment as the word was passed from unit to unit. Fortunately my fears were unfounded and a little two-by-four Japanese read the proclamation, which ran:

'You are forbidden by the Japanese authorities to escape. You may be shot in the act of escaping. If you are recaptured, you will be tried by Japanese military law. Reprisals may be taken against your comrades.'

This told us nothing which we did not know already. The Japanese then took further precautions to strengthen the perimeter wire, which we were able to watch with a high degree of smug satisfaction. Thank God they never thought of taking a look at the camp from a boat! But in my mind was still a nagging fear. Did they know? Even if they did, we were going to have a go.

I suppose, to some extent, it strengthened the hand of those set on discouraging any attempts, but generally speaking, the attitude among the prisoners was one of complete resignation. There seemed to be no one in the whole of Shamshuipo with the initiative or the will to escape. Reprisals, reprisals, reprisals, that was the big stumbling-block, the psychological gimmick used by the guards. Yet few seemed able to ask themselves: will I even survive the camp? Is it not better to try to get out than to die here? The tacit attitude may have been sad although it was probably to our advantage. There was nothing to keep the sentries on the alert, and in consequence it made it very much easier for us to do all sorts of things under their very noses. Only when someone went too close to the perimeter wire were they aroused.

We used this method to move them along their beat when they happened to be standing in an inconvenient spot. We first did it the evening after we found the drain because one sentry stood almost permanently at the south-west corner of the officers' building and, besides being within thirty yards of the manhole by the cookhouse, he was almost on top of the entrance to John and Duggie's quarters. It was vital that many of our comings and goings should not be seen, especially when our planning was to reach its final stage.

Now our planning revolved around one main point—how long it might take us to drag ourselves plus a pack from the manhole to the sea wall. Duggie said, 'I will pop down and drag myself along part of the way to see just how difficult it is to make progress.' We all agreed that it was a good idea, but sure enough there was the sentry leaning against the wall. We all walked past and stopped around the other corner of the building.

'John, go round the side of the cookhouse, stay fairly close to the wire and look out into the harbour. See if he moves towards you and is hidden from us. David and I will manage the manhole. Try and keep him on your side of the cookhouse for as long as you can,' said Duggie.

John disappeared and in no time the sentry had moved. We whipped off the cover, and down went Duggie while I leant against the corner of the building, as if nothing was happening. After two or three minutes I peered into the manhole. There was no sign of Duggie. Again I did so but still no sign and I wondered what John was doing and how he would let me know when the sentry started to move back to his old position.

There was still no sign of either of them when suddenly Duggie's head appeared.

'OK?' he called, and just as I was about to say yes, round the corner came the sentry.

'Stay for God's sake,' I almost shouted. He stayed and the sentry obligingly moved on out of sight behind Jubilee Buildings.

'Out, Duggie, now,' I called, but there was no movement. I called again. Still he did not appear. I knelt down and put my head immediately above the manhole and told him to come out. This time he came out and the cover was back in place in a flash.

When we were safely away, I said to Duggie, 'What the hell were you doing? You stayed when I told you to but I called twice for you to come out before I put my head almost into the manhole.'

'Didn't hear a thing. Once you are below the rim, you can't, you know.' Of course, we did not know that but we realized how important it was that we had found out at this early stage.

'How did you get on?'' said John.

'It is quite hard going. I found the best way was to lie flat and pull myself along moving both elbows together.'

'It looks as though it was a bit damp in there,' said John, looking at Duggie's soaking front.

'Yep. That's why I didn't stay down longer. The water seemed to be building up behind me. I let some of it go by pressing myself against the top of the drain and then backed into the inspection chamber. Going backwards isn't all that funny, I can tell you. The rough concrete of the drain is damn hard. We will have to pad our knees and elbows somehow.'

We then asked how far along the drain he reckoned that he had been and whether he had been able to calculate the time. He just couldn't tell. We might have missed out on this aspect of the exercise but we had learnt a lot, of which perhaps the most important was that one could not hear what was going on above ground once one was in the inspection chamber. We were also concerned with the near miss of the sentry appearing and John being unable to warn me of his movements. While it gave us a good deal of satisfaction being able to get in and out of the drain with a sentry so near, a single slip could spell disaster, and that had to be avoided at all costs. After a long debate we decided that, since we would have to enlist the help of a number of friends for the actual night, there could be good purpose in approaching one of them immediately. The question was, who should it be?

John's brother, Alec Pearce, was also a Gunner subaltern in the camp and, of course, knew of our intentions. We had asked him to join us originally, but he had been so lukewarm to the whole idea that we never broached the subject again. For that reason we thought of others to give us an immediate hand. A fellow officer called Lynton White was proposed. I hardly knew him although he had arrived in Hong Kong at the same time as Duggie. Perhaps it was that he had other pastimes than games. He was a quiet, rather retiring person, but as soon as the others suggested him, I was delighted and he readily agreed.

Although we now knew quite conclusively that we had a ready-made tunnel, there were some tough problems which had to be resolved before we made an attempt. We had to get our haversacks to the end of the drain. We could not put them on our backs, for the drain was not big enough. In any case not one of us thought we could swim any distance weighed down by their weight. As it was, John was a very moderate swimmer under ideal conditions—fifty yards in a pool was about his mark—and ever since it had become certain that he would have to swim, the prospect had caused him considerable alarm.

As he said, 'There doesn't seem much sense in getting out only to drown because I can't make it. And I can hardly expect either of you to perform a life-saving act under such circumstances.' We told him that he need have no worries because he would have two army water-bottles strapped to his chest. He would find that, once the felt covering had been removed, the air in them would act like water-wings and in any case we would require no more than a slow dog-paddle from him. He was not entirely convinced and nor were we, but we were not going to leave him behind. His guts would pull him through, so that problem was ticked off the list! But what to do about our packs? We tried wrapping them very carefully in gas capes and putting them in a bath to see how long they would float. The best time achieved was forty minutes. That might give us time enough to get ashore, but much depended on how far out into the bay we might have to go before striking for the beach; in any case, everything inside would be soaked in that time. Apart from that, however, there was still the little matter of getting them through the drain intact. To drag them behind us on a rough concrete surface would rip the gas cape to pieces in less than twenty yards, and the drain was all of 160 yards long from the first manhole.

We racked our brains but could find no solution until Duggie finally made the suggestion of using his valise. The packs could be waterproofed, put in line on the valise and the straps pulled over the top to make the whole contraption secure. That seemed to solve the problem of transporting them down the drain but we were anything but happy about the sea-crossing.

'We have to be able to float them on something,' John said. 'Pity no one has an inner tube which could be made into a raft!'

'I've got a much better idea,' said Duggie. 'Thanks for putting it into my head. I happen to know someone who is sleeping on a lilo. He's a good friend of mine, and I believe that I can persuade him to part with it.'

'He must be a bloody good friend,' I said, to which Duggie retorted, 'It will be at a price, and between us we will leave behind quite a lot of clothes which will be at a premium all too soon—I won't ask him just yet but wait until we know when we are going.'

'It had better be soon,' I said, 'or we will be driven out by sheer starvation. It is all very well being told that the General has been working on the Japanese to raise our diet above pig food but if nothing happens, we'll have no energy to escape. And speaking of pigs, doesn't Tokunaga remind you of a Middle White—that fat breed of English pigs?'

Someone laughed and said, 'I know exactly what you mean.'

I quickly added, 'On second thoughts, perhaps I owe an apology to that distinguished breed. They are far too kindly to be bracketed with Tokunaga.'

It was almost as if, talking of the devil, he had heard us, for shortly afterwards we were told on muster parade in the morning that we were to receive another visit. Since he had come but a comparatively short time ago, we wondered whether it was just another ruse on the part of our guards to get us on extra parade in the middle of the day, leave us standing for hours and then to dismiss the parade without anyone appearing. Further humiliation techniques, we thought, but whatever lay behind it, extra parades were dreaded and men went down like ninepins if it was hot.

On this particular occasion the parade was called at one o'clock but it was not until 4.30 that Tokunaga arrived. When the parade was called to attention and he began his inspection accompanied by our senior officer, every unit had men falling flat on their faces from sheer exhaustion due to lack of food.

We heard afterwards that Tokunaga was furious and told the General through his interpreter that it was an insult to His Imperial Japanese Majesty, whom he was representing. It was a put-up job and he demanded an explanation. We gather that he was given an explanation there and then by the General and told in so many words that, if men were expected to stand for hours on end through the middle of the day, they should be fed, not starved.

Rather naturally this incident caused an air of expectancy which culminated in a real stir some three days later.

'There is meat in the camp,' came the rumour. This reaction was very understandable because there had been so many rumours for so long, but in this case it was no rumour: there was meat in the camp.

Even though the ration per head worked out at no more than an ounce and a half including bone, real excitement built up as the time approached to draw the evening ration, and this was hardly surprising since the very great majority had had no means whatsoever of supplementing their bowl of rice.

Because this first meat ration was so small, and because every man could not be guaranteed an actual piece of meat, the Volunteers elected to chop up the whole of their allocation and put everything into one large cauldron to make a meat soup. I was fortunate, for in my bowl I found a piece of fat the size of my thumb nail. Anything but a hungry animal would have turned its nose up at this brew. We did not, but we were hungry animals, very hungry animals.

Meanwhile, we were making progress in our preparations, all done in the officers' quarters in Jubilee Buildings. It was eventually impossible to keep our activities entirely secret. The others took little notice and never objected to the almost constant sight of me, a mere sergeant, in their quarters. It was necessary to do a great deal of packing and unpacking—to plan meticulously so every cubic inch of space was used. Yet the valise still had to go through the manhole easily.

We had accumulated a dozen tins of food by barter. We lacked a compass though. But luckily for us the Japanese expected such absolute obedience that they double-crossed themselves. They issued instructions that all torches, electrical equipment, compasses and cameras were to be handed in to the guard-room by noon on Monday. The camp was officially administered by our own officers under Japanese orders, and the instructions went out that everything was to be taken first to the adjutant's office. It has never ceased to amaze me how much equipment poured in. It underlined the dreadful defeatist attitude of a lot of the men. In any case, Duggie knew the adjutant and we had our pick before the Japanese! We got our compass.

Then we nearly blew our whole operation through carelessness. All this packing and unpacking became excruciatingly tedious, and one evening when we had been at it for hours I was still in Jubilee Buildings at 'lights out'. The sleeping-bag was still stuffed.

It had by now taken on a distinct personality. It looked like a rather well-fed, fat Egyptian mummy. We had come to call it the 'the body'. We were all very tired and we decided to break our golden rule of unpacking and hiding our precious belongings. That night I borrowed one of John's blankets and ended up with the 'body' on the floor. There was plenty of time in the morning to unpack the 'body', to disperse our valuables and for me to get back to my hut before muster parade. The floor beside John's bed was just as comfortable as anything on which I had slept for the past two months. By 2 a.m. I was sound asleep.

Quite suddenly the door burst open, and there were four Japanese in our room. It took me some time to realize where I was and what was happening. God, everything is in the 'body' and I am lying on it! It was not that I was really afraid. It was worse. It was a mixture of utter despair and anger that we should have allowed ourselves to be in such a position. There was nothing to do but lie sprawled out as much over the 'body' as possible and hope I could remain looking dazed with sleep. Never had I prayed so hard.

It was not a large room. There was John, Alec and two others all in beds, and the 'body' and I taking up much of the remaining floor space. I saw one of the Japanese pick up the torch beside Alec's bed. Another tripped over me. I grunted and a second later he was trying to prise open the end of the 'body'. The game seemed up. I could only mutter 'Tin food. Tin food.' As though he understood, he stopped searching! He kicked the end of the 'body' and found it hard. He hesitated, picked up the torch by John's bed, kicked the end of the 'body' again and made for the door. His hand twisted on the knob. Then he quickly left. He was followed by the others.

I could hear them in the next room and the room after that. Would they come back? The strain was appalling. After what seemed ages, I felt I could stand it no longer, but I daren't move. Suddenly one of them came back and started to prod the 'body' again. I lay doggo.

Duggie was in the next room and he had to suffer the agony of listening to the noise next door. We never knew how the Japanese could have missed the 'body'. A German would certainly have spotted it as escape equipment, especially when it was being hugged by someone who was not supposed even to have been in the room. I put our luck down to the one-track mind of the Japanese private.

As we talked about this later, Duggie, John and I felt that their missing the 'body' was a wonderful omen and a typical example of the contrast in the Japanese military mind which seemed to vacillate from clockwork efficiency to total blind, unthinking duty.

It was now the middle of March. We calculated that the moon and the tide would be favourable on the 20th. We planned to leave that night. J.J. had been unable to give me any more information about an escape as seen from the senior officer' mess, except that it was still very much frowned upon. Despite this we felt we must make an attempt to get official recognition before leaving, and again Duggie went off to see his CO. As a result he was instructed to have us all in his quarters at four o'clock that afternoon so that Colonel

Newnham could speak to us. The Colonel was still Maltby's chief staff officer. As he came into the room, he took on a formal military attitude. He began by giving us the official reasons why we should make no attempt. It was galling to listen to him. Newnham's reasons were: 1) There was no useful information which we could convey to the outside world at that particular time. 2) The escape of three young men, even if it were successful, would make little or no contribution to the war effort while it might undermine all the General's efforts to improve the condition under which the whole Hong Kong garrison now found itself. 3) Every able-bodied man would be required when release came. In short, we were acting irresponsibly and without consideration.

'If we think we can do so, is it not a duty to escape, sir?' Duggie asked.

'In most cases the answer must be yes,' said Colonel Newnham, 'but there are other cases when it may not be so, and the General considers that the present is a special situation. Anyway, you haven't told me how you plan to get out?'

'We are keeping that a very closely guarded secret, sir,' said Duggie, 'but we believe it to be as foolproof as any means could be.'

'All right, let's suppose that you do get out,' said the Colonel, relaxing his formal tone quite markedly. 'How well do you know the country even as far as the border? Which way do you intend to go? Have you any idea of the likely Japanese dispositions? How and when do you intend to contact the Chinese? Do any of you speak the language? And what are you going to do for food?'

Duggie took a deep breath. 'None of us has an intimate knowledge of the country between here and the border. We spent most of our time playing games instead of walking over the New Territories. But we are not total strangers. Now, because we will not be covered at the muster parade next morning, we have to pick another route. Our original plan was that, if we'd had two, perhaps three days' start, we could have got across the border in that time. Now that we are down to ten hours, we have been forced to take a more complex route likely to be free of Japs.'

'I suppose you mean east of Tolo Harbour,' said Colonel Newnham.

We could hardly believe our ears. Could he be getting interested?

'Yes,' said Duggie.

'Then avoid Sai Kung. If the Japs are not actually there, you could run into a pocket of Wang Ching Wei's supporters,' he said, mentioning that they were Chinese traitors who fought for the Japs.

68

'Thank you, sir,' we all said in chorus.

Then Duggie went on, 'We think we can last on very reduced rations for fourteen days without contacting anyone. If we aren't a long way farther than Sai Kung by that time, we will be in real trouble.'

There was another pause, quite a long one, while we watched Newnham's face.

'Have you got a map?' he asked.

'Well,' said Duggie, 'we were able to make quite a detailed tracing of the area to the west of Tolo Harbour from a map which one of Colonel Ride's party brought into Shamshuipo in the very early days, but we only have the eastern part of the New Territories in outline. That area is a bit of a problem.'

By this time Colonel Newnham was sitting on the edge of one of the beds and we followed suit. Suddenly he got up and said, 'What am I to tell the General?'

Duggie continued to be spokesman: 'Please tell the General, sir, that we have listened to the argument against an escape but we're still determined to go.'

We then indicated that we were sorry if it did bring reprisals but could not believe that they would be severe because only junior ranks were involved. Surely the Japanese were likely to take the same attitude as the General and consider that three of us at large were of minimal importance, warranting only token reprisals. In fact, there might even be none at all. The Japanese, to save 'face', might simply announce that we had been shot evading capture and that would be the end of it.

The Colonel got up and as he reached the door he turned, undid the top button of his battledress, pulled out a carefully folded piece of paper and said, 'There is a map. I will be back in twenty minutes to collect it.'

Even after the door had closed behind Colonel Newnham, we continued to stare at the folded map. This action was almost impossible to believe and yet there it was, an army ordnance map of the New Territories. God! What could we do in twenty minutes? It would take hours of patient work to get the detail that we wanted. Our precious map had already been sealed into a tobacco pouch but we took it from its hiding-place, carefully unsealed it and added a little detail to the outline. Clearwater Bay and Hebe Haven, where I had often spent happy weekends surf-boarding behind Henry Lo's launch, were carefully marked and, of course, Sai Kung. Much of that twenty minutes was spent poring over the map in the hope that we could memorize at least some of it. It was not easy because the areas around Ma On Shan (Horse Dung Mountain) and both sides of Tolo Channel were totally unknown to us. We had seen them only from a distance. I know that we did not make the most of those twenty minutes in tracing more detail but the valiant switch in attitude by Newnham did more for us than any detail could ever have done.

Colonel Newnham proved to be a fine man. Towards the end of the war he was taken out of the camp by the Japanese, accused of signalling, receiving and sending clandestine messages. He suffered many months of the most brutal torture, but they never broke him and he was finally shot at Stanley Prison.

Chapter 9

There was still a lot to be done in the forty-eight hours before we hoped to leave. My job was to fill the packs and prepare the 'body' so that it would fit through the manhole and pass along the drain. It also had to be easy to break open once we reached the sea wall. Duggie and John organized the helpers who were to watch sentries and make diversions if necessary.

Lynton White started on his job as the key helper. He was to follow us through the manhole and remain in the inspection chamber so that he could tell us what was happening above ground. Lynton was passed his information from a man in the shadow of the Gunners' cookhouse. The man would be able to watch the movement of the sentry at the corner of the officers' quarters.

The man at the manhole could also see the sentry on the parade-ground side of the hospital whose beat took him to the very point at which the drain emerged. However, he could not see the sentry at the south-west corner of the perimeter fence until that sentry moved towards the mouth of the drain. Knowledge of the movement of these two sentries was so important that another helper was posted at the west end of the cookhouse so that he could observe both together.

Duggie had persuaded his friend with the lilo to let us have it. It would be possible to float the packs across the bay by just pushing the lilo in front of us. Someone else very generously let us have half of his flask of brandy. We put it into a large vaseline bottle. All in all, we had just about as much as we could afford to take, thanks to our friends.

The day before we were leaving, I went to Jack Manley in the Volunteer cookhouse. Jack was a Jardine's man who had spent a lot of time in Tientsin in North China.

At the cookhouse door, I paused. Should I tell him? I could trust Jack but we'd all pledged not to say a word because nothing spread faster than camp gossip.

'Hello, Jack,' I said breezily. 'Still putting on weight I see?' Actually he was far from fat, but anyone who could wangle a job in a cookhouse was a kingpin at Shamshuipo.

'Maybe. And what are you after, you old scrounger?' he replied. He was usually ready for a joke or some crack.

'Jack,' I continued, 'this is serious. I want your help. You once told me you'd give it.'

He turned to me from the rice he was washing and said, 'Does this mean you're off, David?'

'Yes, Jack and we wish we had your knowledge of Chinese.'

'But for my gammy leg you wouldn't see me for dust, David. Don't ask for caviar or roast beef, but I'll fix up something for you.'

'Thanks,' I said.

Jack had to spend the war in the camp and when he was released in 1945 he weighed only eighty pounds.

We went outside so as not to be overheard.

'How many of you are there?'

'Three,' I said, as at that time Lynton had not joined us to escape. He was only a helper.

'Bring me a couple of flat mess tins . . .'

'Mess tins? Here? It'll start a riot.'

Jack grinned and shifted on his bad leg, 'Got a spare pair of trousers?'

I nodded.

'Then stick the mess tins in the legs and I'll come to your hut and pick 'em up. Half past seven, OK?' He hobbled back into the cookhouse. 'Good luck. I wish to God I could come. Your pants will be ready here by eight.'

By early afternoon next day (20 March), the 'body' was ready. I hid it under John's bed. 'I'm going to get some rest. Hope muster parade is short,' I said. I went down the stairs and in my over-excitement nearly bumped into the sentry. 'God help us if I am such a clumsy fool tonight,' I thought to myself.

I had not seen J.J. since our interview with Colonel Newnham and I wondered whether I should tell him of the map incident. I decided rest was more important, and by that time I had reached our hut.

I was half dozing when our corrugated iron door creaked as someone opened it. 'Bill Dudman about?' said Sergeant Major Walker. He had taken upon himself the role of organizing all the Volunteer Gunner working parties. He was always trying to get people to do things, and I was always ducking out of the jobs he organized. He was a small, elderly man and had been a regular soldier early in his life. Seeing only me, he said, 'It doesn't matter about Dudman. You will do.'

72

'Do what?' I asked.

'I have to organize a working party to go out of the camp tomorrow and I want you to be in charge.'

'I am very sorry, Sergeant Major, but I'm afraid I can't do it. I have a job to do for Lieutenant Clague tomorrow. And in any case I have a strong aversion to working for the Japs. I hope you will understand.'

'Understand? I understand only too well about you. You haven't done a hand's turn since you came here. You're the worst sergeant I've ever had anything to do with.'

'Really, Sergeant Major?' I said. 'Well, I am sorry. I'll try and make amends very soon. This job tomorrow is important. Please believe me.'

The worst sergeant! The nerve of the man, I thought, but he was probably right.

That evening, as we all lined up as usual to collect our ration of rice, I could not help wondering if this was really the last time that I would be doing this. Pray God it might be.

After we had eaten, I washed my mess tin next to Bill Dudman. 'Bill, I know you have been wondering what I have been doing lately, why I wasn't in my bed the other night and why I'm only in the hut so little. Well, the reason is that we have a little operation on tonight.' Bill looked at me and nodded knowingly. 'God knows how it will go but I thought I'd tell you. The less you know, the less you have to lie. Agreed? Actually, I don't think you and the others will be questioned. We're all small fry. Anyway, could you leave my bed and all my things just as I leave them tonight? It will look better.' I paused. 'And if things go wrong, I *could* need them again.'

Bill was taking it all as a matter of course. He hardly made a comment except a nod of understanding. We returned to the hut in complete silence. The others were all talking round the table. Bill joined them. I sat on my bed. I made an effort to chip in, but my mind was elsewhere. I pretended to doze off, and before I knew it, it was time to join the others.

I sat up on the edge of my bed, found my canvas shoes, put them on my bare feet and started for the door. Bill got up and came outside with me. 'Good luck,' he whispered. 'I hope you all make it.' And by the time I turned to thank him, he had darted back into the hut.

Chapter 10

We were all in John's room. Lynton, Duggie, John, me, two helpers and the 'body'. A tight squeeze. The other helpers were already in position. We were a little tense. We had worked out each stage of the scheme like a mathematical problem, exact and precise. At least we thought we had. I pulled the 'body' up and stood it in the corner. It was much heavier than I thought.

The plan began like this: the two helpers got ready to take up positions at the cookhouse and they left. We carried the 'body' out of the door and down to the small hall to wait for the 'all clear' from one of the helpers. We got it and whipped the 'body' to the side of the building. Duggie made straight for the manhole and took the cover off. He must have done it a dozen times in practice.

He signalled and I came to the edge of the manhole. Out of the corner of my eye I could see the sentry on the move. It was the last thing I saw. The next second I'd dropped into the blackness of the inspection chamber. Lynton and John still had the 'body'. I recovered myself just in time to miss the 'body' being hurled down on top of me. I had it on the floor of the drain as Duggie arrived. Together we pushed it up the drain away from the sea wall to allow me to go ahead of it.

I started to pull myself along on my elbows. I had a rope twisted round my wrists. The other end was at the head of the 'body'. I could feel Duggie shoving at the other end.

'Are the other two down?' I said.

'All present and correct,' said Duggie. 'Just keep pulling.'

'Christ! It's as heavy as a two-hundred-pound corpse,' I groaned.

'Hold it a second, David.'

Perspiration was pouring off me. Already my elbows were raw and my head was pumping like an engine. The trouble was that I could see nothing ahead, and my rear-end view was blocked by the 'body'. I felt like ink in a fountain pen.

'Let's get some rhythm into it,' Duggie panted.

Duggie was right. I found that by yanking the 'body' along with my arms and then tucking up my knees, while I pulled and Duggie pushed, we began to make some headway.

After every five or ten minutes we had to rest. There was no way of telling how far we'd gone. Along the passage of the rough concrete I could hear Lynton carefully calling out the exact movements of the sentries. The communications were working.

I knew we had 160 yards to go before my head would hopefully pop out into the fresh, free air on the side of the sea wall. God, what a thought—160 yards! Might as well be 160 miles.

The temperature seemed to have risen about forty degrees. We dropped into the drain wearing only a shirt, shorts and canvas shoes. We had shivered. Now it was an oven.

We dragged ourselves along. I was almost certain that there must be an inspection chamber below the original manhole we had found out in the open beside the parade ground. By this time we ought to have reached it. Why hadn't we? We couldn't go any faster. For John, who was bringing up the rear, our slow progress must have been worrying.

We were taking a rest when a call from Lynton came down the drain. I could not hear him properly but Duggie told me that Lynton was giving up.

'Why?' I asked him.

'They've sounded lights out. All the helpers have had to go. He has to go too.'

This news was shattering. There was nothing he could do for us without his helpers.

Duggie and I waited, trying to clear our thoughts.

Lynton called to us finally that when he got out he would only half replace the manhole cover so that we could get out ourselves if we decided to return. He wished us luck should we continue but warned that we were already hopelessly behind schedule.

While we were debating what to do, I pulled myself further along the drain and quite quickly found myself beneath the second manhole. I turned round and came back to the 'body' facing the way we had come.

'Duggie,' I said, 'we are almost half way. Surely we can't go back now, and what in God's name do we do with the "body"?'

'It's no use going on,' he said, 'the "body" can stay where it is.'

'Thanks, but I happen to be on the wrong side of it.' We argued back and forth and in the end I had to concede that it was madness to think of emerging into the water without knowing where the sentries were, and equally mad to go on when we knew that we would have much less travelling time than planned once we did get ashore. I conceded with rather ill grace, I fear, but they were kind enough never to hold it against me when they were proved right and I so wrong.

John started going back while Duggie helped me to get the 'body' into the second inspection chamber. Before we started our return, I pulled the 'body' a few yards behind me into the drain itself so that anyone removing the second manhole cover could not see it.

It seemed to take us no time at all before we were back at our starting-point. Clearly it was the 'body' which had beaten us.

Duggie very slowly pushed aside the manhole cover and gingerly put his head out. He pulled it back again to say there was no sentry visible. He would get out, lie in the shadow of the cookhouse, and we were to watch his hand. When he was clear of the manhole, John was to come out and get across the road into the darkness of Jubilee Buildings. As soon as John was clear, I was to follow unless I saw his hand. Duggie would replace the cover and join us. All went well, but we still had to get into our quarters, and that could be very tricky unless the sentry was at the far end of his beat. We crept along the wall to the south-west corner, feeling that the perimeter lights were shining specially upon us, but we were in luck and soon safely upstairs.

Even if our attempt had failed, at least the Japanese were in total ignorance of the affair, and the way out was still open to us, but it could well have been a very different story because almost imme-diately after 'lights out' a Japanese patrol passed between Jubilee Buildings and the cookhouse within yards of the first manhole.

Fortunately the chap passing messages to Lynton saw them just in time and was able to warn him and avoid being seen by flattening himself against the darkened wall of the cookhouse. Fearing that the patrol might come back the same way and knowing very well that we were making extremely slow progress, Lynton had no qualms at all in closing down his operation after giving us due warning and leaving us to make the final decision to go on or return.

As we went to bed that night, I again on the floor with one of John's blankets but with no 'body' to cuddle, it was blatantly obvious that there was much work to be done to get our timing right. However, it was not until the next day that we were to realize just how much we owed to our helpers and to Lynton in particular. It was because of this that we invited him to join us in our next attempt. He jumped at the chance.

In the morning we woke rather stiff and sore from our exertions, otherwise we were none the worse, but it was raining. Even though the rain was not torrential at that time of year, it was quite enough to make it important that the 'body' did not remain as we had left it.

'Let's meet as soon as we have eaten and then decide what to do,' suggested Duggie, so I went back to my quarters just in time to form up for the morning muster. After it, we went off to collect the ever-recurring bowl of rice. Jack Manley looked at me as I came into the cookhouse and I just smiled. On the way back to the hut Bill Dudman caught up with me and asked, 'What went wrong, David?'

'Our timing was all to hell,' I said, 'but by the grace of God no damage has been done.'

'Good,' he said, and we all sat around our table in the hut and ate our rice just as we had done every morning since we had arrived at Shamshuipo. By the time I got back to the officers' quarters, I knew we had to start an 'immediate' rescue operation on the 'body'.

Since the 'body' was close to the second manhole and there was ample room to dismantle it below ground, we saw no purpose in running any risks by trying to bring up the packs in broad daylight. All that was needed was to raise them off the floor of the drain so that the water could flow beneath them. Having decided to do this, the question remained should Duggie and I, who were to do the job, enter the drain by the first manhole and drag ourselves along until we came to the 'body' or pose as a working party and enter through the second manhole, even though it was in full view of the two sentries at the western end of the parade ground? Neither of us relished the thought of having to drag ourselves some seventy-five yards so soon after the exploits of the previous night unless it was absolutely necessary—our knees were very sore—and this gave us the idea that John should march a small working party to the vicinity of the second manhole where we should all busy ourselves doing some fictitious job. If the sentries took no notice, first one, then the other would go into the inspection chamber, while the others, all our previous night's helpers, would continue to mill about. In the unlikely event that one or other of the sentries did decide to come across and see what was going on, there would be ample time for the gang to warn us to disappear down the drain itself. So under John's command a little party of six marched out to the manhole in full view of anyone who cared to watch.

As we judged, no one took the slightest notice. We all fiddled around for a little time before we lifted the manhole cover, and when it was obvious that neither sentry thought it in the least bit strange, Duggie and I dropped into the inspection chamber.

We had brought odd pieces of iron, some of them broken window latches, on which to rest the packs. We pulled the 'body' into the inspection chamber but having done so there was not all that much room to move. We were in fits of laughter at the antics we had to perform to get our legs out of the way while unravelling the valise, but as we got the packs free and saw what the rough concrete had done to the valise, we soon stopped laughing. A great hole had been worn in it. This in itself did not matter: our concern was for the lilo. Both the top and bottom surfaces of the lilo had been worn away.

We were sitting one each side of the inspection chamber with the lilo across our knees. We just sat and looked at it and then at each other. The same thought passed through our minds. 'My God, what a mess we would have been in had we gone on last night.' There was no need to say anything. The lilo had to come out with us. Somehow we had to find a means of repairing it. We safely stowed the packs and wedged the valise between them at the top of the drain to keep them firm, while the water flowed gently beneath them.

These antics had taken a very long time, and John had long since withdrawn his working party.

Once again we sat looking at each other. What were we to do? We waited for some considerable time, hoping that John would return to help get us out but he did not. Later we discovered that he seemed to think that to go through the same performance all over again might attract attention and that, when we were ready to surface, we would do so by going back up the drain to the first manhole. That thought did not strike us (although perhaps it should have) but by that time we had had enough of the bloody drain in the last twenty-four hours and all we wanted to do was to get out.

I was greatly relieved when Duggie took the lead. 'Let me take a look and see what the sentries are doing; they will never spot my head from this distance,' he said. Cautiously he looked out. The sentries appeared to have little interest in what was going on within the camp, which was not exactly surprising for, as Duggie looked around, there was absolutely no one about. It was decidedly wet, and the sentries, having nothing better to do, were watching the movement of junks in the harbour and sampans in the bay.

As he scrambled out of the manhole, he called to me to throw up the lilo and to follow immediately. He caught it and was gone. I was half out of the manhole when suddenly I realized that I had to replace the cover. I dare not look to see what the sentries were doing, and while I struggled with the cover, which was damned heavy, I felt that every Japanese in Hong Kong had his eyes fixed on me. It seemed to take ages to get it in place.

'Good God, this is awful,' I thought, and as soon as it clanged home, I wanted to dash for cover but something told me, 'Put your hands in your pockets and shuffle off as unconcerned as possible.' I feel sure it was a rather fast shuffle, but there was no shout behind me and at last I reached the sanctuary of the buildings. To this day I have never understood why John and Lynton did not expect us to emerge from the second manhole, especially as they and other friends in the Gunner officers' quarters kept watch from a window in Jubilee Buildings. Their hearts were in their mouths when first Duggie appeared, then the lilo, and as he made off, I started to emerge. As they told us when it was all over, it was bad enough seeing us emerge one by one but the tension became intense as they watched me wrestle with the manhole cover. Everyone used all the will power he had on the sentries, willing them to remain interested in whatever was going on in the harbour. For Duggie and me the feeling of satisfaction was immense, not only because we had accomplished our mission under the very noses of the Japs but also because we were warmly congratulated by the spectators for the nonchalant manner in which we left the manhole. Luck was on our side. In retrospect I do not believe that we should have taken the risk we did when it was not absolutely necessary.

The more we thought about our attempt, the more forcibly it was brought home to us how ill-prepared it had been. Far too many assumptions had been made, the chief of which was timing. To be successful we had to be out of the end of the drain and preferably one hundred yards away from the sea wall before 'lights out' sounded. Therefore it was absolutely vital to know the precise time needed for each stage of the operation, the half-crawl, half-drag, down the drain, the inflation of the lilo and the loading of it in the water at the mouth of the drain. The rescue of the 'body' by the use of the second manhole demonstrated that the Japanese had no conception as to what their prisoners might be up to, and consequently with care it should be possible to carry out various time-checks using this manhole.

We estimated that there would be no moon between the 9th and 13th of April when, as far as it was possible to judge, there would also be an incoming tide. This gave us three weeks in which to perfect the operation and above all to find some means of repairing the damaged lilo. It had two ugly holes an inch or more in diameter where both the top and bottom surfaces had been worn away.

At first it seemed that nothing could be done without a proper repair kit. All we had was a small roll of elastoplast, and that on its own would never hold. Somehow the whole area around the two holes (which, perhaps fortunately, were one above the other) had to be isolated, if only a means of clamping the two surfaces together could be found. Days went by with the problem unresolved until quite by chance we saw what appeared to be a discarded inner tube behind the Japanese guard-house. We borrowed it!

The lilo was spread out on the floor; the elastoplast was cut into strips, and with infinite care, since there was only just enough, the strips were spread over each hole so that it stuck to itself where each surface had been worn away. Pieces of inner tubing were cut to fit two round cigarette-tin lids which were to form the clamps by screwing them together—a nut and bolt had not been difficult to find. This done, a hole was carefully pierced through each lid and each piece of rubber to take the bolt. Equally carefully a hole was pierced in the elastoplast. A tin lid and a piece of rubber were put onto the bolt. The bolt was then passed through the elastoplast and the same process repeated on the other side. Having screwed up the contraption as tightly as possible, we began to inflate the lilo. It seemed to hold even when it had been blown up harder than necessary, and we left it piled high with anything heavy that came to hand. Some hours later, hardly daring to inspect our handiwork, we returned. The repair had held.

The next priority was to determine accurately the time needed in the drain. I agreed to carry out tests, providing I was given proper cover when I wanted to come out. There was to be no question of repeating the performance suffered by Duggie and myself when rescuing the lilo after the abortive attempt.

It proved so easy to get in and out of the second manhole, operating with a group of five or six helpers, that the first manhole was not used again. Indeed, the decision was taken that our final departure would be from the second manhole—80 yards in the drain as against 160 made all the difference in the world!

Having made my way to within some ten yards of the mouth of the drain, this first full reconnoitre was rewarded by the discovery of yet another inspection chamber. Until I reached it, it had never entered my head that, had it not been there, I would have been forced, on the return journey to my point of entry, to back all the way. It was arduous enough to drag oneself forwards but to move backwards was tenfold worse. My God! I thought, had it not been there, we would all have had to back down the drain since it would have been quite impossible to enter the water silently head first from the mouth of the drain—a point which had been totally overlooked as we set out on our abortive first attempt.

As I sat pondering over all these things in the third inspection chamber and working out just how it should be used on the night, it suddenly struck me that the manhole cover to this inspection chamber must be almost directly on the beat of the sentries. They probably walked over it time and time again and stood on it as they met each other.

In the third chamber I could hear the gentle lapping of the water, which made me forget the sentries and turn my attention to thinking of some means by which to gauge the height of the drain above the sea bed. If it were possible to stand and still reach into its mouth, our exit would be comparatively easy but, on the other hand, to be forced to tread water while inflating and loading the lilo would greatly complicate matters. I moved as close to the mouth as I dared without running the risk of being seen by some passing sampan but it helped little.

As far as I could judge, the water level was some two to three feet below the mouth, but there was no means of telling how deep it was against the retaining wall. I lay there for quite some time, enjoying the view of the bay and Lai Chi Kok beyond unsullied by an electrified fence. I backed once again into the inspection chamber and listened for the tramp of sentries' feet. There was none. Perhaps, I thought, they were wearing the Japanese army issue of rubber-soled boots with the big toe separated from the others.

By this time I had been underground all of two hours, and dragging myself back the seventy-five yards to the second manhole was quite hard work. It was necessary to rest quite often. I was thankful that the cover had not been replaced, for the light it gave was something to aim at rather than working one's way along further and further into inky darkness. Nonetheless, I began to feel very alone in the dark, dank, claustrophobic tunnel, although it was a relief to know that it would not collapse. It had never entered my mind on the way to the mouth because, I suppose, there was a job to be done. The return journey seemed so different; there was altogether too much time to let my thoughts wander. Until that moment working and planning the escape had seemed a perfectly normal thing to be doing. Suddenly it became difficult to believe that I was actually engaged in a story-book escapade.

It was a great relief to get out of the drain into the fresh air of a warm spring day and be able to wash under a tap in the sun but I felt tired and spent the rest of it lying on my bed. The strain had been considerable so I was hardly surprised to feel tired. However, the next morning I felt as though there was a ton weight on me. It lifted after muster parade and I gave no more thought to it. The same thing happened on the next two mornings. My eyes and face felt puffy; in fact someone remarked that I was getting fat and wondered how I could look so robust on the prison diet! It became increasingly difficult to open my eyes in the morning, and I had a nasty shock when my feet would hardly go into my shoes. I pressed my swollen ankles, and my fingermarks remained for an appreciable time. There was fluid present, and this could only mean one thing. I had beriberi.

Very sick at heart, I went off to tell the others. I knew that, unless something could be done, there was no way in which I could go with them. Beriberi is caused by lack of vitamin B. In layman's language, this tends to destroy the red blood corpuscles, and water collects in the extremities, gradually spreading all over the body so that the sufferer swells like a balloon. In the end the heart can no longer stand the extra work pumping blood around the body, and the patient dies of heart failure.

All this I knew for already there had been quite a number of cases, and only after a great deal of pressure had been applied to the Japanese did they allow a limited supply of vitamin B into the camp. This was administered to the more serious cases by injection. Duggie was wonderfully reassuring. 'Leave it to me,' he said. 'I will find the answer.' He went off in search of a medical officer whom he knew well. Apparently he explained the position and said I was a vital member in the party. His MO friend was a Regular and fortunately all in favour of our escape. He immediately went with Duggie to the senior Volunteer MO, who listened sympathetically to the story, and as a result my name was added to the list of those receiving injections. When he came back and told me to report that evening, I could only say, 'Duggie, how marvellous of you.'

No questions were asked when I reported to the MO. I received my first injection that evening and was told not to take any exercise and to rest as much as possible. I was excused from all formalities. I could not attend muster parades. This was indeed a bonus.

After a comparatively few injections, the swelling began to subside; yet I was told that I must continue to rest and not to exercise because it could affect my heart. This was not good news. I could not afford to relax the training which we had all maintained for so many weeks. I had to be fit enough to undertake an hour in the water. I had to climb about a thousand feet or more to the top of the Kowloon Hills. I had to be ready to force march for several miles to put some distance between us and the camp the first night out.

The going could only be very rough for many nights. Yet I had no choice but to do what the doctor said.

The weather was warm at the beginning of April, and I did a good deal of sitting in the sun. Apart from having nothing else to do, I thought perhaps the sun would help cure the concrete burns which had become sores on my legs.

Victor Nunes, my Portuguese friend who had worked with me in Jardine's, saw me. He pointed to my legs. 'You ought to do something about that,' he said.

'It's improved since I've given it as much sun and air as possible.'

He left me without saying any more and was soon back with some ointment. He did this three or four times during the next few days, and within a week the sores began to heal. It was typical of the kindness which the firm's Portuguese staff gave me in the camp. Life wasn't all black. The greatest generosity of all was to come from J.J. very soon afterwards.

He burst into the hut one bright morning and said, 'David, why didn't you tell me you have beriberi?'

'I have been receiving vitamin B injections. Look, the swelling's reduced,' I said.

'I only found out because the sick list goes to the camp adjutant's office, and when I saw your name on it, I was afraid that it would mean the end of your plan.'

I thanked him very much for being so concerned.

I said, 'I start exercising again soon, and in the meantime I'm not holding the others back because the moon is not right.' I then told him about the abortive attempt. It seemed to fascinate him. He listened intently to every detail and said, 'I am delighted to find you in reasonably good shape but there are others who may not be so pleased.'

I looked at him enquiringly.

'Oh yes, there was quite a sigh of relief when some saw your name on that list. I find it highly amusing that the health of Volunteer Sergeant Bosanquet should arouse so much interest among the brass hats.' We both laughed. Then he said, 'Now don't be stupid and ignore the doctor's advice. Here's a tin of fish and a small bottle of yeast tablets. They should help to put you right.' He dropped them on the bed.

'But sir, please . . . I'm getting injections,' I said, trying to hand them back to him. He would have none of it.

'I really don't need them and God knows they could be very important to you later on.' No one could have made a more unselfish gesture. But he was that kind of man.

I'm afraid I did not stick rigidly to the doctor's orders. As soon as the swelling had disappeared, I began to do exercises each morning in the hut when the others were on muster parade.

A few days later I said to the MO, 'Let me start taking real exercise again, sir.'

He gave me a rather quizzical look as if he knew what I'd been up to. 'I'm going to give you a thorough test. If you pass it, I advise a gradual exercise build-up, and I should see you again after a few days.' I think he knew we had set a firm date and was recommending a build-up which would help me get fit for it. I came away much encouraged.

Duggie called a meeting in John's room. A decision had to be taken to leave within the next four or five days or to wait another month. I had exercised strenuously for three consecutive days without any ill effects. I felt fine. We set Sunday 12 April as the day. I think it was a relief to all of us. The waiting was getting us down. Then there was a sudden change of plans.

On the Saturday conditions seemed ideal. A gentle off-shore wind blew. Enough to make the water choppy and any object in it less easy to distinguish. Enough to carry any sounds made at the mouth of the drain away from the sentries. It seemed too good an opportunity to miss, and we prepared for an escape that night.

The packs were already in the drain but stacked near the second manhole. To save time once the operation was under way, I volunteered to move them to the inspection chamber below the third manhole within a few yards of the mouth of the drain.

I entered the drain that morning clutching our precious lilo which had been carefully repaired. It proved no easy task to drag all the packs single-handed and at the same time to protect the lilo. But I completed the mission and emerged feeling rather pleased with myself. There was no problem getting out of the second manhole as John and other friends were sitting beside it watching a game of cricket.

'Have you made the rope ladder in case it is necessary to be lowered out of the drain into the water?'

'Yes,' he replied, 'only it's not made of rope but of strips of material cut from a spare pair of Duggie's trousers.'

'Let's hope we won't have to use it. By the way, where is Duggie?'

'He's over there playing cricket.'

'What!' I said, jumping to my feet. 'The bloody fool!' I ran straight across the parade ground to where he was fielding.

'Duggie, what in the name of hell do you think you are doing? You've only got to fall and twist an ankle and the whole operation is in danger. For Christ's sake, stop this bloody nonsense. I've just slogged my guts out in that damn drain. Doesn't it mean anything to you? Have you gone mad?' I was over-reacting perhaps because I was tired and very preoccupied with the scheme. Duggie was taken aback, but he had the grace to follow me off the ground.

The wind remained unchanged. We decided to go that night. All spare tins of food specially put aside for that moment were opened and I gorged myself, and so did the others. We lay back to rest. For me, it was quite impossible to sleep.

Duggie decided he would make a final attempt to get an official blessing on the plan. He spoke to the Colonel. Colonel Newnham spoke to General Maltby. Then he came to our room.

'The General has no message he wants taken out of the camp,' said Newnham.

'Nothing about the conditions?' said John.

'How about the food, sir?' said Lynton.

'He has no message,' repeated Newnham. 'He doesn't even believe you will make it. I'm sorry. He hopes you will all think again and come and see me in the morning. He wants nothing reported to London.'

We could tell from his face that Newnham was angry. So were we. However, we had better things to think about. We wrote a letter to the Colonel saying we could not make the appointment in the morning and that we were disappointed to be leaving without the blessing of the General.

Then I went to have my name taken off the sick list. I didn't want anyone on the medical staff to be blacklisted by the Japs because they had co-operated in the escape. Lastly, I made my way to the officers' quarters to meet the others. I had eaten a bowl of rice at supper and added to it a can of cold, almost solid pea soup. My stomach's unaccustomed reaction to this was to swell out as if I were pregnant. I wished I hadn't eaten half of it.

This time we had rehearsed everything to top pitch. It was like being in an orchestra. John's brother, Alec, was to start diversions. He had mustered a party to chop wood on the seaward side of the cookhouse, near the first manhole. Each man was to make as much noise as possible.

Another group of diverters was to keep the sentry occupied in the south-west corner of the camp by constantly getting near the wire, which would provoke the Japanese into chasing them away.

Yet another group was to congregate near the huts used as a hospital. There was a path nearby which ran from the parade ground round the hospital building on towards the huts behind. It ran very close to the perimeter fence, and after dark the sentry there would stop people using it. The idea was that, if people exercising approached the path first from one direction and then from the other, the sentry would plant himself on the path and remain there, thus diverting his attention and presence from the second and third manholes. Duggie's battery commander had a concertina in the camp. He posted himself on a balcony of the officers' quarters from which he had a clear view of the two sentries. As long as the sentries remained apart, he was to play loudly in a major key. He was to change to a minor key should either begin to converge upon the mouth of the drain. A cacophony of sound and a plethora of movement!

Finally, our most trusted helper was positioned near the first manhole itself. He was armed with a brick attached to a piece of string. He was to sit on the edge of the parade ground with the string and brick down the manhole. By pulling the string and releasing it, the brick made sufficient noise on the drain floor for us to hear it the length of the drain. One clang denoted danger, three, all clear.

To be quite sure that no interest was aroused among those exercising on the parade ground, no move could be made before 8.15, by which time it was dark. This gave us just under two hours to be clear of the mouth of the drain and take maximum advantage of the help all our friends could give us. It was a tight schedule but it could be done providing nothing went badly wrong.

We rehearsed our roles just one more time: Lynton was to be last and hold up our communication lines; John was to keep ahead of Lynton; Duggie was next, with me leading. If we got separated in the water, each one of us knew that there were two rendezvous. A ten-minute wait at the first stop. Then we'd push ahead, all there or not. One hour at the second, and no grace was to be given there either. The life of each of us was in the hands of the others, but in the final moment it was each man for himself. There were a few of the butterflies which any athlete or actor knows full well before 'going on'.

Duggie said, 'Come on, David! Time to go. John, you and Lynton follow but give us a lead of two or three minutes.'

The butterflies were gone now. We trotted down the stairs, out through the doorway, and instead of turning left past the cook-house, we walked into the middle of the parade ground and from there to the second manhole. The cover had already been removed by our helpers. They stood chatting as on any other fine evening. We thanked them all and disappeared into the drain. John and Lynton came on cue.

Progress was comparatively quick and much less painful than our first attempt. We had put on knee- and arm-pads. We heard the brick clang three times behind us. In the inky, clammy darkness it was reassuring to hear it. We seemed to be enveloped in the dark as though we were battling through a porous blanket. Suddenly I was in the third inspection chamber.

'Hold it, Duggie,' I whispered. 'I've got to turn!' I groped around to find the lilo without disturbing the packs. After what must have seemed ages to the others, I started to back towards the mouth, clutching the lilo. I waited, panting with the exertion in so confined a space. I heard Duggie turn. He passed me the makeshift ladder through his legs. I passed it under my tummy and out into the sea. I hung on to his thighs.

'Back a bit, Duggie,' I whispered again. His backside was smack against my face as he braced himself on the side of the drain. My legs went down into the water as I balanced on my tummy on the lip.

Cold, not too cold. A shock though. Knee deep, thigh deep, waist deep. My feet touch bottom! Wonderful, the mouth is no more than chin deep. I help Duggie as he lowers himself into the water and crouches as close as possible to the wall. I start to inflate the lilo. We freeze as the brick clangs and the concertina wails into a minor key. Quite suddenly the key changes; our aides are doing well, God bless them. Duggie gives John a hand out. The lilo is ready. Lynton hands out the packs one by one. We tie them onto the lilo. Lynton goes back to turn. John helps him out. Another alarm. We freeze once more and wait and wait. It is ten minutes to ten. 'Please, boys, do your stuff quickly.' As if in answer, we hear three clangs of the brick again.

John moves away from the wall; so does Lynton, a few yards apart. Slowly, very slowly, they paddle away from the wall. Duggie and I wait. There is an ominous sound above us. It turns out to be nothing. He launches himself with the utmost care, leaving me with the loaded lilo still close beneath the wall. Seconds seem like minutes but I must wait, butterflies in the stomach! The lilo and I must be fifty yards clear before our helpers have to stop their diversion tactics because the lights on the boundary fence shine on the sea for this distance. Once beyond their light we shall be swallowed up in the darkness on this very dark night.

I give the lilo a gentle push, and it begins to drift away. I pay out the string which is attached to it. If it is seen and the sentries open fire, it still gives me a chance to get away without being hit. It seems gigantic as it glides silently towards the darkness. The rope is round my wrist as I sink slowly into the water on my back, keeping my hands and feet as deep as possible. I barely move them but the water is full of phosphorescence which flashes. A damn beacon! The distance between me and the wall increases. Quite suddenly the lilo and I are in darkness. I am aware of the others beside me.

What a sight! We see the whole western perimeter of the camp ablaze with light and the monkey-like figures as if upon a stage standing in front of the footlights while we wallow in the water. Then the bugle sounds 'lights out'. Immediately a Japanese patrol appears from the direction of the hospital area. We watch the changing of the sentries. Voices from the parade ground die away. The prisoners return to their quarters for the night. The concertina blares out the final chords of 'Happy Days Are Here Again'. Then silence. What more dramatic curtain-drop could there be to Act One of the drama?

Chapter 11

Slowly we continued to swim on our backs out into the middle of the bay, hardly making a sound. Judging that we had gone far enough, we altered course for the shore. As we did so, the lilo turned turtle. Thank God Duggie had insisted that the packs be tied on. He and I set about righting it. We refused to let either John or Lynton help. They had always been worried by the distance they had to swim. They needed all their energy. We each got a pack on the lilo. We started to fish for the other two, but one of the others flopped into the water. Somehow we got all four back and made some headway. Then the same thing happened again. Another brief spell of progress. The packs slipped into the water again.

By now the packs were getting waterlogged and heavier—too heavy. Each time we rescued one, we also got waterlogged ourselves. The strain was almost intolerable but Duggie was magnificent, taking the lion's share of the salvage work. It inspired me to greater efforts. John then gave a hand as the situation grew ever more desperate. Duggie and I were almost dead beat. After a moment of frantic activity we suddenly realized that Lynton had disappeared. How could he have missed us when he had nothing else to do but keep in contact? Was he so intent on making the shore that he had continued to swim on, not thinking that we would drift with the tide? Whatever it was, there was nothing we could do. He would have to catch us at one or other rendezvous if we ourselves ever got there. Now we were actually holding the packs in position. We seemed to be making some headway. The lilo also gave us some much-needed support. The two empty water-bottles strapped to John's chest were his life-savers.

At last we saw some shapes ahead. Junks! Soon we were among them and quite near to the shore. We touched bottom with our feet and this gave us a chance to take a look where we were landing. My God! Not fifty yards away there was a Jap sitting under a light. We slipped back into the water and swam away among the sea-going junks. As we took a short cut under their anchor chains, dogs barked. We had forgotten that most junks have dogs on them, and someone stirred. There were muffled voices. Damn those dogs!

Eventually we struggled onto a comparatively clear patch of very muddy beach. We landed exhausted and perished with cold.

We were so cold we could hardly move. I found the precious vaseline bottle with the brandy in it. We each had a gulp and silently blessed the donor. None of us had ever been so cold but we deflated the lilo, rolled it and tied it to the top of my pack. We gave each other a hand to shoulder our water-sodden packs. They weighed a ton but Duggie insisted on carrying Lynton's as well as his own.

We started to creep forward, trying to make no noise, but the slimy black mud on the beach made this impossible. We fell about like drunken men. One and a half hours in the water. It had taken all the guts out of us. To make matters worse, there were large bits of wood embedded in the mud. We tripped over them or slipped when we trod on them. The noise we made might have woken the dead! We stumbled on, making for a small wooden hut immediately beneath the embankment, which carried the road. We were almost there when someone came from behind it. We froze. There was nothing else we could do, and the figure, a Chinese, passed within ten feet of us. We reached the embankment. I fell flat on my stomach, thankful for the respite this gave me. The others followed suit. Slowly we crawled to the edge of the road, lay there again and listened. Duggie raised his head and looked in each direction. There was not a sound, not a soul about. Immediately opposite on the other side of the road there was a gap in the houses, two rows of them, then the comparative safety of the hills behind. Duggie whispered, 'Come on, flat out across the road between the houses and don't stop running until we are clear.'

Our dash was a drunken totter. We were almost defeated by the cold and nervous exhaustion. Somehow we managed to keep going until we were clear of the houses. John reached the path leading up the hill among the Chinese terraced gardens. Duggie and I were close behind. There we stopped to listen but heard not a sound. No one seemed to be following. We pushed on up the path towards the first rendezvous.

We waited where we judged it to be. There was no sign of Lynton. We sat down, panting, and looked back. The lights of the guard-house and the camp perimeter were still uncomfortably close. 'We can't wait too long,' I said. 'We're all too bloody cold.' The others insisted that we give him a little longer. 'C'mon, for God's sake. If he's made it, he must catch us up at the second rendezvous,' and I stomped off.

We continued to follow the path which wound its way up steeply, and just as we were beginning to make better progress, we rounded a corner. Four dark figures were ahead of us. We spotted each other at the same moment, and to our great relief they fled down the hill, obviously thinking we were Japanese.

We plodded on and came to a rocky ravine which in the wet season carried rainwater directly down the hillside. Reluctantly, we decided to abandon the path and climb up the ravine, since we dared not risk another encounter. The going was tough, but at least the effort started to generate some warmth within us.

The ravine ended in a culvert under the embankment of the inland road from Kowloon to Taipo and beyond to the border with China. We wormed our way up to it, rested at the top and listened for any movement on the road. Again we heard nothing. 'Damn!' Duggie said. 'Look at that cutting on the other side of the road. It is sheer. We can't climb that.'

'No, of course we can't,' I said. 'Let's move down the road a bit. I know it's not all sheer.' We soon found a gap through which we could see, silhouetted against the sky, the saddle in the top ridge between Eagle's Nest and Beacon Hill, the point chosen for the second rendezvous. We were on course at least, but this last section of the climb to the top of the Kowloon Hills was very steep. We rested frequently. Just short of the saddle we heard a noise behind us. We moved apart and sank into the scrub. The noise got closer. We held our breath. A figure appeared out of the darkness. 'Lynton!' We almost shouted. 'Thank God it's you.'

'What the hell happened?' Duggie asked, handing him his pack.

'I lost you in the water. I am sorry but it was bloody dark, wasn't it?'

'Never mind. You caught us up. That's the main thing,' said Duggie. 'Tell us about it later but we won't waste more time here. Let's make the ridge and then rest.'

It was only a short distance to the saddle in the ridge at which we had gazed so often and lovingly from the camp. Once there we set down our packs, found the vaseline bottle of brandy, gave Lynton two gulps because he had missed the first and took a swig each ourselves.

Here, Lynton tried to explain further how he had missed us but had little to add except that when he found himself alone quite suddenly he gave a soft call. When there was no answer, he made for the shore. Like us, he had some difficulty in finding a place to land. However, eventually he made it and set off for what he thought was the first rendezvous. When he found no sign of us, he continued towards the ridge where, if he did not find us, he knew it would be safe to call out.

As we rested, sitting on our packs, I allowed myself to indulge in a little smug satisfaction. Although ill-fed for months, we had achieved a lot since entering the drain less than five hours earlier.

We were all together. We had survived the nightmare swim when total disaster so nearly overcame us. We had climbed the Kowloon Hills in pitch darkness. I had reached the point at which I had let my mesmerized stare rest morning and evening, on those hated muster parades.

Still wet from the swim and the added dampness of the perspiration, we began to shiver. 'Let's go,' said Duggie.

We were glad to be on the move again. We walked quickly over the ridge, and Kowloon disappeared from view.

Chapter 12

We dropped down on the other side of the ridge where we knew that a catchwater ran round the hills in the direction we wanted to go. We also knew that it would be dry, for it was built to catch the heavy summer rains, then the only source of Hong Kong's water supply. We soon found it. This huge concrete culvert was large and deep enough to hide an army truck. We had to lower ourselves by an overhanging tree branch and drop into it.

The going was easy inside and we made good progress until Duggie, who was leading, suddenly stopped. 'Did you hear anything?' he whispered. We listened. He moved forward a few paces. We followed. A dry twig snapped under my foot. 'Don't make such a bloody noise,' he hissed. 'I'm sure somebody or something's ahead of us.' This made us all jittery. There was nowhere to hide in the catchwater, and no means to get out in a hurry.

'Do you think it could be patrolled?' asked John. No one answered. We all had the same thought.

'We won't have a dog's chance if we are seen in here,' I said. 'There is an iron ladder let into the concrete wall further back. For God's sake, let's get out there.' We retraced our steps, found the ladder and climbed out.

There was no convenient path beside the catchwater. The hillside was covered in thick undergrowth. Every hundred yards we gained was a nightmare of hidden gullies or sudden drops in the land. We had to claw our way out of them. I was leading and was waiting for the others to catch up when Duggie disappeared into a gully I had just missed. We pulled him out, luckily only scratched and bruised, but that was enough. We had to find a path but we couldn't. The catchwater was the only alternative. We clambered back to it, climbed in and, throwing caution to the wind, hurried along to make up for lost time.

The inky blackness began to turn a pale grey. The cold damp mist swirled around us. It grew lighter. We had to find a place to lie up for the day. Where were we? At that moment the cloud lifted slightly and we recognized a landmark. Above us towered Amah's Rock, so called because this craggy piece of the hills resembled a Chinese woman carrying a baby on her back. This gave us our bearing.

We climbed out of the catchwater to find that the thick undergrowth gave way to a large area of coarse grass around the base of the rock which presented little cover for our day's rest. Then we spotted a slit-trench among a small outcrop of rocks which would give us fair protection against anyone who might pass by. We spread our sweaters beneath the rocks and prayed for the sun to disperse the cloud. The early morning chill bit into our bones. We huddled together beneath a mackintosh groundsheet and a gas cape. There should have been another. We couldn't find it. 'We must have left it on the beach in our frantic efforts to get away from those bloody dogs,' I said. 'Hope a Chinese and not a Jap found it.'

'Yes, so do I, but where are my boots?' Duggie added.

'I never saw them on the lilo, Duggie. They must have been left in the drain. What a give-away as to how we got out. Pity.'

'John and I'll go back for 'em,' quipped Lynton.

'Like hell we will,' said John.

'Not even if we guarantee to wait for you?'

'Damn the boots,' said Duggie. 'I can walk in my sneakers. Besides, we have spares.'

'Then it's OK,' said John. 'Let's forget 'em.'

'No, it's bloody well not. There was a tin of fifty Players in one of them, and do you realize, David, that only you and I smoke!'

'God! What a waste, Duggie.'

'Yeah, especially when I'd saved 'em from the beginning. Think what I could have bartered 'em for.'

'Don't! I bet those two non-smoking pack-passing clots left your boots behind on purpose, just to deny us an after-breakfast smoke!'

'And talking of breakfast, let's have some.' John chose one of our precious cans of bully beef, solemnly opened it and with scrupulous care divided it into four. It seemed so little after such a night's work. It was and felt as if it was, after we had slowly eaten it.

'Now, John, since you are the dispenser of all good things, except cigarettes, how about rustling up the sun,' said Duggie, trying to make light of our extreme discomfort.

'No chance before midday, I reckon,' he replied. 'Midday! That's hours.'

'By the way, what is the time?' asked Lynton and as if in answer the sound of a bugle came wafting across the hills.

It sounded ominously close but unmistakably it was the eight o'clock muster parade call. In half an hour the Japanese would know that they were missing four prisoners. It was a great moment even though we knew that we were barely three miles from the camp as the crow flies.

Each of us, deep in his own thoughts, savoured the thrill which the bugle call had aroused until Duggie broke the silence which had again returned to the mist-clad hills. 'I wish our escape had been given official blessing.' We all nodded but said nothing.

Minutes later the silence was broken again by the chattering of some twenty Chinese women as they approached over the brow of a hill in front of us. We watched, expecting them to pass by, but to our dismay they stopped and began to cut the coarse grass no more than fifty yards from where we were hiding. They worked all day while we remained trapped.

The sun made a few feeble attempts to penetrate the mist. When it did, we were able to see across Tide Cove to the village of Shatin, where there was considerable Japanese Army activity. An occasional train puffed its way along the western shore of Tide Cove. Otherwise we sat and listened to the incessant chattering of the women which, combined with the cold, the cramped slit-trench and our inability to sleep, tested our endurance to the limit. One day, I thought, there should be some glamour in escape. On that day there was none.

Late in the afternoon the coolie women began to collect the grass into large bundles. Each would carry two by means of a bamboo pole across her shoulders. Often the bundles were so large that the woman carrying them was entirely hidden. It looked like two giant grass balls walking on their own.

At long last the women left, still chattering. We opened another can of bully beef and again cut it into four. We were stiff and aching in every limb as we shouldered our packs but our spirits revived as we began to move. It was almost dark when we picked up the path which the women had taken.

All too soon it came to an abrupt end. We were baffled. We had seen no real fork which we might have taken, but again the evening was very dark. We slipped, slithered and sometimes fell down the hillside into a valley that had to be crossed if we were to maintain our bearing of north by east.

Suddenly some huts loomed out of the mist. We were edging round them when dogs started to bark furiously. We heard voices and beat a hasty retreat, luckily finding a path, but it led in the wrong direction. We were losing time again, which worried us. We could not go on retracing our steps. We had done it too often, so we cut straight up the hillside. The going was diabolical. Our nerves were on edge. Imaginary figures moved ahead of us. Fireflies became torch flashes as we hit barbed wire. We were seized with the idea that it might be patrolled. We retreated.

'C'mon,' said Duggie. 'We'll still be here at first light unless we pull ourselves together.' He was right. 'We'll search for a path. Find one and stick to it.'

We did and struggled to the top of the ridge, only to find that there was another depression before the next. We pressed on and finally made it. Horror! The eastern outskirts of Kowloon and the harbour lay before us. Walking all night in our foolish panic, we had almost completed a circle. Exhausted, we collapsed and sat huddled together for warmth. We cursed our own stupidity.

That second day, like the first, was spent in an L-shaped trench among some rocks. It was damp but the sun did break through at times to give us some warmth before the swirling mist enveloped us again. At least there was no marauding Japs or chattering women to disturb our peace. We even dozed. I wouldn't say we were relaxed. Relaxation was a long way off. We were like animals resting on the run.

During the afternoon we took stock and pored over the sketch map we'd made from the one Newnham had lent us. It told us almost nothing. Our aim had always been to reach the coast near Sharpe Peak. It was at this point that Tolo Channel, which ran inland to Taipo Market, emerged into Mirs Bay, and across Mirs Bay, which lay to the north-east from Hong Kong, was the mainland of China.

We had to make Tolo Channel. There were two possibilities. The first was to persuade a fisherman to take us across Mirs Bay. If that failed, we had to get across Tolo Channel itself by stealing a sampan if need be and walk into China, crossing the border wherever we could.

But the first problem was to reach Tolo Channel. At our present rate of progress it might take a week. The limiting factor was our food supply. To maintain our strength to travel on only two ounces of food every twelve hours was another matter. As there had been very little activity around us all day, we decided to set off early and travel for an hour while we could still see.

We made excellent progress, but as darkness fell, so did the mist, and again it was impossible to see more than a few yards. Again we floundered about on that terrible terrain. Again we wasted hours before finally ending up in one of our pillboxes. It was not much help. We could find no reference points in it, and on our map only the top of the hills was shown. The mist was hiding those. 'We're in one of our defence positions,' said John, 'and all the damn paths lead up and not down.'

'I know,' said Duggie. 'We ought to have realized it sooner. But we've got to get below this mist.' We headed on down the hill. Then we lost Duggie. It wasn't difficult to find him because of the flow of vitriolic language which issued from a deep gully. We helped him out. He hadn't broken any bones but had twisted his right knee. 'This is madness,' I said. 'We stay put until it begins to get light.' When we did, we found ourselves hard by another pillbox. We helped Duggie to it. We opened another tin. We were famished.

The mist still enveloped us but every now and again we caught glimpses of the coastline, so John and Lynton went off to find a point from which they could investigate the lie of the land.

'Duggie,' I said as we sat with our backs against the pillbox wall, 'how's your knee?'

'A bit painful,' he replied. 'I'll get along all right.'

'I'm sure you will. But another fall like yours and one of us is going to break a leg. If that happens, either the game is up for all of us or the crippled one would have to be dumped in the nearest village and take his chance.'

'That's an unpleasant prospect.'

'Of course it is. Don't you think we've got to travel by day?'

'Well, I think you're right, David. Perhaps we should talk to the others.'

'We must. I bet John'll take some convincing,' I said. 'But we've just got to do it. Take the risk and pray to God any Chinese who sees us doesn't want to get involved with the Japs at any price.'

'I agree. These two and a half wasted nights gall me.'

'Me too, Duggie, but they are all country or fishing folk in this area.'

'Maybe, but both J.J. and Newnham warned us about Sai Kung.'

'I know and I respect John's cautious attitude, but the thought of being abandoned . . .'

At this moment John and Lynton came back with the news that they had found a good path leading down towards the sea but they were still by no means sure of our position.

Duggie and I told them of our discussion and we hoped they would agree. Although John was not wholly convinced that we were right, he fell in with the idea of moving to a lower level without further delay.

Lynton led us to the path which he and John had found, Duggie limping with us. The sun came out and we moved easily down it, enjoying the real warmth of the sun for the first time (a lovely spring day). The hillside seemed deserted until, rounding a corner, we ran slap into a little knot of grass-cutters. Except for a casual glance, they took no notice of us. We had passed the first test, I thought, but dare we risk passing through the centre of a hamlet to which the path was leading? We decided not. Almost immediately we were struggling through undergrowth up to our waists. We were seen again. This time there were no casual glances: the villagers stopped and stared. There was far too much interest to be healthy. We changed course and hurried out into the open, hoping this would allay any suspicions they may have had.

In doing so, we found ourselves on a broad path and, judging by the constant flow of Chinese in both directions, it obviously served as a main thoroughfare to places of greater importance than the hamlet which we had so assiduously tried to avoid.

We sat down beside it to gauge the reaction to our sudden appearance but few took much notice of us, and to those who did we nodded politely. When one man stopped, John tried out his Cantonese and was quite overwhelmed by the torrent that was thrown back at him. The one-sided conversation went on and on and we could do nothing to help except smile benignly. At last he went on his way, and we pumped John to learn if he had understood anything of significance. The whole conversation had been of the whereabouts of Sai Kung.

'According to that chap, we are already north of Sai Kung.'

'Can't be,' I said. 'I'm almost certain that the bay ahead of us is Hebe Haven. I've been there on one of Henry Lo's Sunday launch parties.'

'Wherever we are,' said Lynton, 'well done, John. I'm sure it did us a helluva lot of good to be seen talking to one of those folk. The chap you talked to seemed friendly enough.'

'Yes, indeed. He was trying to be helpful. The trouble was that I could not really understand him.'

We moved on up the path and turned off to a headland where we could see the whole bay but remain unseen. The midday sun beat down on us relentlessly. There was no shade. We were tired after eighteen hours on the go without sleep, hungry and very thirsty. We could not afford any bully to eat until evening. Stupidly we ate some tinned cheese, and that made us more thirsty.

Three villages lay around the bay, and scattered between them were a few houses standing on their own, but of special interest to us were two large sea-going junks anchored off a promontory at the narrow entrance. 'There's a chance,' I said. 'If only we could persuade one of them to take us across Mirs Bay.'

'And how,' echoed Duggie.

'But it's better not to approach them until it's nearly dark just in case we have to get away in a hurry.'

Lying in our hide-out waiting for the sun to go down, we tried to sleep but our craving for water kept us awake. How we had longed for the sun on the previous days. Now that we had it, we longed to see it disappear behind the hills.

An hour before dark we went in search and found a spring where it bubbled out of the hillside. We drank heavily of this nectar, filled our water-bottles and headed to where the junks lay within fifty yards of the shore.

John hailed them. A man stirred on the nearest. We waved. Our hearts sank as he turned away. We stood for a few moments wondering whether to call again when a sampan rounded the stern of the junk with the man in it. 'My God, he's coming ashore,' murmured Lynton. We tried to control our excitement.

'Good for you, John. Your Chinese worked!'

'Not my Chinese, just our arm-waving,' he grunted. 'God knows how I'm going to explain what we want.'

The man stopped the sampan ten yards off shore, and a long and very one-sided conversation ensued. We kept asking John what he was saying, which did nothing but make it more difficult for John. Eventually I saw the man begin to draw away.

'Stop him, John. For God's sake stop him.'

'Shut up, David. I can't. He says the Japs have confined him to these waters. If he's ever found in Mirs Bay, they'll rip his guts out.'

'Ours too if that's the case,' added Lynton.

'No doubt, but he wasn't being unfriendly. He was in fact trying to tell me something but I couldn't make out what it was.'

We retired from the beach out of sight of the junks to plan what next to do. We had another look at the map before it became too dark. I was now sure that the bay was Hebe Haven where I had come with Henry Lo, and John agreed with me. This confirmed that Sai Kung lay to the north and was all too near the direct route to Sharpe Peak. While John had been talking to the junk man, Duggie and I had noticed a row of three little houses. They were set back from the beach about a hundred yards further along. Moored in front of them was a sampan. 'Duggie, your knee's not well enough to try walking all the way round Hebe Haven tonight,' I insisted, although I didn't relish the walk myself. 'Why don't we pinch that sampan we saw? It would save us miles.'

We considered the idea but thought it wiser to try to persuade the owner to row us across himself rather than stirring up a hornet's nest for ourselves in an area where no one so far had been in the least antagonistic. By the time we had made our decision it was too late to approach the house. We did not want to frighten anyone by appearing suddenly out of the darkness, so we decided to sleep where we were, stay put the next day and try our luck once again an hour before dark. We didn't sleep much. The mosquitoes saw to that. We covered ourselves as best we could but still they attacked. The next day we were covered in geat circles of our own blood where we had squashed them with our hands. There was no sign of the junks.

'Can't blame 'em,' said Lynton, 'for not wanting us anywhere near 'em if the Japs really are breathing down their necks.'

'Sure,' replied John. 'But I wish I'd understood what the man was trying to tell me. I am sure he was trying to be helpful.'

'Never mind, John. You did bloody well. I just hope you'll turn on the charm to such an extent that the sampan owner won't be able to turn us down.'

We lazed in the sun, content, with a plan firmly in mind. Evening came. The mist settled on the hilltops. It was clear and still beneath. There was not a ripple on the water and no one about as we stepped out onto the beach and walked slowly towards the three houses. Not until we stood ten yards away did an old weatherbeaten fisherman step out of the first doorway. He was smiling. We made a slight bow to each other, and John, pointing to the sampan, asked whether it was his. He nodded. John continued with the aid of signs and his limited Cantonese to make him understand that we wanted him to take us across the bay. Without hesitation he said he would. Decorum demanded that we keep our mounting excitement in check. John manfully struggled on, offering as payment the prodigious sum, to any such as the old man in those days, of ten of our precious $25. He told John that dollars were no longer any use in Hong Kong. We knew this to be nonsense. He pointed at Duggie's watch. He would take that. No, he could not have it.

By this time the family had gathered round to stare at us and enjoy the bargaining. Through them a little old woman pushed her way, bearing a cheap thermos and one cup. '*Cha*,' she squeaked and poured a little green tea into the cup which she handed to us in turn until there was no more.

Had we entered the house, the gesture would have been common courtesy but we had not. Our thanks were profuse, and all of them knew they were genuine. They also knew we were ravenous. She went into the house and came back again with a bucket, at the bottom of which was a small handful of cooked rice. They had just finished their evening meal, the old man told John apologetically. They had no more food in the house. Chinese are not renowned for compassion, but what else prompted this little old peasant woman to bring us the dregs of the family's evening meal? If it were not compassion, it was the nearest thing to it and how we blessed her even though three small spoonfuls of rice each did nothing to appease our hunger.

It was now dark and the old man urged us into the sampan although the financial arrangements were not resolved. He stood in the stern working the single oar back and forth while we sat facing him and listened intently as he spoke to John. Using his few words of English, he repeatedly said, 'This place all belong good men. Japanese belong no good.' He then lapsed into his own tongue, telling us, as far as John could make out, that there was a 'good man' with a boat who might take us across Mirs Bay. However, beyond the fact that it would cost money, John could not understand how contact might be made with this 'good man'.

So absorbed were we by what the old man was trying to tell us that we did not notice until too late that he was putting us ashore among a fleet of sampans, some of which were being prepared for a night's fishing. We hastened to find some suitable reward for our friendly boatman in the hope that we might slip away in the darkness. It was to no avail. We had been seen. Those preparing the sampans left them and surged round us. Oh God! This was exactly what we wanted to avoid. Others appeared from nowhere. We were soon surrounded by an ever-growing crowd of all ages. Their curiosity was not so much that they had never seen any 'round-eyed foreign devils' before but rather that none so downtrodden and dirty had ever set foot on the shore in front of their little village at dead of night. But this apart, how had they arrived now that the Japanese ruled the roost?

We were having difficulty in paying off the boatman when one man pushed his way to the front. 'All belong good men here,' and he waved his hand around the staring faces. 'Good.'

Pointing to the boatman, I said, 'Our friend velly good man. He say good man here have sampan take us more far. China side, can do?'

'Sure can do,' said the man.

Ever cautious John heard this and, leaving Duggie to settle with the boatman, whispered, 'For Christ's sake, David, be careful. All they've got to do is to delay us while they contact the Japs. I'll bet there's a reward on our heads.'

'Of course, I'll bet there is too. But why all this talk of a man with a boat? First the boatman, then this chap. They couldn't have been in league with each other. There must be something in it.' I turned to the man, 'More better one man come now, look see this man night time not morning time.' He shook his head and as I turned away he held my arm. 'Maybe after chow,' he said.

The boatman left, presumably satisfied with what he had been given, and as we argued among ourselves we began to move up the beach. The crowd slowly but surely were sweeping us towards their living-quarters. It was typical of the walled villages in southern China. The houses were built in a square facing a courtyard, with no windows in the outer walls and a great wooden door as the gateway which could be barred against intruders. It was here we stood, fearful of the dilemma which faced us. Was it a trap or were we foolish not to accept their hospitality? I felt a tap on my shoulder. I turned to find a diminutive figure looking at me intently. 'You belong soldier?' he asked. I hesitated. Was there still any magic left in the name of Jardine? I decided not to try. 'Yes, all soldier.'

The young man beckoned to me to follow him. He led me through the gateway and into his house. With the aid of a small oil lamp, he burrowed to the bottom of a chest and brought out a tatty piece of paper which he handed to me. On it I read, 'These people have housed and fed me and helped me on my way.' It was signed by a naval officer whose signature I could not read and dated just after capitulation.

I dashed out, waving the note. John, and to a lesser extent Lynton, did not share my enthusiasm but in the end were persuaded to accept the offer of a meal, especially when both Duggie and I made it clear that to show further distrust at this stage might be more dangerous than taking an opportunity to slip away later.

We were ushered to a corner house watched by a thousand and one pairs of eyes as we made our way into a small room which faced the courtyard. There we were given the seats of honour while as many as were able pressed in with us and others stood in the courtyard clustered round the door. The packed audience watched us drink green tea and listened to our feeble efforts to make some kind of conversation while the meal was being prepared. It seemed to take forever, especially since delicious smells of cooking began to waft into the room. We could hardly bear to wait. It had been so many months since we had had a full meal yet we continued to smile and nod and drink everyone's health in the tea.

At last two women pushed through the throng carrying steaming bowls of rice and various small dishes of fish and vegetables. Had there been nothing but rice, it would have been no less welcome. I hate to think how many bowlfuls each of us ate. Our appetite certainly intrigued the audience, but it was unlikely that they had any conception as to how we had lived since the fall of Hong Kong or, for that matter, how little had passed our lips during the last few days. Slowly the aching void in the pit of my stomach began to disappear. I have never forgotten it going. John remained apprehensive about their intentions. I still had no such qualms. Perhaps the food dulled my senses. But the naval officer's note seemed proof enough. After the most profusive thanks there came the problem of payment for the meal. We had so little to offer.

I turned to our host, who seemed to understand a little English. 'Please tell me your name and the name of this village. I will write a letter like the one given to you by the naval officer.'

He replied that the village was called Ho Chung and he was Mr Loo. I then told him I was from Jardine's and that in my letter I would ask the company to give him $200 upon presentation of the letter at the end of the war. (This was accepted and Mr Loo presented the letter very soon after the Japanese surrender. He received payment.)

Chapter 13

We moved out of the room where we had been given our first square meal in four months and into the courtyard, still surrounded by all those who had jammed in to watch us eat.

It was quite obvious that nothing was going to hurry the Chinese, and I drifted to the door in the village wall. Standing there for a few moments by myself, I looked out upon the bay which we had just crossed, now dotted with pinpricks of bright lights. An occasional figure could be seen crouching over the bow or stern of a sampan— John Chinaman peacefully fishing beside a pressure lamp. The sight relaxed for a few moments the tension within me. Above, the night was dark, the clouds thick on the hills. I shuddered and offered up a little prayer of thanks that we were no longer enshrouded in them, struggling to find our way.

Two men came to the doorway and disturbed my thoughts. It was time to go. After much bowing and more profuse thanks we set off, one guide in front with a lantern and one behind us. We walked in silence. The going seemed so easy with a swinging lantern to follow. At length the path from Ho Chung merged with a much wider track, and ahead it was just possible to make out a cluster of houses. The leader stopped us all under a large banyan tree and in a jumble of Cantonese and English asked us to wait there, while he and his pal went off to the village to make contact. I began to wonder if John's misgivings were right. There was something secretive about the way the man was acting. 'John, ask our friends the name of this village.' From the babble of Cantonese I heard Sai Kung. I had suspected as much. 'Sai Kung. This really puts us on the spot,' but before I could say more, John interrupted.

'Let's thank these men and tell them we'll go on from here on our own.'

'God, that won't do us much good,' said Duggie. 'In fact it is almost inviting them to contact the Japs if there are any about.'

'And make them lose plenty face,' I added.

'No, thank you, not at this stage. We would not have a cat in hell's chance of avoiding a determined search.'

'John,' said Duggie, 'tell the leader that we will hold his pal here while he goes alone to make contact.'

Somehow, John made the man understand. He did not demur and we waited until the lantern disappeared among the houses.

'Grab that lantern, Lynton, blow it out and force "our friend" to hide with us in these bushes,' ordered Duggie. 'We'll club him and run for it if we have to.'

It was not long before the lantern reappeared with two men. They stopped under the tree, surprised to find no one. Then we stepped out of the darkness. What was said between the three Chinese, John could not understand, but the leader beamed at us cheerfully and seemed to take our obvious distrust in good part. He relit the second lantern and made signs for us to follow him.

Soon we were walking on cobblestones between the houses. There was not a light, not a sound, except for our own footsteps. The little street was so narrow that it was claustrophobic until we emerged onto the waterfront where junks and sampans were tied up to the sea wall in front of a row of Chinese shop-houses. There was not a soul about.

One of the Chinese walked silently up to one of the doors and pushed it open. Its hinges squeaked. I looked about me but still nothing stirred. He beckoned. Through the doorway there was a steep flight of stairs and as I started to stumble up them, through the dark, thoughts flashed into my mind. Were John and Lynton right? Had we thrown caution to the wind? We all climbed the stairs which led directly into a big room ill-lit by an oil lamp.

Three men were sleeping in chairs. Another lay on the table in the middle. The man on the table sat up. The others stirred, while we stopped dead in our tracks. On the wall facing the door at the top of the stairs were two flags and a photograph. It was the flags which hit us because one was the Rising Sun of Japan and the other was not the Nationalist flag of Free China but that of the usurper, the Chinese traitor Wang Ching Wei, who supported the Japanese. The picture was, of course, a portrait of Wang himself. We were like animals led into a trap. Our only escape was blocked by the Chinese behind us.

The man who had led us up the stairs quickly tried to reassure us. 'Maskee, maskee,' he said. 'Look see, you savvy?'

He then said something in Chinese, which we could not understand, and everyone else in the room burst into laughter.

'Look see ah,' they chanted, 'belong look see, very good look see ah?' and they went on chortling, obviously delighted that we had been taken in. But had we? That was just what we wanted to be quite sure about. Our guide from Ho Chung could do no more than pat us on the arm and suggest we sit down on the floor.

'OK, OK,' he kept saying, 'good man come,' and he backed out of the doorway quickly—perhaps too quickly for our comfort. We sat down, feeling there was nothing else to be done.

The original occupants of the room continued to doze.

'Surely,' I said, 'if these birds intend to hand us over to the Japanese, those left to watch would hardly ignore us in this dozy way.'

'Pray God, you're right,' said Duggie, 'but if only we knew what was happening.'

'Perhaps it's better not to know,' interjected Lynton dourly.

We sat and waited for what seemed an unconscionable length of time.

'John, prod that chap on the table and see whether you can understand anything he might be able to tell us,' suggested Duggie.

John resignedly got up and as he did so there were footsteps on the stairs.

We were all on our feet in a flash. The door was rudely pushed open, and into the room burst a stocky little Chinese followed by another man who slammed the door behind him. Standing with legs apart in a somewhat aggressive manner, the first man to enter looked at us. He was dressed in a shabby green pin-striped suit with a grey slouch hat pulled over one eye. He had a Mauser slung at his side which he handled in the most casual manner, swinging it on his forefinger by the trigger guard. We did not laugh but it was ludicrous. We waited for this little thug to make a move. At length he nodded at us, and we responded, whereupon he and his sidekick proceeded to search us, feeling us bodily to see whether we were armed. Satisfied that we were not, he signalled us to pick up our packs and follow him. Down the stairs we trooped, out onto the waterfront and through the main part of the village. On the outskirts he stopped in front of a house while his aide hammered on the door, which eventually opened slightly. After a brief word the door shut again. We waited, sitting on a pile of stones. I asked John, 'Can you understand anything they're saying?'

'Not a word.'

We continued to wait and comforted ourselves that at least they did not seem in league with the Japanese. At last the door opened again. A tall, gaunt Chinese emerged. He walked over to where we were sitting and in near perfect English said, 'I'm sorry to have kept you waiting, but I was in bed asleep when you arrived and until then

I did not know that you were in Sai Kung.'

'Thank God you speak English and can tell us what is happening!' said one of us.

'Yes, I can understand your bewilderment,' he said, 'but I am a schoolteacher and I have been roused tonight because you do not speak Chinese,' with which John would have been the first to agree. 'You are in good hands and have nothing to fear because we are all members of a guerilla group fighting the Japanese. I am your interpreter.'

We told him about the old boatman who ferried us across Hebe Haven and how he had tried to tell us about a good man with a boat. He took it all as a matter of course and said, 'You are now being taken to meet the guerilla leader of this area. I will come with you. I think we should start. It is already late.'

The path we followed was extremely rough, and our guides, who obviously knew it blindfolded, set off at a cracking pace, moving with great agility while we stumbled and fell after them. Once clear of the houses we seemed to turn towards the sea and at length arrived at a big building, which apparently had been used as a school, but judging by its dilapidated state, that must have been a long time ago. We were led through an entirely empty ground floor, up a staircase at the back and into another small room where we were greeted by the guerilla leader. He was introduced as Cheung Ming. Again, he was dressed in a green pin-striped suit rather down at heel with a slouch hat pulled down over one eye, and he too had a Mauser which he swung round his finger by the trigger guard. Cheung Ming was small, thickset and looked as strong as an ox. From his moon-shaped face beamed his continuously smiling eyes, and he jabbered away while the interpreter did his best to translate.

There are some people to whom I take an immediate liking. Cheung Ming was one, and although we could not converse directly with him, it did not matter. An understanding seemed to develop automatically through signs and smiles.

Of course, it would have helped had the interpreter stayed more than a few moments after the initial introduction but, having told us he would not be away too long, he left with Cheung Ming's second-in-command to perform some mission which was not disclosed to us. Meanwhile, Cheung Ming continued to beam at us as he remained perched on the edge of the table swinging his legs and twirling the Mauser round and round by the trigger guard.

By this time we were feeling the effects of all that we had experienced since making contact with the old boatman. It seemed so long ago that we had made that fateful move because so much had happened that it was hard to believe that it was only seven hours. As we waited and wondered what the next move was going to be, we tried to keep awake, but each time our heads began to nod, Cheung Ming would throw both his arms in the air and shout, 'Up the ABCD Front! Up the ABCD Front!' This was the only English he knew. We had no idea what he meant. We simply repeated, 'Up the ABCD Front.' Then he roared with laughter and twirled the Mauser round his finger more ferociously, saying again, 'Up the ABCD Front.' Gradually the twirling would subside and for a bit all would be quiet and we would start to doze again, but not for long as the room was filled with the same roar. This and all the laughter that followed must have happened three or four times, until at last the second-in-command returned with a collection of buns, Chinese cakes and cigarettes, which he dumped on the table. Cheung Ming had despatched these two to knock up the local shops in Sai Kung despite the time of night because, as he said, he thought we must be hungry and would wish to smoke. This unexpected thoughtfulness simply warmed our hearts towards him.

Later, as I lay back, having again eaten too much and enjoyed the luxury of a cigarette, I asked the interpreter the sigificance of 'Up the ABCD Front'. We were told that it stood for America, Britain, China and the Dutch and their future campaign to annihilate the Japanese! Such a prospect seemed a long way off in April 1942, even to us who had yet to discover to just how low an ebb the Allies' fortunes had sunk. I rather suspect that the guerillas were little better informed than ourselves, and it was most encouraging to witness their attitude after the short, inglorious defence of Hong Kong.

By this time it was between three and four o'clock in the morning, and the interpreter told us that he had to return to Sai Kung. We were to move just before dawn to a more remote spot where we would be quite safe.

Cheung Ming would take us there and then leave to make arrangements for the next stage of our journey. 'You are in good hands. Good men. Just do what they tell you,' said the interpreter.

It was almost light when we set off with two guerilla escorts including Cheung Ming. We were led across the paddy fields towards the sea north of Sai Kung. We passed a lot of peasants already working who stood and stared at us. Cheung Ming seemed unconcerned by this. We eventually reached the sea. At the beach was a fair-sized sampan with a crew of two who wasted no time in getting us under way. It was a perfect morning, not a cloud in the sky, and the water, a deep blue, was like glass.

The sampan headed across yet another inlet towards a single row of houses tucked away in a remote corner under the hills which rose behind it. We hoped we were to be given a chance to rest in these blissful surroundings.

We landed and walked a couple of hundred yards from the beach to the end house. Cheung Ming told the owner we were to be housed and fed. The man was a middle-aged peasant farmer who, without any surprise or apprehension, bowed and invited us to enter his humble abode. Each house in the row had a frontage of only ten to twelve feet. The door led into a room with an earth floor. There were strips of red paper over the door to bring 'good joss' and help keep the devils away. There were no windows, only another door at the back of the room leading to the equivalent of our scullery. It was used for storage and for cooking. One corner was partially partitioned off for washing.

Although the sun shone bright outside, it was dark within and smelt of stale smoke for there was no chimney above the cooking stove. The whole family lived in this tiny area and slept in a loft in the roof.

During the next four weeks we were to stay in many such houses. It became easy to accept the conditions in which they lived. There was dirt but never squalor. Even in the most extreme poverty the Cantonese have a wonderful propensity to keep themselves immaculate. But when we walked into that small house, we were in no position to talk about cleanliness because we had not washed since entering the drain in Shamshuipo. We were filthy.

My shirt was in ribbons, and my shorts had a large rip which could have exposed most of one buttock except that my jockey shorts were still intact. We smelt filthy to the Chinese, I'm sure, because we were taken immediately into the scullery, shown the corner where we could wash and provided with a small hand-towel each. The womenfolk began to heat water.

John went first, followed by Lynton. Duggie and I sat on the ground just outside the front door and sunned ourselves. At length, Duggie said, 'God! They are taking a helluva time. I can't wait. The sea looks too inviting. I'm going in.' He jumped up with a piece of soap and the minute towel. At the edge of water he stripped, walked in knee deep and began to wash himself, presenting a white backside to all who cared to watch him. The water glistened in the sunshine, but the thought of being able to wash in hot water again dispelled any temptation to follow him.

John reappeared, 'all spruced up'. I walked into the scullery. Lynton was still pouring hot water over himself by dipping a small enamel saucepan into the bucket which the womenfolk provided. There was no door to the walled-off corner, just big enough for one person and a bucket.

'Get your clothes off, David. I will be out in a moment,' he said. I hesitated. 'There is no need to be shy. None of the women have taken the slightest notice of either John or myself, and there is no point in trying to kid yourself that you have something we haven't.'

I smiled. 'Any one of them would come and wash you at the drop of a hat,' he went on.

'How come that you are such an authority in these matters, Lieutenant White, sir?' He grinned.

'Try it yourself,' I said. 'Invite one of 'em to come and dry you with that pocket-handkerchief towel. You'll enjoy it! Only get out of there.' He got out but I noticed he had no nerve to invite assistance in drying himself!

I was brought a fresh bucket of steaming hot water and, having washed from head to foot, I plunged what remained of my shirt and pants and socks into the bucket and was given some more water in which to wash them. I kept my shorts, thinking that I could wash them later when the sun had dried my pants.

When all of us were clean and thoroughly refreshed, we sat at the round table in the main room and were brought steaming bowls of rice, eggs, a few chopped vegetables lightly cooked and green tea to drink. Later we discovered that Cheung Ming had sent one of his men all the way to Sai Kung to try to find some coffee. 'You like vely much after long time no have.' There was none to be had, but we marvelled yet again at the thoughtfulness of this splendid little man.

After the meal we sat in the sun and studied the hills in the direction of Kowloon, arguing about our route. It looked so easy in the bright sunlight.

'It doesn't really matter. All that matters is that we can relax in reasonable safety,' said Lynton.

'That may be so,' replied Duggie, 'but when you think of the actual ground we covered to put so little distance between us and the camp after five nights, we would have been in dead trouble but for these kindly folk.' There was nothing to be said. We all knew it.

We sat in silence, happy just to look at the loveliness of the country and the serenity of the land-locked sea.

The sense of safety brought on an overwhelming fatigue.

110

Somehow, somewhere, we had to sleep. We found a heap of drying grass in a small yard and sank into it in blissful oblivion. Two hours later we were woken by some young Chinese whose curiosity had got the better of them. Quite obviously most of them had come from some other settlement. It was not surprising, I suppose, that many in the area were aware of us. These young men meant no harm. They were simply intensely interested in our experience. Although awake now, we had to rouse ourselves to answer innumerable questions. They insisted on examining our packs and were intrigued by the cans of bully beef, intrigued also by how little we had existed on for so long. In the end, we invited them to open a tin. First one tin and then another was shared among them, much to their delight and our hope that the food would not again be needed.

Somehow or other Duggie had managed to extricate himself and slip indoors. When we tried to go inside, the young men followed us. We found Duggie engrossed in conversation with a cadaverous and very earnest Chinese.

His name was Henry Tam. He shook us warmly by the hand and much to our relief told our admiring followers to leave.

'I am sorry that my young friends disturbed your rest,' he said in perfect English, 'but the news of your arrival here has provoked much interest and they wished to see these brave English who have eluded the Japanese. I felt I could not deny them the privilege.' We thanked him for these kind words and for coming to see us himself.

'As I was telling your friend,' he said, pointing to Duggie, 'I am the propaganda administrator of this particular guerilla group. It is our policy to help anyone safely to reach Free China. It was my duty to hasten to see you the moment I was informed of your presence here.'

Again we thanked him and sang the praises of all those who had already given us so much help. 'That is good,' he said. 'I am very pleased to hear what you say, but you are not the first. Only quite recently we have been able to help a police officer and a lady who managed to escape from civilian internment at Stanley. The lady has been passed on and is now in Free China. The officer is still in the neighbourhood.'

We looked at each other, wondering who it might be, while Henry Tam continued pedantically to describe his work with the guerillas. Later, a Chinese entered and handed Henry a note. He looked at it. 'It is for you,' he said. Duggie, who was sitting next to him, read it aloud. To our amazement it was from the police officer to whom Henry had referred so short a time ago. It was signed

Thompson. None of us knew him. He suggested a meeting if we were able to follow the messenger. We looked at each other. One of us laughed, then we all roared. Eighteen hours earlier we had been struggling desperately to survive, to avoid the Japanese contingents scattered throughout the New Territories. Now we were invited to a rendezvous with a compatriot not quite, but almost, under their very noses. The change was hardly credible.

We recovered ourselves as Henry asked, 'Do you want to meet him?'

'Yes, please,' we chimed. Henry consulted Cheung Ming.

'If you leave at once, it is possible,' he said. We were ready in minutes.

Everyone gathered to bid us goodbye. They all remained to watch our progress until the path into the hills took us out of sight of the tiny settlement, which was called Tai Wan Ho.

That first, unstinted demonstration of genuine enthusiasm and good will from those who could so easily have turned us over to the enemy for a reward, aroused in me an emotion of both pride and humility. Pride that we had defied the Japanese, humility that we needed their help, help which was given so readily without regard to the risks involved. We did not know at that time, but to many of them an escape was looked upon as heroic.

As we moved across the New Territories, the legend seemed to follow us. We were unique oddities. An aura of interest surrounded us. To meet men who had escaped from the actual grasp of the Japanese fascinated them. What powers did we have which had enabled us to outwit the mysterious, diabolical strength which, in their eyes, the Japanese seemed to possess? Alas none, were the truth but known, except a determination not to waste away in a vile prison camp. Life was precious.

We met Thompson high up in the hills. He was a tall, dark, serious-minded man, as acutely interested in our experience as we were in his.

He began by explaining that he had been in a house not far from Sai Kung when early in the morning he was told that the Japanese had been seen near Tai Wan Ho. He took to the hills immediately, and it was some hours later that he learned that we were the intruders, not the Japanese, whereupon he decided to make contact.

'Sorry we were the cause of a little added excitement for you,' said Duggie.

We all laughed but the remark raised only a faint smile from

112

Japanese machine-gunners on the attack near Kowloon under command
of a 'Gunso' (Sergeant) with his traditional short sword in hand

Japanese landing at North Point on the Island

Japanese mountain guns near Jardine's 'Lookout' on the day before the
Hong Kong garrison fell

No flags herald the victor. Lt-Gen. Sakai passing through the Chinese
Quarter en route to the city of Victoria

A mixed bag of dejected prisoners being marched to the infamous camp of Shamshuipo where many hundreds were to die of starvation and disease

Primitive villages dotted the countryside; some afforded shelter but some contained Japanese collaborators

Kukong, 14th November 1942.

Letter from P.C.M. Sedgwick to
T.J. Fisher, Chungking.

A Lance Sergeant named Cheung Wing Kam
(   ) who was a detective attached to the Larceny
Squad, of the HongKong C.I.D., has reported here.
He states that he was forced by the Japanese Gendarmery
to work for them as a detective from the 27th March to
the 17th April.
He produced a photograph of David Bosanquet, which I
attach.   He tells me that he was instructed by the
Japanese to try and recapture Bosanquet and the three
other who escaped with him.   Luckily he failed to
do anything about it, but you may care to pass on the
photograph to Bosanquet as a souvenir.
I do not know, what the writing on the back is.
it might be a misspelling of Tai Lee, of whom I presume
you know.

A photograph of the author issued by the Japanese for use in their
efforts to recapture him

The author, immediately after the first
opportunity he had to remove his beard;
Yunnanfu, June 1942

In a walled village such as this the escapers received their first substantial meal for months

Sampans at Taipo. In one such sampan the author and his companions were taken across Mirs Bay

Large seagoing junks and inshore fishing sampans are a common sight
but nonetheless picturesque in war as in peace

Three generations aboard their junk—the permanent floating home
chosen by many thousands of fisher folk

Sai Kung, in spite of its dangers from enemy activity, was a place of
great beauty

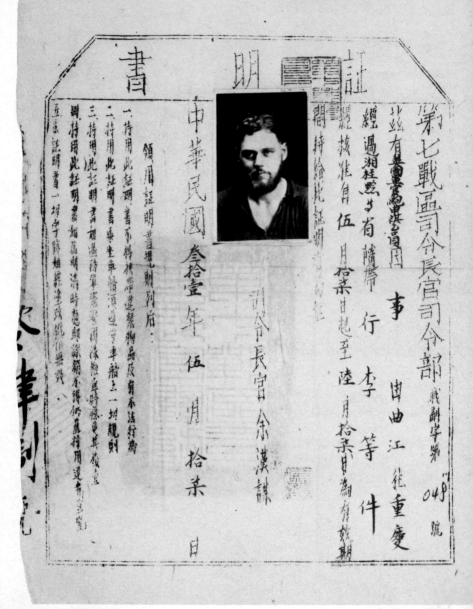

Chinese wartime passport issued to David Bosanquet in KuKong after his escape

Thompson. 'The explanation's easy. I'll bet those who saw us on our way to Tai Wan Ho passed the word that foreigners were about. To those having the news and who hadn't seen us, foreigners could only mean Japanese.'

Apparently it had been easy to get out of Stanley, where all the civilians were interned. The difficult part had been getting across to the mainland, but since he spoke good Cantonese, he had had none of the problems which we had encountered. The girl he had escaped with was Gwen Priestwood. I knew her and asked, 'Why did you choose Gwen?'

'It just happened.'

'Didn't you think any girl might be a liability?' I persisted.

'Yes,' he replied. 'But she was going anyway and I admired her determination. As it turned out, I couldn't have had anyone better. My God, that girl has guts.'

'Why didn't you go on through with Gwen?' Duggie asked him. He hesitated.

'I'm staying in this area to build up contacts. I shall try moving closer to Kowloon and get a message into Shamshuipo. Perhaps even Stanley.' He did not want to say more and we did not press him.

Anyway, we had to move on. Our destination, according to Henry Tam, was a junk which we presumed would take us across to Free China. We were glad of our brief encounter with Thompson. It raised our spirits, especially his information that the Chinese forces now controlled most of the approaches to Waichow, a large city fifty miles inland from Mirs Bay. He also said there was a British post there, run by Dr Scriven, who had practised medicine in Hong Kong before the war.

We travelled swiftly over the route which Henry Tam and yet another able aide, Fong, chose. Just after dark we swung off the path through a bamboo gate and into a farm. The house was rather larger than, and obviously superior to, any of those we had left. It stood back from the gateway through which we had just come. It was constructed in the same way except that the whole front of the house was open and the side walls had been projected from the eaves to form an inner courtyard open to the sky. The only break from the courtyard was two steps so that the floor under the roof was at a slightly higher level. Through the double doors of the inner courtyard which stood open we could see in the dim light a number of Chinese sitting round a table drinking tea and talking their heads off.

Fong, whom we were told had been a house-boy, walked straight up to the round table, and in trying to follow him we fell over unseen objects. Coming out of the darkness towards the dim light in the house, we could not see that the ground in front of the steps was littered with sleeping animals. As we tripped over them, another moved slightly, but none particularly resented our clumsinesss. A calf lay on the floor beside the round table, and chickens roosted on any convenient perch.

No surprise of any kind was shown as we stepped into the light. We were simply ushered to a stool when womenfolk appeared out of the background to offer hot towels—so refreshing—and to disappear again as quickly as they had come. We sipped tea while Henry Tam talked to the men round the table, having explained to us that Fong was collecting torches. It was not long before he appeared with bundles of dry bamboo sticks. 'Put two or three together and light them,' said Henry. 'You will find they will do no more than glow in here but as soon as we start moving they will burst into flame in the wind. Take plenty of spares. I don't know how long we will have to make them last.'

We paid our respects, waved the torches to make them flare, held them above our heads and stepped over another calf and a couple of pigs as we made our way out of the inner courtyard, through the bamboo gate and onto the path by which we had come. The going, once again, was quite easy and it was not long before we reached a few houses clustered together at the head of a small cove. As Fong approached one of them, he indicated that we should douse our torches and stand back in the shadow. He hammered on the door. Nothing happened. He went on hammering and after a considerable time two men appeared. A great deal of talk ensued. It seemed that Fong was arguing with them, and I whispered to Henry Tam, 'What is going on? Those men seem very disgruntled. Are they to be trusted?'

'They are telling Fong,' said Henry, 'that he is late and they do not wish to sail the junk tonight. They might not have time to get back before it is light. Don't worry. Fong knows what he is doing.'

'I am sure he does,' I said, 'but I hope he won't take any risks.'

Henry did not answer for just then the men moved off. Fong beckoned us to follow. As we did so, I said to Duggie, 'Don't like the look of these two chaps after everyone else we have met.'

'They don't exactly inspire confidence, do they?' he said. 'But Fong's all right. And I am sure Henry is.'

'He certainly knows what he's doing.'

114

A large junk loomed in front of us, and the moment we were aboard it slipped away from its moorings towards the mouth of the cove. The darkness closed in like a blanket round us, and our apprehension about the two crew faded as we sat below deck on rattan mats, listening to the gentle movement of the junk. Had we really left behind us the New Territories of Hong Kong? Were we actually heading for China? The thought was most exhilarating, even though there was still a long way to go. It had been quite a day. No matter how exhilarated we were, sleep overcame us.

Chapter 14

The junk lurched. We half woke. It lurched again. We were wide awake, groping about in the dark. There was another thump which made us stagger as we tried to collect our packs.

'We must have hit something,' said John.

'God, I wish I could see,' said Lynton, as we all fumbled for the small companionway to get on deck. As we emerged, Henry Tam and Fong were together.

'Henry, have we hit something or run aground?' I asked.

'We've just run ashore,' he replied, quite unconcerned.

'Where are we? We couldn't have crossed Mirs Bay so quickly.'

'Of course not,' he said. 'We were not trying to. That was never the plan. We have crossed into Plover Cove, and we must now make our way to the village of Chung Mei before it gets light.'

We stood in silence, looking at each other with the same thought in mind. We were still in the New Territories. God, what a let-down. I had been so sure we were on our way to China.

Fong and the crew pushed out a long plank from the bow. One man jumped into the water to improve the angle of the plank so that we need only go into the water up to our knees instead of our waists. Fong led the way. 'Please,' said Henry Tam, 'we must hurry because the junk has to return and we have a long walk.'

Sure enough the moment we were ashore the junkmen disappeared. They were delighted to be rid of their dangerous cargo.

It was a long walk to Chung Mei. It seemed to take hours, yet it was still dark when the first house appeared. Fong once again marched up to a door and hammered on it. His head went from side to side, nervously watching in case anyone saw us while we waited, to the sound of shuffling footsteps inside. A small, middle-aged man eventually put his head out and nodded casually, yet again totally unconcerned about being so rudely disturbed at four o'clock in the morning.

Once inside the house, Fong relaxed. We were standing in a small store. We were led to the back of it, and there, separated by a screen, were the usual living-quarters. Four o'clock in the morning or not, we were to be given a meal, true Chinese hospitality given to

116

weary travellers.

It was light outside by the time Duggie and I climbed the ladder into the loft. John and Lynton took the benches we'd sat on to eat. In the loft I found what must have been the bed of our friend, a couple of boards and a Chinese pillow—a small block of wood shaped to fit the nape of the neck. All right for those who sleep on their backs like the Chinese, otherwise useless. We both chose the floor.

We were tired enough to sleep anywhere, so we thought, but by noon we could stand the persistent attacks of mosquitoes no longer. We were bitten to death. We roused the others, suggesting a walk through the village, when Henry Tam appeared looking worried.

'Please don't go outside,' he said. 'You must not let anyone know you are here until it is time to move on. It is very dangerous. There are some bad Chinese about, men who rob people going to Taipo market. Brigands you call them, I think.' We nodded. 'If they saw you, they would tell the Japanese, who are not far away, hoping for a reward.'

'I bet they would,' I said. 'When do we move on, Henry?'

'I cannot tell you when or where until Fong gets back. Please be very careful. We don't want any trouble, do we?'

'No,' we said almost in unison. It was not just our skins. We knew that the whole village would be slaughtered if we were caught.

'Have no fear, Henry. Only over my dead body will any of these three jokers put their noses outside,' said Duggie.

'Well, prepare to die,' Lynton said without a trace of a smile. 'I've got to go out right now.'

'What the hell for?'

'I'm bursting. Haven't peed since we arrived. I'm no bloody camel.' We all laughed, including the ever-serious Henry Tam, who said, 'You would not be seen in the bushes outside the back door.' We remained penned in the tiny room for two more whole days. It wasn't such a bad existence but by the second morning we were getting a little agitated. 'Calm down, for God's sake,' said Duggie. 'You're being well fed. What more do you want?'

'A lot,' added John. 'There aren't any girls!'

'Seriously,' broke in Lynton, 'I wonder if Henry's unsavoury characters live in Chung Mei? I thought I heard some people outside last night.'

'It was the rats,' I said. 'This place has nearly as many rats as mozzies.' I hated rats. They repulsed me.

However, Duggie was right about the food, and all our joking did not take away that fact. It was fascinating to see it prepared—from nothing and out of nothing, it seemed. In the corner of the room was a large metal cauldron set in an earthen fireplace, shaped to take it. The fuel used was the dried grass the peasant women had been collecting, with a few sticks thrown in to keep it going.

Two meals a day were cooked. First, the cook thoroughly washed the rice in many changes of water, all of which had been brought from a spring far beyond the village. Then he put just sufficient water to cover the rice and boiled it until the water had evaporated. Immediately the beautifully separated grains of rice were put into a wooden tub with a lid on top. The cauldron was ready to take meat of some kind or fish.

In our case it was chicken—meat was a rare delicacy for any peasant. The chicken was chopped into small pieces, bones and all so that nothing was wasted. It was then fried in its own juices and put into small porcelain bowls ready for the table. Another method was to boil a whole chicken and cook it until the flesh fell off the bones when prodded with chopsticks. In this case it was served whole in its own soup. With the chicken out of the cauldron, it was the turn of the green vegetables to be very lightly boiled. The cauldron was never taken off the fire. If any water remained, much was allowed to boil away and the remainder was flicked out on the earth floor with a brush made of thin wood-shavings tightly bound at one end.

As soon as the first dish was ready, we were given a bowl of rice from the wooden bucket steaming hot and we started to eat. The second dish and the third, if there was one, each came in quick succession. Best of all was a delicately fried egg which cooked in seconds from the moment it touched the hot cauldron.

This simple meal was very different from the formal Chinese dinners we had been used to, where rice was only served afterwards and it was bad manners to eat a lot—which, of course, we did in the village.

The next morning Fong arrived and had a quick word with Henry Tam. Then he left in a hurry. The eager little man was always running, nervous like an animal. Henry stayed and told us that we would leave that evening to go to guerilla HQ in the hills. It was taking time to arrange the dangerous passage across Mirs Bay.

We were glad that we were soon to get away from our cramped quarters and the fear of being surprised at any time.

'Thank you, Henry, for taking so much trouble,' said Duggie.

'That's OK.' He looked even more serious than usual.

'Do you know the movement of the Japs round here and in Mirs Bay?' Duggie went on while we all waited expectantly for the answer.

'And that's part of the problem only,' said Lynton.

We did not ask what the other part might be. We could guess: frustration.

We sat in silence for a long time. The day dragged on, and just when I felt it would be nice to eat again, there was a commotion at the front of the house, then hammering on the door. We leapt to our feet. Should we bolt through the back? We heard the door open. It was then too late, and we stood at the ready, armed with nothing! But it was Fong who appeared. A broad smile spread across his face as he saw our consternation. We relaxed but could only muster a faint smile in response.

Wasting no time, he stepped aside and waved us out. As we emerged, a small armed guard sprang to attention. Four stepped forward to relieve us of our packs. We resisted but Fong made it very clear that we should not.

There were ten in the escort, some of them little more than boys, armed wih an assortment of weapons, dressed in coolie vests and the usual Chinese trousers—a motley bunch if ever there was one. And yet each one exuded enthusiasm. Each one had a beaming smile and seemed silently to say, 'You are one of us. We are proud to be your guard.'

From that moment, until we were forced to say goodbye to our guerilla friends many days later, we were never permitted to move without an armed escort.

If we were surprised that evening in Chung Mei, as indeed we were, it was only a small demonstration of what was in store for us but an hour or so later.

Beyond the outskirts of the village the path rose steeply into the hills, and while it was a great relief to be on the move again, we were soon puffing and panting in an effort to keep pace with our vanguard. We had to stop from time to time to catch our breath and in doing so, before the swirling mist cut visibility to a few yards, were able to gaze over Plover Cove, across Tolo Channel to the hills through which we had come. But for the odd cluster of peasant houses with wisps of smoke hanging over their roofs, there was nothing man-made to mar the natural beauty of that small corner of the vast China Continent. Few knew of the beautiful little valleys which existed between those austere hills and the streams which gently wound in and out of rocky beds suddenly, at times, to cascade over a small cliff to a clear pool beneath, or of the small, isolated paddy clothed in the vivid green of young rice growing in its sodden bed. How we had cursed the mist when struggling on our own. Now, no longer alone, it held no fears. Instead, as it came and went, it gave an ethereal look to everything about us.

As the path became less steep, our escort suddenly burst into song. Then in unison they stopped singing as abruptly as they had started and we could hear the song being repeated in the distance. We marched on and the same thing happened again but the answer now sounded quite close. Clearly our arrival was being heralded. The path became very narrow, with high banks thickly covered with scrub meeting overhead.

At the end of this natural tunnel the leaders stopped, waiting for the mist to clear a little. As it did, we saw below us two or three acres of paddy fields. On the far side was a row of the usual houses set into the hill behind them. In front, an earth terrace had been built to separate them from the paddy. Then our eyes met an incredible sight which took away our breath. Drawn up on that terrace in three ranks was the main body of the guerillas of which our escort was a part.

A tremendous cheer echoed round the hills. Fong, who had been behind us all the way from Chung Mei, took the lead, and as the path widened where it made its way round the paddy, the escort formed up on each side of us.

Our progress was watched in silence until we were almost on the terrace, when there was another cheer which continued until we ourselves stood to attention before the group to pay our respects. This fantastic greeting with its sheer enthusiasm told us that here at least there was no resentment for the poor showing of the British against the Japanese. It was also fantastic that a people generally so undemonstrative as the Chinese should show such emotion. I do not know about the others but there was a lump in my throat, and my eyes were decidedly moist. The Chinese broke ranks and swarmed around us to shake our hands or just to get a closer look at us.

Somehow we were extricated from the throng and led into a small, cramped room in the end house, where, after we had been given a chance to recover, various members of the group came to talk to us while Henry Tam acted as interpreter.

The group consisted of fifty or sixty men and boys. However, there were also some women, both old and young. One had returned from Malaya to join the group; another, a formidable species of womanhood, appeared to be the right hand of the leader.

120

After we had eaten, Henry told us that the whole group had gathered in one of the other houses and were waiting for us to honour them with our presence.

The room was packed. Some were sitting, others standing, and somehow we had to make our way to a small, round table which had been set in the traditional place of honour at the furthest point from the entrance.

No sooner had we appeared in the doorway than everyone started to clap, and the clapping continued until eventually we managed to reach the table. As we threaded our way through the gathering, those sitting on the floor patted our legs as we passed. Those standing patted us on the back. This reception, like our earlier arrival, was charged with emotion.

Once we had taken our places round the table and the gathering had settled down, different members of the group from all quarters of the room continually jumped to their feet to make speeches of welcome. They were all the same pattern of how clever we had been to escape from the Japanese and how, together, we would drive them from the mainland of China back to their own islands, never again to pillage, rape and plunder the good people of China and all their friends.

It was a long performance because each speech had to be interpreted, no matter how repetitive. In the end we were called upon to reply. Duggie did so. Henry interpreted. The speech got an ovation. This was followed by songs and again we were called upon to perform. We were not very good. Neither could any of us remember the words of any song. We staggered through some kind of repertoire which included *It's a Long Way to Tipperary*, and just as we thought that the proceedings were drawing to a close, one of the Chinese who had spent some time in Latin America rose to his feet and told the assembled company that he would sing a song in 'English'. He then proceeded to sing *It's a Long Way to Tipperary* rather better than we had done. We applauded loudly, having recovered from the initial shock, but there was no need for embarrassment since there was not a soul in the room who realized that it was one of the songs which we had just sung.

Were we at last allowed to leave and go to bed? Not a bit of it. Back in the house at the end of the row Henry said, 'Mr Choi is on his way to see you and should arrive quite soon.'

'Henry,' I asked, 'who is Mr Choi?'

'Mr Choi is very important,' he replied. 'He is our leader in the whole of this southern area.'

'Oh,' I said, 'he does us great honour by coming so far into the hills just to see us.'

Then a tall, spare, intellectual-looking Chinese walked into the room. We got up and shook hands, bowing almost imperceptibly as we did so. Mr Choi was very earnest and after the usual pleasantries began to tell us all about the activities of his particular guerilla group which, since the fall of Canton to the Japanese in October 1938, had been operating in the southern part of the province of Kwangtung.

At that time we knew little about Chinese internal politics. We were four young men in our early twenties who had come to Hong Kong to do a job. Our thoughts had not been concerned with internal Chinese politics but with the war in Europe, the survival of England and, for the past year in particular, the menace of Japan to the whole of Asia. We knew, of course, of the ideological split in China, that Sun Yat Sen had been a Cantonese and that a new rebellion, led by a so-called people's party, was in the north. Therefore, as Mr Choi began to unfold his story, the full significance and its political implications did not strike us. We found it hard to understand why Kuomintang forces and these guerillas could not operate together against the Japanese, which surely both recognized as the common enemy. Mr Choi went to some pains to explain that, while his group was labelled Communist by the Chinese Central Government, his members did not consider themselves as such and in fact yearned to be recognized for what they were—men and women committed to do all within their power to lift the Japanese yoke from China.

It was now the early hours of the morning. We were allowed to go to bed. Mr Choi left us, saying that he would come again to continue the talk next evening and, in true Chinese fashion, hoped we would accept his apologies for the meanness of our quarters. We smiled and assured him that there was no need for any apologies since to have a roof over our heads and to be among friends who had given us such a welcome was a luxury we would never forget. Mr Choi in offering us his apologies was in all probability doing no more than conforming to the Chinese custom of the host belittling anything and everything he might give his guests. We, on the other hand, meant everything we said.

We looked at each other. We knew what we were saying, yet our lips never moved. 'Yes, we have escaped. We can feel it in our bones. We have made it to friends, who will see us through the next critical stage of our long journey. Thank God.'

We climbed the ladder into the half loft, arranged our packs as pillows and lay down on the bare boards, huddled together for warmth. It was remarkable that we slept as well as we did, for the loft was full of my hated enemies—rats, who not only sniffed around the packs but appeared to set themselves a steeplechase course using all parts of our anatomy as the obstacles.

That night and the one following, their capers in that loft, despite my intense loathing of them dead or alive, did not worry me. It was still luxury, despite them, to be under cover and in the care of these good peasant folk.

Immediately we appeared the next day, the whole troop engulfed us, eager to show their weapons and their proficiency in handling them. They had Chinese rifles of a quite unpredictable vintage, some of our service rifles and a remarkable number of Mausers such as our friend Cheung Ming had twirled by the trigger guard while he entertained us at the school outside Sai Kung. In addition they had a Vickers machine-gun, a Bren and two Lewis guns, of all of which they were very proud, but nothing could induce them to tell how they came by these weapons. I could not conceive how the Vickers could have been of any use because any of their operations had to be a hit-and-run affair, and yet, of them all, it was a prize possession, and some time that morning was spent setting it up to attack an imaginary target in the paddy from various strategic points on the terrace in front of the row of houses.

That evening Mr Choi returned, and once more we were closeted with him for hours while he told us in minute detail of all the problems which beset his group. Money was running low because the group had relied largely upon remittances sent from Chinese living abroad through banks in Hong Kong. Now their only income came from fees extracted from people in Hong Kong who wanted protection while they travelled to relatives in Kwangtung Province. Those who did not solicit the aid of the guerillas laid themselves open to attack by robbers who would strip them of everything they had. The railway between Kowloon and Canton was tightly controlled by the Japanese, and very few locals were allowed to travel by it. The road was similarly controlled, which forced the average individual to make his way across country or find passage by junk across Mirs Bay. Although a number did seek the protection of Mr Choi's men, it could not have been a very lucrative source of income, yet it was clearly evident that anyone called upon to help us was promptly paid. We were determined to have them repaid in full when we got safely through. Indeed, we promised Mr Choi that we would do everything to get support for his group. The session ended on this note, and we retired to the loft for the rats to have their fun for the second night.

I remember that night so well that it could have been yesterday. I could only sleep fitfully. For the first time my thoughts were riveted inexplicably to the camp and not on our next move. What had been the Japanese reaction? What reprisals they might have taken preyed on my mind. We knew there had to be some. They had lost 'plenty face', for which only our mutilated bodies exposed for all to see could atone. I hoped the guards had got it in the neck but that reprisals against the prisoners had been irksome rather than vicious. It was a long time before I knew what did happen after we escaped from Shamshuipo. The first personal account was from John's brother Alec after the war.

It was then that Alec told how he was taken out of the camp just after the morning muster parade at which we were missing. He was questioned at length and beaten, although not badly enough to break any bones.

'After that they made no move for a month,' Alec recounted. 'Then suddenly, when I thought the hue and cry was over, ten of us were rounded up, for no sensible reason. We were taken out of camp and made to strip. We were then thrown into minute cells in pitch blackness. They left us there for days to wallow in our excreta and never able to wash. At times we were taken away for further interrogation. It was a relief just to get out of the cell, in spite of the beatings. I was made to kneel on a concrete floor naked and in front of a low table on which a Japanese officer put drawings of different escape routes which they said had been done by one of you. Of course, I knew they were not yours but I did not argue. I was just thankful that I had no idea which way you had gone and could profess complete ignorance without having to lie. Looking back on the whole affair, I think the worst thing of all was being smothered in lice and not being able to get rid of them.'

Alec had to endure this appalling treatment for three weeks, during which time he had to listen to one of his fellow prisoners, Peter Lloyd, being beaten to death.

Peter Lloyd was a sergeant in the Volunteer Force, and he, like the others with the exception of Alec, knew nothing of our plans, although both John and I knew him.

Whatever any of us may have felt about the apathy in Shamshuipo, a tragedy of this kind disturbed us greatly. Could he have survived, as did the others taken out for interrogation? Was Peter Lloyd arrogant or did he argue? No one knew. Being very arrogant themselves, the Japanese took a particular delight in beating the so-called arrogance out of the British. Post-war reports of the treatment of POWs confirm this. In many cases it was enough to give the appearance of arrogance, no matter how unintentional it may have been, to bring about a beating. The problem remained for every Japanese POW throughout the war. How could you best behave and yet maintain some dignity?

At the end of three weeks the remaining eight prisoners in the 'special treatment' cells with Alec had to face a final and terrifying ordeal. A road ran the full length outside the eastern perimeter of the camp and finished in a dead end at the harbour. It was to this point that the Japanese took any citizen who had offended, for punishment or execution. There had been quite a few soon after capitulation who had been run through with a sword in full view of the camp, and the bodies, sometimes still twitching, kicked over the sea wall into the harbour.

Alec, among the last nine, was dragged out of the cells, herded to this very spot under guards with drawn swords and made to kneel on the edge of the wall.

'We waited for the first blow to be struck as the guards stood in front of us. After minutes which felt like hours we were forced to our feet, but still no blow was struck. Oh God, did this mean a sword through the stomach? I would rather have my head cut off,' said Alec. Then swords were sheathed and this ill-clad, emaciated, lice-ridden party was marched back to the guard-house at the main gate to Shamshuipo. There they were all given their clothes and returned to their quarters.

I can think of no more shattering experience for anyone. For Alec it was a nightmare beyond description, because the gnawing thought must have been ever present, 'Why, in the name of God, didn't I go with them?'

These nine men were lucky. Mercy is not something which has figured prominently in Japanese military history. For the losers there was honourable death in battle. If they did not choose to take that course, no death was too ignominious for any captive. I'm sure it was this attitude, inculcated for generation after generation, which accounted for the treatment that was meted out to all their prisoners during the war in Asia.

Chapter 15

The next morning the clouds were very low and it was still raining.

'I wonder what the weather is like down below,' I said to anyone who cared to listen as we stood in the doorway of the little house which had been allotted to us since our arrrival.

'It's bloody wet and miserable here,' said Lynton. 'Why do you wonder what it is like down below?'

'I was thinking about conditions for us to cross Mirs Bay. We don't want a clear night,' I said. Mirs Bay was a direct route to the Chinese mainland and thus to Free China. 'It would also be nice to know whether the guerillas have any information on how the Japs send out patrol boats from Sha Tau Kok,' I said, referring to a village set in a small harbour occupied by the Japanese navy to the north of us.

'I think they are pretty clued up,' said Duggie, 'and poor visibility and a good tail wind will be a great advantage.'

'I'm sure they know what they are doing, Duggie, but we'll be sitting ducks in a boat in Mirs Bay.'

There was nothing to be done about it. Clearly it was the best way to get us into Free China, and none of us felt we had any right to suggest the only other course of trying to cross the Sumchung River between the border points of Lo Wo and Sha Tau Kok.

That morning we all sat around dragging out the time until noon, when Fong appeared. Then we went in search of Henry Tam to translate for us.

We found Henry lying in a corner of a hut, wrapped up in a blanket, very ill. His whole body was shivering with malaria. He listened to Fong and through chattering teeth then told us that all necessary arrangements had been made for us to go. We would be leaving during the afternoon, and Fong would see us aboard the junk. Henry added that Fong was very sorry but he himself would not be able to accompany us all the way, as had been his original intention. This was bad news because he had proved such an efficient guide and we had confidence in him. We must have shown dismay because Henry immediately said, 'I will come with you. This fever will pass by the time we will have to leave.' It was a brave gesture but while we desperately wished that he could have come, it was quite obvious that he would not be fit to travel anywhere for two or three days.

'No, Henry,' said Duggie. 'You obviously can't move. We'll have to manage without you. We'll be in good hands with any of your friends.'

Henry's face showed relief, but as we left him we began to worry that the language barrier would make communication almost impossible for this vital leg of the journey.

In the middle of the afternoon an escort of guerillas formed up, took our packs and waited while we went to say goodbye to Henry, but he was asleep.

'We must thank him for all his help,' said Duggie. Eventually we left a note on the floor beside the huddled figure.

We retraced our steps to Chung Mei and passed through the village to a spot on the shore where some sampans were moored. In front of them were ranged thirty or forty members of the guerilla troop. Fong indicated that our singing friend, the Spanish-speaking Chinese Alberto who had returned from South America, was in charge of a party to accompany us. We clambered aboard one sampan with six, and the half remaining leaped aboard two others. Those left on the shore waved vigorously as the little flotilla put out to sea.

It was another fantastic scene: a motley bunch waving their weapons in the air on shore; four of us standing in one sampan, flanked by our guard, and an equally motley bunch armed to the teeth in the sampans on either side of us. It only needed a large sea-going junk to have been riding at anchor out in the cove for it to have become a perfect film sequence of Chinese pirates returning with four captives. The only trouble was that 'the victims' were hardly acting the part since they were waving as merrily as anyone else.

Long after the shore party was out of sight, the two accompanying sampans continued to sail with us until we began to wonder whether they intended to escort us all the way and whether we could possibly make them understand that so many men should not be put at risk since they could not defend us were we unlucky enough to encounter a patrol boat. However, there was no need for concern because at the mouth of Plover Cove the two sampans altered course; the men gave a cheer, waved again and again and left us to sail out into Tolo Channel alone.

Alberto, our new commander, made signs for us to go below to ensure that we were not seen. This meant crawling aft, where a section was covered by matting stretched over curved bamboos from one side of the sampan to the other. Alberto was tall and swarthy with long black hair--a Latin American influence, no doubt—and was not one to look you straight in the eye. He lacked, so we thought, the stable character of both Cheung Ming and Fong and consequently did not command our confidence.

The cabin, for want of a better description, was windowless and no more than six by five feet, and in it were a young Chinese and his wife, who was suckling a tiny baby. This little family were obviously 'fee-paying' passengers and, although they put a brave face on the situation, were anything but happy to have us as fellow passengers. Somehow we all crammed into this minute space and remained there as long as daylight lasted.

As soon as it was dark, we emerged from the cramped quarters into the air to see how far we had got. We were in Mirs Bay but the breeze which had taken us swiftly and happily down Tolo Channel had died away.

The sampan was making no headway. This was one thing which we all had dreaded might happen. We were sitting ducks. Our anxiety was shared by everyone aboard, not least the old boatman who sailed the sampan. He knew that he carried a dangerous cargo, a cargo far more dangerous to him than dynamite, a cargo which could bring appalling, lingering death. Small wonder that all he could say in his sing-song Cantonese was '*Mo Fong . . . eh, Mo Fong . . . eh,*' 'No wind . . . no wind.'

Indeed, there was not a breath of wind. The boatman began physically to propel the sampan towards the China coast hardly visible in the dim distance, while the sail hung like a lifeless rag.

However, very slowly we got farther and farther out into Mirs Bay. We could see bright lights at the dreaded village of Sha Tau Kok. They must be Japanese. We sat in silence listening to the creak of the oar as the old man manœuvred it in the waters.

Suddenly there was a roar of an engine being started. We all froze. Even the boatman stopped *yuloing* for a moment. Nobody said a word until he started again with renewed vigour. There was nothing we could do. None of us could take over from the old man to give him a rest for there is a great art in *yuloing*. We'd probably have upset the boat.

The engine spluttered and stopped; everything was quiet again. We looked over the side of the sampan to see whether there was the slightest sign of a bow wave indicating we were making headway. It seemed to be so, but the lights of Sha Tau Kok were still menacingly close, and the dark land-mass ahead appeared to get no nearer. By now we were seized by another gnawing doubt. Would we make the crossing before daybreak?

The engine started again. A light from Sha Tau Kok flashed seawards, or was it our imagination? We prepared to go overboard at a moment's notice if the patrol boat's searchlight caught us. To jettison our packs and to try to remain hidden in the water on the lee of the sampan seemed the only hope.

The throb of the engine continued. But it got no nearer. There was another flash of light. I was sweating now, although the night was cool. Suddenly the engine on the still invisible boat cut. We all remained tense, frightened it might start again. We were so tense that it was some time before anyone noticed that the sail had begun to fill. A breeze (oh so gentle), but it was a breeze. We felt the sampan respond. The old boatman held her into the breeze and gradually, very gradually, our tension eased. It lasted until we were quite close in to the shore. Why were the lights at Sha Tau Kok still visible? Surely Sha Yu Chung, the predetermined landfall, was further up the coast? We were coming into a small bay by a tiny peninsula which jutted out into the sea. We all strained our eyes to see a sign of the village. I could make out nothing much, although we were very close to the beach.

Suddenly the old boatman whipped the sampan round and began rowing out to sea again as if all the devils in China were after him.

'What the hell is going on?' asked Duggie as we all picked ourselves up from the bottom of the boat.

John spoke to Alberto, who only gesticulated with his arms, which told us nothing.

'This man's no bloody good,' I said. 'I wish to God that Fong were here.'

The old man and his mate in the bow worked feverishly until we were clear of the point of land jutting out to our left. Then he slackened his efforts. We began, once again, slowly to creep up the coast, until we came to the entrance of another small bay where the old man left his oar, hauled down the sail and hurled the anchor over the stern. We rushed up to him, vigorously pointing in the direction of the land, and by every possible demonstration indicated that we wanted to be put ashore. The boatman would not budge, and when one of us seized the long oar, he simply tightened the rope by which it was held so that it could not be moved.

I turned my attention to Alberto and pointing to the shore said,

'Sha Yu Chung? Alberto, Sha Yu Chung?' He did not answer and as he was about to turn away, I seized him and shook him by the neck.

'Answer, you silly bastard. Is this Sha Yu Chung?' He just looked at me and gaped. I was about to shake him again when my arms were grasped from behind.

'David, don't be a bloody fool. It's no damn good doing that.' It was John. He was right. And in seconds I felt thoroughly ashamed at such a lapse of self-control. I attempted to apologize but his pride had been so sorely damaged that no apologies could make amends. It was an incident of which I have never been proud, and I am afraid that Mr Alberto Chiang, lately returned to his native land from Argentina, now had a very different attitude towards his English friends. We were no longer '*Ho Pung Yau*'—good friends. We had to be content to be simply '*Pung Yau*'. The attack did nothing to relieve the nervous strain. We sat in silence, each one lost in his own thoughts, still listening for an approaching boat.

Lying at anchor the sampan dipped and bobbed in the swell. Soon the movement was too much for the young Chinese girl, who struggled to the side and was sick. Her baby started to scream as she hung there almost toppling into the water in a desperate attempt to escape the feeling of seasickness. Meanwhile, the father's efforts did nothing to quell the screams of the child. God! How long could this be endured? Would this terrible night never end? And, when it did, would we be at a point on the coast where it would be safe to land?

As the screams of the baby continued, the girl dragged herself back, crept under the bamboo cover, lay down as best she could in the cramped space beneath it and let the baby suckle. Once more there was silence. Heaven be praised! Despite our anxiety we could only feel sorry for the poor girl.

Streaks of light began to appear, and it was possible to see a few shadowy figures near the beach. However, it was still too dark to tell who they might be. They did not look like Japanese; neither did they act as if they were, also it was too far away to hear what they were saying. As it grew lighter, two figures climbed into a small boat and rowed towards us. No one on the sampan moved. We were transfixed by uncertainty. Then one of those approaching hailed us, and the suspense was over. They were guerillas who had been expecting us.

We were taken ashore, landing on the golden sand of a beautiful beach, and were greeted by others who immediately led the way to a small village nestling among some huge spreading banyan trees.

130

Around the village a kind of stockade had been built which was patrolled by guerilla sentries. It was some kind of a stronghold with hidden escape routes because being so near the coast it was vulnerable in the event of an attack with which they could not cope.

At a large house in the middle of the village we were introduced to a venerable old gentleman who spoke English with a broad American accent. He told us that he had spent many years in San Francisco and had only in the last few years returned to Kwai Chung, to make sure that he would die in his native village.

'Kwai Chung! Is this village called Kwai Chung?' I asked.

'Yes,' he replied.

'But we were told when we left Chung Mei that we would land at Sha Yu Chung.'

'Come,' he said, ignoring my question, 'the meal is ready. I expect you are hungry.' We nodded. 'While you are eating, I will tell you all about it.'

He led us to the usual Chinese round table. On it were a few dishes of vegetables, fish and chicken, and a great steaming bowl of rice in the middle. While we ate this excellent food, the old man told us that a small force of Japanese had raided Sha Yu Chung only two days before but that very little damage had been done by the raiding party because it had been attacked by the guerillas and driven off. 'Our boys did very well,' he said, 'but it was lucky that you did not cross Mirs Bay two nights earlier. You would have landed in the middle of it all!'

'That's why the preparation for our crossing took so long,' said Lynton.

'Yes, probably, but why weren't we told about the switch to Kwai Chung?' said Duggie.

'It might have saved Alberto from my attack upon him!' I added.

'Look at my house,' said the old man, seemingly ignoring our talk. 'Once it was a fine home but now I must apologize for it and all the cheap furniture. Some time ago those goddam bastards came to this village, burnt some of the houses, raped some of our women and took nearly everything I had.' He went on raging about the Japanese. He never called them Japanese but 'those goddam bastards' or 'those goddam sons of a gun'. It was a joy to listen to him! Finally he said, 'More better you rest. You go Sung Tong by and by. Now you lie down upstairs.'

We went upstairs but got precious little rest. We were the object of much curiosity, for half the village found some excuse to come and look at us, until finally a small group of young men arrived,

131

triumphantly bearing a Japanese flag with blood on it which, we were told, had been captured at Sha Yu Chung during the raid two nights earlier. It was a great prize. We agreed but we wondered what future retribution it might bring. This was the problem, or so it seemed to us: retribution against innocent and defenceless people for a pinprick which caused the enemy no more than mild irritation. The bravery of these ill-equipped people could only be used to real advantage when the Allies were in a position to back them.

That afternoon we moved on to the headquarters of the 3rd Division of the Kwangtung Guerillas at Sung Tong. We were subjected to the same lengthy talks with the leaders as had been the case with Mr Choi in the hideout above Chung Mei. We were asked to carry pamphlets to various towns and villages through which we must pass on our way to Waichow. Blissfully ignorant of their content and true political substance, we consented happily.

During these talks a large dish of *wong tong* was put on the table before us. *Wong tong*, literally yellow sugar, is sugar in its unrefined state pressed into slabs and then cut into fingers so that it is easy to eat. We had been starved of anything sweet for so long, apart from the cakes which Cheung Ming had produced in the schoolhouse outside Sai Kung, and we all fell upon this rare treat. We gorged ourselves, I am ashamed to say.

Early the next morning we set off along ribbon-like paths across the rice paddy fields. The paths were no more than the walls of mud which had been built up around individual plots. Within the plots were smaller fields but generally speaking the walls of mud between these were not wide enough to walk on. They were built so that it was a simple matter to breach any one of them to allow the water to flow from one to another as required.

In half an hour or so we left the flat paddy fields and all those working in them who stopped to stare as we passed. We began to climb the range of hills which stand sentinel between the hinterland and Mirs Bay. The morning had been cold at first, and each one of us was glad of a sweater, but by the time we reached the first spur we were equally glad when the leading guerillas called a halt and we could remove them. Having done so, we turned, sat on a rock and gazed at the breathtaking view of the land and sea across which we had just travelled. Clearly could we see the golden sand of the beach at which we had landed and to the east of it the village of Sha Yu Chung. Beyond the village the land swept far out to sea past the island of Ping Chau. To the south-west lay Sha Tau Kok, Tolo Channel and the hills of the New Territories. Mirs Bay, which so little time ago held us in a terrifying grip, lay calm and peaceful as though nothing could disturb the tranquillity of its beauty as it shimmered blue and silver in the morning sun. Not a junk, sampan or boat of any kind could be seen upon it. We lingered, knowing that this was the last glimpse which we would have of Hong Kong. Now that the moment had come, its magnetic charm held me. It was like leaving some secret love, yet I knew that I must leave to fulfil another yearning—the determination to try to get home. The guerillas were agitating to press on, which snapped us out of our day-dream.

'Goodbye, Hong Kong,' I said, turning to follow them. 'I don't know when I will see you again, but I will be back.' (I was to be back within months of the end of the war.)

We crossed the first ridge and passed out of sight of the sea. Another ridge lay ahead of us. We crossed that only to be confronted with another and yet another. These uplands seemed never-ending. However, we knew that at some time we must drop down into a valley because the city of Waichow was on the East River.

The country was attractive. Large areas of rich red fertile loam grew various cereals between one ridge and another. It was a change from seeing rice. Also there was no lack of water for we had to negotiate streams almost continually as they poured off the hills above us. I particularly remember one of them, since we had been following its bank for some time, climbing all the way until rounding a corner we were faced with a cascade of water falling as if from heaven over a sheer rock face thirty feet above us.

The going continued to be steep, and when at length we walked into a village where our escort called a halt, we were thankful for the chance to rest. We sat on a wall in the sun while the guerillas talked to some of the village elders. At first the place seemed almost deserted.

It had not escaped the attention of the Japanese: burnt-out buildings and other destruction around us told a tale. Gradually one or two people began to emerge from some of the houses, and then more and more appeared. They formed a half-circle around us to stare rather blankly until a woman came forward to inject some life into the proceedings.

Like the venerable old man in whose house we had been fed at Kwai Chung, she spoke English with an American accent. She told us that she had lived for some time in Honolulu before returning to Hong Kong, but immediately it had fallen to the Japs she had left and made her way to this village where she had been born. She too

133

had no love for the gentlemen from the islands of the Rising Sun, and their defeat could not come too soon.

It was interesting, at a time when the Japanese were going from one conquest to another, that no one to whom we had spoken had any doubt about their ultimate defeat. It was just a question of how long it would take.

The guerillas reappeared. We said goodbye to the woman with the American accent, waved to everyone else and marched out of the village much refreshed.

We had walked for only fifteen minutes when the leading group halted. The leader explained that the country beyond the pass—just ahead—was under the control of Central Government troops, and if his armed section was seen, it would be attacked. Attacked? Chinese fighting Chinese? I wondered if we were to meet more of these conflicting groups.

The leader said that he and his men could take us no further. He went on to say that we still had a guide who would lead us to Pingshan. We had not noticed that a man from the last village had joined the rearguard, and when he came forward, we bowed to each other, while being assured that everything had been arranged with this man for whom the government troops would make no trouble.

This division of territory seemed beyond comprehension. It was not until many months later in Chungking, after I had been able to see the Chinese Nationalist regime in its true light, that I began to understand. At the time we were angry and resentful that these guerillas, who had done so much for us and who possessed a passionate hatred of the Japanese, should be treated as enemies by their own government.

And so it was we left them. I for one was going to make damn sure their case was heard not only by their own authorities but by the British and US forces supposedly supporting them.

Chapter 16

Before reaching the pass, we turned to wave at the little party making its way back on the path by which it had come. Despite the guide standing beside us, we felt alone, very much alone. We had become too accustomed to the presence of a cheerful escort. But having emerged from the pass itself, we were immediately so absorbed with what we saw that all else was forgotten. The ground fell away sharply, and as far as the eye could see there stretched to the north-east a green, fertile valley intersected by streams and a river winding its way into the distance.

This was the sight for which we had been waiting. Directly below was a fair-sized village.

'That must be Pingshan,' said John, 'and if you look over to the right, that town must be Tamsui.'

'You're probably right. By God, it looks a bloody long way. I feel as though we have already done a day's march. Do you think we can make it today?'

'Don't know,' replied Duggie, 'but there's not a cat's chance in hell if we stand here gaping, great as the view may be.'

With that, we set off down the steep hillside path and, as we passed a number of folk toiling up it, thanked our lucky stars that it was now our turn to be travelling downhill.

We reached the bottom quite quickly and there ran into the first Chinese military post. It consisted of no more than a tattered flag on a stick beside a derelict hut. It was manned by three or four surly-looking ruffians in uniform armed with age-old rifles. If this was any kind of sample of the Chinese government forces, small wonder that no attempt was made by the Chinese to relieve the pressure when the Japanese attacked Hong Kong.

In fact there were similar posts at varying points all the way to Tamsui, and the only purpose of them, it appeared, was to extract a toll from the local population travelling between one district and another. No one asked for whom the toll was collected. It was all too obvious. No one who relied on Chinese Army pay alone was likely to grow fat.

The men at this first post did not trouble us and were frankly uninterested in what we might be doing, although one of them saw fit to fall in with our guide and accompany him to Pingshan.

We had made good time from the pass and arrived at this straggling village in the early afternoon. Houses were dotted about in no semblance of order, which seemed odd until we saw the remains of the old walled village which had been completely gutted soon after the Japanese had arrived in Kwangtung Province three and a half years earlier.

Our guide stopped outside some houses where he and the soldier from the military post, totally ignoring us, became engrossed in conversation, and although John could not understand a word of what was going on, it seemed a little sinister. The conflab went on and on while we became more and more concerned.

'What the bloody hell do you think those two are up to, Duggie? I don't like it. I think that bastard from the military post is putting ideas into the head of our guide.' Just as I was saying this, an elderly Chinese, whom I had seen walking in our direction, came up to us.

'You belong Englishman?' he said.

'Yes,' replied Duggie.

'I many years belong Chinese crew English ship.'

'What ship?' I asked.

'Many different ship, Blue Funnel.'

'Then you Butterfield man. I Jardine man.' We grinned at each other, and I felt sure that he was aware of the rivalry which existed between the two great companies, Butterfield & Swire and Jardine Matheson.

'You come Hong Kong side?' he asked.

I tried to explain what we were doing.

He went on. 'Big trouble Hong Kong side, big trouble. Japanese no good.'

We readily agreed to that and, pointing to the remains of the old walled village, I asked, 'What thing Japanese do?' The old man told us how the Japanese had periodically swept through the valley but we gathered that they had not been seen recently, which was reassuring. Duggie asked if anyone from Pingshan would go with us to Tamsui. The old man shook his head as he looked round the small crowd that had gathered while we were talking. The old man seemed friendly enough but we did not like the look of the others and had no wish to spend a night in Pingshan. Tamsui, as far as we could judge from the rough map made in the camp, was some fifteen miles away, and fifteen miles further from where any Japanese might be. If we were to get there before dark, we had to start immediately.

Our guide and the soldier were still engrossed in their own affairs, so, pointing in the direction in which we believed we had to go, we said to the assembled company, 'Tamsui?' They pointed in the same direction and we marched off. To our consternation the crowd followed. We quickened our pace. They quickened theirs, but as soon as we reached the last house they stopped. We felt that we could not put too much distance too quickly between ourselves and the people of Pingshan. They didn't seem friendly, and none of us trusted them.

Our concern proved quite unjustified, but it was probably the effort which we made during the first hour on leaving Pingshan that enabled us to get so far on our way so quickly.

Crossing the range of hills from Mirs Bay had taken a good deal out of us. When Tamsui was only a few miles ahead, it required a supreme effort to keep going, especially for Lynton and Duggie who, by this time, were not only weary but also horribly footsore. Duggie was particularly sore-footed because he had nothing but old tennis shoes on his feet.

There were many small clusters of houses every so often, not immediately beside the road but standing back among the fields. There were also a number of attractive walled villages which had escaped destruction. The traffic, but for a few bicycles, was entirely pedestrian. There were shacks in which tea, cakes and an assortment of Chinese sweetmeats were available. We marched on, trying to avoid the temptations of any wayside foodstores.

Finally we were too tired and too thirsty. We'd had little since early morning. We prayed that the stall vendor would accept Hong Kong dollars because we had nothing else. However, $2 bought all we needed and they were accepted without question. The hot green tea was wonderfully refreshing, and we wolfed the fly-covered cakes and sweetmeats as if they had been caviar.

Sitting on the ground under the shade of a bamboo-leaf shelter, Duggie turned to John and said, 'Your Mama would have fifty fits if she were to see us guzzling away at these dirty little cakes.' John's mother was fastidious about the 'do's-and-don'ts' of living in China.

'Perhaps she would,' John replied rather pensively, and looking at him I wondered whether this casual remark of Duggie's had set off a train of thought. His mother was imprisoned by the Japs in Stanley. I also wondered how she had taken the death of John's father. The war had dealt the Pearce family a shattering blow.

We finished our tea and plodded on. Our pace got slower and

stops were more frequent. Almost every time we did so, people appeared as if from nowhere. Many had been in Hong Kong at one time or another. One or two had received their education there and it was from them that we heard the first words of criticism at the Hong Kong garrison's poor showing against the Japanese.

What were we doing? Running away? Yes, we told them, at this particular moment, we were running away but by doing so we hoped later to be of some use. Anyway, what did they do when the Japanese appeared near their villages in such force that they could do nothing against them? Generally speaking, the point was taken and there was no real animosity. Often these Chinese, who collected at each stop, would walk with us some way along the road—their incessant chatter was a bit irksome, but the very fact that they did walk with us spurred us to greater efforts to keep going. We needed that spur.

Just as we began to despair of reaching Tamsui, the gates came into sight. By this time the light was fading fast but we saw that the look-out post was set on a mound so that each sentry was beautifully silhouetted against the sky! Ready to be picked off by any would-be attacker, Japanese, Chinese or what-have-you. It was typical of the untutored and ragged group that made up the government army.

One of the guards at the gate took us to the police station. The walk through the town did nothing to cheer our weary souls for there was desolation at every turn. Apart from the occasional building which remained more or less intact, the others were shells in which the unfortunate inhabitants had built makeshift homes. At the police station our reception was none too cordial but we were allowed to sit down—and later to wash. We already missed the genuine friendliness of the guerillas.

The Captain in charge of the small military garrison in the town told us that we would be fed and that we might stay the night in the police station. He had little else to say except that we might call on him if we should need any assistance. With that he left, but his interpreter remained on duty with us.

The whole atmosphere of the place was uninviting, and we determined to move on to Waichow as quickly as possible, but Duggie's feet were in such a painful condition that there was no way in which he could walk anything like the thirty miles that still had to be covered. Lynton's feet were none too good either. In fact the tremendous effort which we had made in getting from the coast to Tamsui in one day had worn all of us out.

When we had eaten, we explained our problem to the interpreter, and he told us that we could probably go down the river on the next flotilla of barges, but he had no idea when this might be. The journey would take a minimum of two days.

'Is there no other way?' Duggie asked.

'Are there no vehicles moving on the road?' Lynton added. Certainly we had seen none between Pingshan and Tamsui despite the road being in quite good condition.

The interpreter explained that the Japanese had destroyed large sections of the road and blown all the bridges. Therefore, if we did not want to go by river, the options were to walk or go by bicycle. Bicycles! That was an idea! How on earth could we return them?

'Oh,' said our adviser, 'that is no problem, for you ride on the back, and when the men get to Waichow, they will stay there until they find a passenger to take back.' We felt much better at this news, and the idea of hiring bicycles took hold of our imaginations. We asked the interpreter to set it up. Later we were told that everything had been arranged and that we should be ready to start at eight o'clock the next morning. Full of hope that our next move had been resolved, we lay down in the police station to sleep fitfully.

Dead on time, at eight o'clock the next morning, we were ready and waiting. At 8.30 there was still no sign of any gentlemen with bicycles. One of the police was sent to find them, and he eventually appeared with four reluctant operatives and their machines, who demanded $80 each for the journey. We possessed no more than $20 between us. Their demand seemed a king's ransom, but there was no way that any of us were able to go on the journey on foot, and after endless wrangling the police interpreter persuaded them to come and discuss terms and payment with the Captain.

The Captain told them quite bluntly that they were to take us to Waichow whether they liked it or not, and only when we had been safely delivered to the British officer who was stationed there would they receive payment. We were delighted by the firm attitude which he adopted, and he rose immeasurably in our estimation. Within five minutes of seeing him, we were wobbling our way out of the ruins of Tamsui, roaring with laughter at the absurdity of the scene. Four unkempt, irregularly dressed, crazy young men, on the back of bikes, with their large, sore feet sticking out like the blades on Queen Boadicea's chariot.

To the Chinese it was an accepted method of transport and did not look out of the ordinary but to us riding pillion we looked grotesque. The main difficulty was to know what to do with your feet. Our legs were too long and because there was no step on the side of the frame which housed the back wheel, the effort to keep our feet clear of the ground put an almost intolerable strain on our thigh muscles, which became excruciatingly sore where they gripped the metal carrier. Needless to say, the luxury of a cushion or any padding did not exist.

The 'jockey' in front of me led the cavalcade of 'sit while you run' machines (for that is the literal translation of the Chinese characters for bicycle), and for the first hour we bowled merrily along the road. Then without warning he veered off, down a steep bank and along a narrow path with rice paddy fields on either side, and from that point onwards we did not rejoin the road until we were almost within sight of Waichow.

We continued to travel through the rich, fertile valley, sometimes across paddy fields, sometimes through orchards and sometimes on the towpath beside the river which we crossed and recrossed many times. It was obviously the recognized route, for the same type of stalls and shacks which we had encountered between Pingshan and Tamsui were dotted along it at intervals which, after the first one or two, we considered all too frequent because our 'jockeys' insisted upon stopping at almost every one.

The Chinese stared whenever we stopped but only one old gentleman spoke more than the odd word to us. It was at one of the ferry crossings. We were having an altercation over the fare and he came to our rescue. On the far bank there was a stall, and while we waited for our 'jockeys' to drink tea, he introduced himself as Hip Foo and told us that he was on his way to Kweilin to report to a British official who was stationed there. Later we caught a glimpse of him in Waichow, but nobody knew anything about him. He was a mysterious old body, benign, kindly and one who should never, I felt, have allowed himself to be involved in military matters of any shape or kind.

Soon after leaving our friend Hip Foo, we had a long trudge up a hill and having got to the top climbed onto the bikes and began a long, gentle decline back to the river, which had snaked its way round the hill. The path was narrow with bushes either side. As usual my 'jockey' was in front and going very well when we rounded a bend to find three 2,000-pound water-buffaloes across the path. We missed the first, bounced off the rump of the second and virtually landed under the nose of the third. Water-buffalo can be very fierce, and they have the weight to back it up. I was up in a flash. I darted past the beast, leaving my 'jockey' to extricate himself and the bicycle as best he could. The buffalo took no notice of the Chinese and the bicycle because he had smelt me. He turned, glared and snorted as though he was trying to make fire come out of his nostrils when Duggie hurtled round the corner, followed in quick succession by John and Lynton. Miraculously they all managed to miss the water-buffaloes but ended in rather undignified postures in one of the several bushes. They too extricated themselves rapidly and retired to a safe distance while the buffalo, totally nonplussed by this sudden onslaught of 'foreign devils', stood snorting ominously.

With the people of the country in which they live, water-buffalo are splendid, passive beasts of burden, but one whiff of a foreigner and they change immediately. The answer is to run.

As we collected ourselves, the 'jockeys' all talking at once at the top of their voices, the buffalo snorting and we roaring with laughter, there was suddenly another disturbance behind us, and an old cock pheasant rose majestically into the air and as he did so added his indignant voice to the cacophony.

This ridiculous incident did us all good because by this stage we were sore of foot, sore of behind and sorely tested by the effort we had sustained over the last seventy-two hours. It made bearable the last few miles into Waichow and our search for Dr Douglas Scriven.

Chapter 17

It was late afternoon when we arrived at the Red Cross centre, where Dr Douglas Scriven worked as the British Medical Officer. We found him immediately. He was short, plumpish, with an aquiline nose and beady eyes, one of which sported a monocle. He had been with the Indian Army Medical Service, but at Waichow, I was later to find out, he held certain other posts in the British intelligence-gathering systems.

'Ah, there you are,' he said, coming forward to greet us. 'I am delighted to see you.' Rather naturally we were taken aback by this greeting and quite obviously showed it for, as he shook hands, he said, 'I knew you were coming. In fact I have already sent a message up the line to say that I was expecting you any day.'

Duggie was the first to recover from the surprise. 'That was a bit risky wasn't it? How the hell did you know that we had got out?' he asked.

'Very simple really,' replied Scriven with a broad smile. 'My wife is Chinese, and she was in Hong Kong when you escaped from Shamshuipo. She left some days later and *en route* was told that you had made contact with the guerillas. She arrived a couple of days ago, so you have done quite well.'

'God! That's an understatement! We think we have done bloody well, especially in the last two days,' and we began to tell him of our forced march from the coast.

He cut us short. 'Yes, of course. It's a damn good effort to have covered sixty miles since yesterday morning, especially after four months of starvation. I am amazed that you were able to keep yourselves fit enough to have done it. All that can come later. Now, I must pay off your bicycle men and then I will take you home. I am living in what used to be the Italian Mission House. It is only just outside the city.'

Fortunately, it was not too far. The building was very pleasant, surrounding a courtyard. Scriven produced an assortment of clean clothes. We washed and he attended to our sores, some of which were beginning to look rather nasty. Then we relaxed for about an hour before being introduced to his wife, whom we immediately asked whether she had heard of any unpleasant reprisals being taken as a result of our escape. She knew, at that time, of none and went on to tell us that, because I was a Volunteer, the Japanese were convinced that we had received help from outside the camp. As far as she had been able to learn, they had concentrated on any likely contacts which I might have had.

When we heard what Mrs Scriven had to tell, we thought no more about reprisals until much later when all the dreadful news became known. The doctor said, 'I think we should celebrate your arrival with a slap-up Chinese dinner. I would like to take you to an excellent restaurant but it does meean walking back into the city. Are you game?' Everyone liked the idea in spite of the effort. We we set off and as we walked, we talked, finding the going much easier after our legs had been treated. We could have talked all night, into the next day and still not told all we had to tell but as soon as we had finished a delicious meal, Scriven, most wisely, would not let us continue.

'There is quite a lot which you will have to do tomorrow. I will tell you at breakfast but now bed is the place!'

The following day we were told that the next stage of our journey was to Kukong which, since the fall of Canton, had become the capital of Kwangtung Province. To get there and to make sure of avoiding the Japanese, it was necessary to travel 170 miles up the East River to Lung Chun. From there to Kukong the mode of travel was to be by lorry. These lorries ran daily, transporting the goods shipped by river to places further inland which could not be served by water transport.

However, before it was possible to leave we had to report our arrival officially to the local Chinese government offices. Scriven also told us that there were a number of other people who would wish to see us, the most important of whom was Mr R. C. Lee, and while these calls were being made, he would make arrangements for our passage aboard a river barge.

Dick Lee had been an eminent member of Hong Kong society before the war. He had been a member of the Legislative Council and prominent in the affairs of the Colony. I could not claim to know him, although we had met at numerous Jardine functions.

Dick Lee was in bed recovering from a fever and was obviously feeling very sick. We told him about our experience with the guerillas and tried to make him promise that all possible assistance should be given to them, but he was most reticent and unforthcoming. In fact he became quite edgy when we made it clear that

143

nothing would stop us from pressing this point at high level with our own military authorities.

He continually referred to the presence of Chinese government guerillas while we, in turn, kept saying that 'our' guerillas wanted to be accepted as government guerillas. 'Why shouldn't they be accepted when they are already on the ground doing the job?' I asked. He did not reply and no matter how often this was repeated, it cut no ice. At that stage we were still totally unaware of the political implications, which I was to learn later in Chungking.

However, from my point of view, the meeting was not wasted for it was Dick Lee who told me that John Keswick was now a member of the British Embassy in Chungking and suggested that I should send him a cable through Scriven's 'network'. We returned immediately to his office, and the following telegram was sent: 'ESCAPED. WILL REPORT TO YOU IN CHUNGKING. BOSANQUET.' Put like that, it all sounded so easy. Whether or not it was so will be seen later, but John Keswick immediately responded by sending a cable to London. It read: 'DAVID B. ESCAPED', and this cryptic message brought to an end an agonizing suspense for Hazel and for my family since I had been reported missing, believed killed, before Christmas.

(At that time, by cruel coincidence, Hazel was stationed at Wye, where she had once spent the hilarious days of the college cricket-week celebrations with me and where we had danced the night through, going in search of breakfast in one of the students' favourite haunts in the countryside . . . and above all where our deep love for each other had blossomed into an everlasting flower. When she heard, Hazel immediately applied for a posting but until it came she had to endure weeks of being reminded at every turn of those wonderful, carefree days with me.)

In the days before the new order in East Asia, which the Japanese attempted to enforce on the people of China, Waichow had been a prosperous and lovely city. It stands on the south bank of the East River at the confluence of the tributary that flows past Tamsui and which we had crossed so many times during our journey by bicycle.

After the fall of Canton to the Japanese, the Pearl River on which Canton stands could no longer be used as the main thoroughfare for goods in and out of southern China. Consequently other waterways became vastly more important, the East River being one.

Inevitably Waichow was occupied by the enemy, but when they eliminated Hong Kong, the importance of remaining in Waichow vanished and they withdrew their forces in early 1942.

'But why the destruction?' we asked Scriven. The city bore grim marks of what we thought to be the old Japanese occupation. It was not so, we were told. The destruction had been recent. Marauding Japanese had earlier moved up the beautiful and fertile valley between Tamsui and Waichow, pillaging and raping the women, and they had been ambushed and destroyed to a man. In revenge another strong force of Japanese came back, and at that time Waichow was sacked, plundered and pillaged.

After hearing these terrifying accounts, it seemed remarkable that there were still so many people about. The streets were congested. There was much buying and selling of produce. River sampans and barges were laden, and although the bridge across the Tamsui tributary had been blown up, it was only partially down and what remained was very much in use by bicycles, rickshaws, sedan chairs and, of course, pedestrians. There were lakes on the western outskirts, and to reach them we had to push and shove our way through a milling conglomerate of humans, dogs, chickens, pigs and even rats, all elbowing for a space of some kind in the narrow thoroughfares.

The lakes were lovely, studded with tree-covered islands. On one there was a massive pagoda, a thousand years old. It had been beautifully positioned so that it could be seen from many points within the city, and connecting the island on which it stood to the shore was a picture-book Chinese bridge. The Japanese had spared the pagoda but had partially damaged the bridge, although enough remained to see what it had been like.

It was drizzling as we made our way to the river to embark for Lung Chun. But we arrived to find that the barge had already left the pontoon. Once again we were stranded, so it seemed.

Even as we stood there, we could see the barge chugging away from us up the river.

'How bloody silly,' said Duggie with some irritation, which I'm sure we all shared. We had made an effort to be early. There was as yet no sign of Scriven, and he would not have let us go without coming to say goodbye.

We stood watching the barge and its tow labouring against the fast-running current and were about to turn away when it seemed to be pulled into the shore again. At that moment Scriven arrived and before we could say anything he told us to hurry back to the Mission House. 'It is obvious that the coxswain has made a mistake and expects to pick you up there,' he said.

The barges had just come alongside the floating pontoon by the Mission House by the time we got there, and we jumped aboard, to save the need to tie up. They moved so slowly that there was ample time to shout our goodbyes and thanks for the first taste of civilization in months. So started the long haul to Kukong and on to Chungking.

Within minutes of being aboard it was evident that the journey up the East River was going to be no pleasure cruise. No sleeping-space had been reserved for us, nor had any bedding been provided beyond a small rattan mat, although Scriven had told us that both had been arranged. We felt a little put out since it would have been so easy to equip ourselves during the two days in Waichow.

Apart from a small section aft and in the prow, the barge was covered by a semi-circular hood made of bamboo and rattan, and it was beneath this that we made our home for the next ten days. When we first saw it, it seemed that every available inch had already been commandeered by the other passengers, thirty-two of them in all. However, the Chinese coolie is an accommodating and cheerful soul, and after a few grunts of mild protest they allowed us to squeeze in. We sat down, contemplated the scene with no great pleasure and hoped that at least the flimsy rattan and bamboo roof would not spring a leak.

The cargo carried by this flat-bottomed, elongated river barge was stowed under the decking on which everyone sat, lay or slept, and any loading or unloading, which often happened at odd times of the day or night, caused a major upheaval. We should not have grumbled, but we did. The river barge was, after all, a cargo-carrying vessel, and we passengers were no more than an added bonus to the operators.

We had lived rough for a long time and should, I suppose, have been able to take these conditions in our stride, but it was not easy, and nights were especially uncomfortable. Everybody slept head to toe. We all had to. And an oriental foot which has never known a sock or a shoe or soap and water is not the ideal object to have within inches of one's nose. No doubt our feet were no less un-pleasant to our fellow passengers.

Our barge was immediately astern of the towing vessel so that the air in the confined and desperately overcrowded living-quarters was permeated not only with the smell of unwashed human bodies but with fumes from the old Ford V8 car engine which had been con-verted to using charcoal 'gas'.

These rugged and wonderfully reliable engines had long been

highly prized by the Chinese lightermen. This one was no exception. It chugged away day after day, night after night, a superb advertisement for its maker, but inevitably, through age and its conversion, its efficiency had been greatly impaired. In addition, it was expected to propel, against a strong current, a load woefully in excess of what might normally be expected of it.

During the first night we tied up alongside, and as it got light we were all turned out into the rain while more cargo was taken aboard—truck tyres smuggled out of Hong Kong, no doubt, and worth untold gold in the interior. By the time the loading was complete, we were all wet and miserable, and to make matters worse a second tow had been hitched behind us.

'For God's sake!' I exclaimed, 'these people must be insane. We will go backwards as soon as the current catches us.'

We did, until men with poles began to punt. Gradually the drift stopped. Then, inch by inch, or so it seemed, we began to make headway. It was so slow that the only way to be sure the vessels were making ground against the current was to fix a point on the opposite bank and watch until it dropped astern.

The prows of the barges were built high out of the water, whereas the stern had a clearance of no more than six to eight inches. Along each side of the craft, from bow to stern, a narrow running-board was set out over the water, and men with punting poles, sometimes two, sometimes three, on each side, would gather at the high point of the prow. The first man would launch himself like a pole-vaulter starting his run before being brought to a standstill as his pole hit the bottom of the river. Then, uttering almost inhuman and quite excruciating noises, he would fight his way to the stern while those behind him followed suit, their faces twisted as if in agony as they strained every muscle to reach the stern. But at the end of each run they would walk back to the prow together, laughing and joking, only to repeat the same performance.

Some of the punt poles had small cradles at one end which fitted into the shoulder, others had none. Those men using poles without this simple device had enormous callous growths on their shoulders where they pushed against the top of the pole. For this muscle-straining and back-breaking job these men received a pittance, and yet they appeared entirely happy, as indeed were all the river folk with whom we came in contact.

Besides the motor-driven barges there were junks and sampans making their beleaguered way up the river close in to each bank to avoid the worst of the current. Some were under sail, but all were hauled by men on the towpath. These men did not make the excruciating noises of the punters but intoned a slow, monotonous, rhythmic song as they strained on the rope and plodded forward as previous generations had done for centuries before them. Against this scene were the barges, junks and sampans which, having delivered their inbound cargo, hurtled past downstream, their sails patched a thousand times, catching any wind there might be, while their crews relaxed.

For three days it rained almost incessantly, and we were forced to remain cooped up with the other passengers. The roofing held, mercifully. At intervals we looked out to gauge any progress which might have been made. At best it was desperately slow; at times there was none, despite the efforts of the punters.

During the afternoon of that third day I could contain my exasperation no longer. 'At this rate it will take weeks not days to reach Lung Chun and by that time I shall be raving mad. God! I wish we could tell this inane coxswain to ditch the second tow. How about it, John? Could you make him understand?' John shook his head, and for quite some time no one spoke. Then Lynton said, 'What the hell are you fussing about, David? We're being fed; we haven't got to walk. There aren't any Japs about. Why should we be in a hurry?'

I was about to agree rather meekly with Lynton when John interjected, 'I know what is the matter with David. He thinks that we are now out of the wood, and his mind has turned to a certain person whose photograph graced his bedside table in Strawberry Hill. In fact, that certain person is probably the only reason he was prepared to escape. All this talk about it being done in the line of duty is so much cod's wallop!' he went on in his rather languid drawl. 'You don't really imagine that she is sitting at home waiting for you? She will have written you off long ago.' He laughed. We all laughed and it broke the tension.

We had come in very close to the river bank. While the old engine ahead of us continued to chug on, there was activity at the stern of our barge. The crew were unlashing the rope which secured the second tow. They cast the rope ashore, and other men made it fast to a bollard on the bank. We could hardly believe our eyes. It was as if the coxswain had heard my outburst and taken heed of it. Even the rain stopped and we were able to sit outside, perched on top of the bamboo rattan roof which had so effectively kept us dry since we had come aboard.

The frustration of our slow progress which had been so exasperating such a short time ago evaporated, and in its place a sudden sense of well-being came over us. For the first time we talked of our good fortune of having the unique experience of travelling as a native across this vast land, of the fascinating activity on the river and of the absorbing beauty all around us.

In the fading light men in wide-brimmed hats, which protected them against the sun and in part against the rain, could be seen leaving the fields; the junks and sampans began to tie up to the banks while the faithful old Ford V8 engine chugged on. We did not move but watched the moon rise. As it did so, the hills and mountains both near and far loomed as severe and imposing sentinels against a now clear sky.

The call of food finally broke the spell, and reluctantly we withdrew from the beauty of the moonlight into the glare of an acetylene lamp hung from a bamboo pole.

The meals, morning and evening, consisted of communal tubs of rice dumped among the passengers, and a few individual dishes of fish, meat or vegetables. It was all very primitive and only just enough to keep the wolf from the door but eggs bought from the local shop at any port of call did help to supplement the fare. Scriven had given us 200 Chinese dollars for the journey.

By next morning we had left the fertile, low-lying country and reached a point where the river began to cut through a range of hills. Large bamboo and giant pampas grass grew in profusion at intervals but always the mountains in the distance dominated the scene.

There is something ominous, certainly austere, about the mountains of China. It is not that they are high but rather that they seem to go on for ever, giving the feeling that, whatever the journey, it will never end. When in China I found that I often longed for the neat, green and orderly countryside of England which gives a feeling of completeness, and yet the fascination of that vast country was magnetic in its majesty.

We were now approaching the small town of Ho Yuen, the halfway port of call between Waichow and Lung Chun, and on a number of high points little square towers had been built, no doubt a relic of times in the not too distant past when strong-points were necessary to guard this important waterway against marauding brigands. Through these cuttings the river narrowed, the current increased and our rate of progress, even without the second tow and the punters working continuously, was almost imperceptible.

John complained of feeling ill and retired to his rattan mat. There was nothing we could do to make him remotely comfortable but when the Chinese understood that he was not well, there were offers of coats and blankets, which were accepted with gratitude. That night we were glad to arrive at Ho Yuen, and when next morning John was no better, we went in search of the local Chinese Relief Agency, where to our great surprise we were told of a Mission Hospital some way out of the town.

There was ample time to get to the hospital. Our barge had been tied up alongside while the powered unit returned to collect the second tow from the point where it had been abandoned. It would get down stream quickly enough but to fight its way back to Ho Yuen would take a further thirty-six hours.

Leaving Lynton to look after John, Duggie and I set off to find the Mission Hospital. It had been built within its own walled compound about a mile from the river, and as we walked up the path from the gate in the west wall to the reception area, we marvelled at its tidiness. We also wondered why this spot in the wilds of Kwangtung should have been chosen as a site for a mission. It was obvious, of course, that it had been foreign-inspired and had been there for some time.

Our sudden arrival in the cool, clean hall of the main building caused quite a stir. All the Chinese looked at us as if we were ghosts. We had not been stared at so intently since the rather unfriendly crowd had done so at Pingshan, but these folk did not appear unfriendly, but curious and perhaps a little apprehensive. When we said 'Doctor?' to a young Chinese woman sitting at a table, they all melted away as she got up and went through one of the many doorways.

'They don't think much of us, do they?'

'I can hardly blame them,' said Duggie. 'I've just caught sight of myself in the mirror over there.' We had become so used to seeing each other unshaven and long-haired, with shirt and shorts much the worse for wear, that it was only when I was able to see myself that I realized what a sight I was.

As we gazed into the mirror in ugly contemplation, a door opened. We turned and there coming towards us was a nurse, a European nurse, in an immaculate, spotless uniform.

She looked so radiant that it made us feel ashamed of our own appearance. If a wall had not been behind us, we might well have backed away but she smiled and we felt better.

'Can I help you?' she asked. The explanation of why we were there gushed forth, that we were particularly concerned with John and how we hoped that the doctor would come with us to see him. Looking at our bare legs and the festering sores on them, she said,

'You need some medical attention yourselves. Please come with me.'

She led us into a small room and told us to sit down while she would see what could be done. We waited. 'I am glad something can be done about our legs, Duggie. Mine have become really rather painful in the last day or two. How about yours?'

'They're not too bad, but I would like to get on with it and get the doctor to see John.' Eventually the nurse returned to tell us that the doctor would see us in a few minutes, but when we asked whether he would come with us to see John, we could get no positive reply from her, which struck us as a little odd. However, she stayed and talked. We were intrigued by her English; she spoke it perfectly but it was obvious that she herself was not English and we were marched in to the doctor before we could find out her nationality.

'I am sorry to hear that your friend is sick,' the doctor said in a thick European accent.

'We would like you to come to see him,' Duggie said. There was a long pause.

'I am afraid I cannot come with you.' Our hearts sank, and just as one of us was about to ask why, he continued. 'You see, I am German and am not permitted by the Chinese to leave this compound.' We looked at him rather blankly, which was hardly surprising, for it had never crossed our minds that we were likely to stumble upon a German Lutheran Mission in Kwangtung Province.

The flicker of a smile lit his face as he saw our obvious embarrassment. 'Is the nurse a German too?' we asked.

'No,' he said.

'Then, please may she come to the boat with us?'

'That will not be necessary,' he replied, 'since I have arranged for my Chinese assistant to accompany you, but first let me attend to your legs.' This he did, while we sat unable to think of anything to say.

When he finished dressing my legs, he asked how long we were likely to remain in Ho Yuen, and as we told him that there was little chance of leaving before the next afternoon, he suggested that I should return in the morning to have them dressed again.

We took our leave of this rather sad-looking but kindly man, still feeling a little embarrassed that we had received aid from an enemy subject but comforting ourselves by the thought that perhaps he had chosen to serve in the back of beyond because he had no sympathy with Nazi Germany.

Outside the doctor's office the nurse introduced us to his Chinese assistant, and the three of us set off for the jetty at Ho Yuen, where he immediately went aboard and gave John a thorough examination. Fortunately, there was nothing seriously the matter with him, just a mild dose of some tummy bug.

The next morning, John still did not want to move from the boat, but since he was content to be left, we again set out for the Mission Hospital. We were greeted by another nurse, and while we had our legs dressed in turn, we were able to talk to her at some length. Hearing that we were not leaving until the evening, Sister Emmy Staub, for that was her name, invited us to return at four o'clock for tea with her and her friend Martha Guggenbuehl, whom Duggie and I had met the previous day.

In the comfort of their sitting-room that afternoon, we discovered that they were Swiss who had trained for missionary hospital duty overseas, and although they had already been in China since 1939, neither seemed the least disturbed by the possibility that it might be years before there would be a chance of returning to Switzerland. For them, our sudden appearance apparently made a welcome change in an otherwise rather monotonous existence. For us, it was a real joy to relax in a room furnished in European style, to drink tea and eat home-made cake *à la Suisse* with two vivacious ladies who took so much interest in our exploits. We returned to the barge refreshed and congratulated John on being sensible enough to have become ill at such a good moment. Kukong was still more than 250 miles away, but perhaps more important than distance was time—the time it would take to reach Kukong and the English Mission Hospital which we knew to be there. This would be where we'd get more treatment for our legs.

We finally left Ho Yuen in the middle of the night, and by early morning we had reached a point where the river divided. On a promontory high above the main stream stood a resplendent pagoda.

In spite of the work by the men punting, our progress was so slow that the coxswain decided, once again, to abandon the second tow. It was just as well he did, because the river soon narrowed and the current raced past us at even greater speed as men and engine coupled in a supreme effort to make headway. It took nearly all day to negotiate this narrow stretch, and as soon as the river had widened and was flowing again through open country, the coxswain tied up near a small village. We went ashore immediately to stretch our legs and followed the towpath downstream to a point where it was some thirty feet above the river. There we stood and gazed at the swirling, turbulent water as it rushed and tumbled towards the sea, leaving little whirlpools in its wake.

On the far bank a line of men were heaving a large junk against the current. Their rhythmic sing-song came clear across the water as they inched their way forward. No doubt they longed for the time when they would reach their destination, discharge the cargo and hurtle downstream on the current which was now causing them to toil almost to the limit of their endurance. As we watched, our own barge appeared with the coxswain at the helm and all the punters relaxing while they were able. We waved and received an answering wave as the boat sped by and finally disappeared in the graceful sweep of the river as it rounded the promontory, with the pagoda in silhouette against the setting sun.

I remained transfixed by the grandeur of what I saw. There were many other times when I was made dramatically aware of the vastness of China, but that particular moment has remained particularly vivid: the men toiling like toys on the far towpath, so small from our vantage point. And as I looked in the other direction, a few lonely figures were working at a more gentle pace in the paddy fields, pushing wooden ploughs behind the leisurely plodding of their water-buffaloes. And again—all round, the same awe-inspiring hills, some far, some near, stood like giants silently observing the rather puny efforts of man to battle against the power of nature, as he scratched a living for himself.

When it became dark, we had no wish to hurry to our cattle-like existence aboard the river craft before it was absolutely necessary, so we made our way slowly into the village in search of any kind of entertainment to shorten the drabness of the evening. Of course, there was none. We sat on stools outside a filthy eating-house, ordered some tea and watched the comings and goings of the few villagers who passed by.

Soon we gave up our search for something to do and went aboard again. For the next two days we continued up river until we pulled into the village of Lam Ho. Here we were told that Lung Chun was sixteen miles ahead. We seriously contemplated setting out to walk the distance but, while John had recovered, the sores on our legs were giving trouble—mine had become particularly painful—and I was thankful when it was decided to wait at Lam Ho while the second tow was, yet again, recovered from further downstream.

The following afternoon we set off on the last lap. The river ran through a particularly lovely stretch of country, and we came on

153

another fine pagoda which had been perfectly placed to set it off against its rich background. That night was to be our last on the boat. At one o'clock in the morning a member of the crew, treading gingerly among the prostrate bodies covering the deck, lit an acetylene lamp. In the sing-song Cantonese dialect he chanted, '*Lung Chun ah.*' We had arrived at Lung Chun. Some, but by no means all, began to gather together their belongings. Apparently this was not the end of the journey for the boats: they were going to Lo Lung, another five miles further on.

We went forward and nodded our thanks to the coxswain before he pulled away from the pontoon. In our haste to get off the boat and our joy at arriving at the end of the seemingly endless voyage to Lung Chun, we suddenly realized we had no idea where to go and what to do for the rest of the night. Douglas Scriven had told us to make contact with the magistrate or, failing him, the director of the local Chinese hospital. Even if we knew where either might be found, eight o'clock was the earliest we could be on the doorstep of either of them. The night felt damp and cold. We began almost to regret leaving our rattan mat aboard the barges. At least it had been dry, even if it had been hard and uncomfortable.

Sensing our predicament, one of the Chinese who had just landed beckoned us to follow him, which we did gladly, and after a short distance he began to hammer fiercely upon a door in what appeared to be the main street of Lung Chun. Nothing happened. He hammered again and again until at last it opened and we were all admitted to what turned out to be a simple but remarkably clean Chinese inn. We slept well and late, enjoying the comfort of a mattress on the bed. After a good and inexpensive breakfast we were told how to find the magistrate. We set off in high spirits only to have them dashed because the magistrate was away and we were quite unable to make anyone else in his office understand what we wanted.

John's limited vocabulary in the vernacular was tested to the full, but eventually by his efforts and by pointing to the running sores on our legs he was able to glean the way to the local hospital. It proved to be some distance from Lung Chun. Here again, we drew a blank. The director had just left for Shui Kwan and would not return for some days. However, his deputy, Dr Wong, spoke English, and while he had no knowledge of how to go about procuring a seat on the trucks which plied between Lung Chun and Kukong, he did his best to be helpful, even to the extent of offering to come and act as interpreter if necessary. It was obvious that he was a very busy man, and we were reluctant to disturb his work. We thanked him and assured him with as much conviction as we could muster that we would manage and took our leave.

Chapter 18

Lung Chun was an attractive little village. The streets, like the hotel in which we had spent the night, were remarkably clean. There were trees which gave some shade during the heat of the day, for it was now May and the weather in South China was hot and sultry. There was far more space between the houses than in most other villages, and the atmosphere of the whole place was friendly. The proprietor of the principal tea-house, an old man in his seventies, sat on a stool at its entrance, dressed in no more than a pair of black silk Chinese trousers and a singlet which was rolled up under his armpits. He beamed benevolently at all passers-by and fanned his ample paunch. As we approached, he climbed off his stool and bowed us into his establishment. In no time at all a delectable meal was produced, and the old man hovered around us continuously, not so much to attend to our needs but rather to air his few words of English. It was a hard struggle to maintain any real conversation, but he seemed pleased by our efforts, and we emerged into the street replete. After much shaking of hands and bowing, everyone, the old man in particular, gained 'plenty face', and we started off again down the street.

If there were to be problems over the next stage of the journey, Lung Chun was as good a place as any in which to be marooned, so we sauntered back to our lodgings to sit at a round table in the shade beside the entrance, there to cogitate the next move.

We were so engrossed in our own business that we gave little thought to our surroundings until one of us looked up and saw a Chinese, accompanied by two scruffy Europeans like ourselves, standing beside us.

The Chinese said, 'My name is Fong Ming. I was a member of the Hong Kong CID.'

The CID was a branch of the Hong Kong police dealing with serious crimes. The man had obviously been a detective.

'What are you doing here?' said Duggie somewhat taken aback.

'I'm on my way to report to Colonel Ride in Kukong.'

Lynton and John had already introduced themselves to the two scruffy Europeans.

156

'D'you realize these chaps have also escaped from Shamshuipo?' Lynton said.

'And they did it before we did,' added John hurriedly.

It turned out that the two men were privates from the Royal Scots. One introduced himself as Hodges and the other as Gallacher.

Fascinated, if not a little sceptical, we invited them to sit down. It was hard to believe that we should have known nothing of their escape, and remarkable that the Japanese had not reacted to it and that Douglas Scriven had not made any mention of these two Scots, for only he could have given Fong his instructions in Waichow. Any doubts were quickly dispelled by what Hodges and Gallacher had to tell us of Shamshuipo and how they got out. Apparently, they were feeling particularly fed up one evening and, while mooching about beside the boundary fences on the landward side of the camp, the urge to get the hell out of it became overwhelming. So, there and then, they wormed their way under the wire and across the allotment gardens which were immediately beyond. This was a method we had contemplated at one time but had rejected as being too dangerous. The Japanese occupied a house on the far side of the allotments, and from our observations the comings and goings were altogether too frequent. Also a blaze of light spread across the allotments. Hodges and Gallacher apparently had no problems, eventually dodging through the outskirts of Kowloon and into the hills beyond, where, according to them, they calmly set off to walk in the general direction of China!

Neither was very explicit in telling us how they reached and crossed the border, so one of us asked what had they done as soon as they reached Chinese territory.

'Och,' said Hodges, 'ye ken yon dirty great hill jiss the ither side o' the border?' We nodded. 'Well, we hiked up it and turned right.'

'And after you turned right?' we asked, keeping straight faces with difficulty.

'We were picked up by guerillas.'

We all knew what they meant when they said 'we hiked up it and turned right', with the whole vast continent of China before them. The simplicity of the statement was particularly appealing, for Hodges and Gallacher were two very simple souls, not given to much imagination. That was their strength, combined with a very full measure of luck. Since they took few, if any, precautions, this accounted for their success, a success which so justly brought them each the DCM.

Having listened to their story and how they had spent their time instructing the guerillas in small-arms drill, we turned the conversation to the more immediate task of getting to Kukong.

Fong said there was a lot of cargo and many passengers waiting for the limited number of lorries which plied between the East River and Kukong. Hodges, Gallacher and he had already been waiting some time and were not booked to leave for another four or five days, so Fong would be glad to help us in any way he could.

He suggested that we should move to Lo Lung, another six miles up the river, since it was very much nearer the point of departure for the lorry, and if there was to be any chance of jumping the queue, it was important to be on hand. He volunteered to come with us, and it seemed stupid not to take his advice. We should have questioned him more closely as to what was needed to secure a place on a lorry before we set out to walk the six miles to Lo Lung. We arrived just as it was getting dark and discovered that the only magistrate empowered to issue us with the police passes and sufficient money to get on the lorry had his office six miles back in Lung Chun.

To be told this was bad enough but we were all the more infuriated to find that the only accommodation available was as filthy as was Lo Lung itself. The streets were little better than running sewers in which chickens scratched and pecked for an existence, children and pigs wallowed, all of which ran in and out of the houses built so close together that it was possible for neighbours living opposite each other to shake hands from one bedroom window to another.

The night was spent fighting bed-bugs. The next morning Duggie complained of not feeling well, so, leaving John with him, Lynton, Fong Ming and I returned to Lung Chun. We did not walk there but hired a sampan and enjoyed the experience of being carried swiftly down river by the current which had caused us so much frustration since leaving Waichow.

The sampan was spotlessly clean. The water folk, whose diminutive floating home it had been from generation to generation, were happy and friendly and we were sorry it took so little time to reach Lung Chun.

As many as three generations live aboard these small craft, for there is an unwritten law that the old are never jettisoned. When each succeeding eldest son marries, the parents give up the best section of the sampan and retire to the stern, where they are cared for until they die; thus the rotation of the family goes on.

Our business with the magistrate was completed easily and

remarkably quickly for China. Had this not been so, there would have been an excuse to stay the night in Lung Chun. As it was, there was none; the six-mile walk back had to be faced. Lynton and Fong set a cracking pace, and I was soon trudging far behind them, counting the eucalyptus trees which lined the dirt road in an effort to keep going. My legs were very painful. I did not feel ill but had an overpowering feeling of slackness, and I wondered if it was the poison in my suppurating legs. It could also have been the after-effect of beriberi or simply reaction to the strain of the last four months. We got back to Lo Lung to find that Duggie had retired to bed with a raging fever. It was obviously malaria, and if he had it, every one of us could go down with it at any time, since we had all been exposed to the same mosquitoes. The next morning, I felt no better myself and began to feel sure I had too much poison in me. Nevertheless, we reported regularly to the lorry station.

Fong acted as our interpreter each time, and after the third attempt, when there was still no success, we began to suspect he might be trying to negotiate for himself a part of the 'squeeze' which inevitably had to be paid. We confronted him and asked the possible cost. He was reticent and most off-handed. A few hours later he could not be found, and we never saw him again.

By the fourth day Duggie seemed to have sweated out the fever. He was resting while I sat with him bathing my legs in a small bucket when a little man walked into the room looking for Fong. He seemed slightly surprised that we did not know where he was or whether he would be coming back. He told us that his name was Chow and that he worked for the Bank of China.

'Do you bankers have any influence with those who operate the lorries running to Kukong?' I asked. He smiled and in correct Chinese manner humbly shook his head. 'No, but I will help if I can.'

That afternoon, Mr Chow called again and took Lynton and John to the station, where he secured places in a lorry due to leave the next morning. The 'squeeze' demanded was 450 Chinese dollars each, a king's ransom! At that juncture almost any price was worth paying to get away from the filth of Lo Lung. To show our appreciation for his help, we took Mr Chow to dinner.

The following morning we were up before it was light, determined to be at the front of the queue. Lynton and John, being sounder of wind and limb, strode on well ahead of Duggie and me to deal with any last-minute arrangements. As it happened, none was necessary, for our friend Mr Chow was already there to make sure no chicanery was meted out to 'those incompetent foreigners' who were able to speak so little of the language. Would we, I wondered, have taken the same trouble at such an early hour as Mr Chow after so short an acquaintance, had the boot been on the other foot?

For two hours we hovered round an ancient Chevrolet, waiting for its driver. It had seen better days but there were few that had not, once they had travelled the roads of China. At least this one had not been converted to charcoal, which we were misguided enough to think would give it enough power to negotiate the rough, hilly and tortuous road which we knew lay between Lo Lung and Kukong.

A locally made, totally enclosed body had been built on the chassis, and in it, stacked almost to the roof, were sacks of salt.

Again, misguidedly, we had hoped to travel in the cab. Not a bit of it. When the time came, we were unceremoniously pushed through a small opening between the cab and the main body, along with fifteen Chinese and their belongings. We perched as best we could on top of the sacks of salt. The driver shared the cab with two of his particular pals, and as we started we were intrigued to notice that a young boy took up a position on the front wing. All too soon we were to discover why.

Within a few miles the road began to wind its way over the first range of hills. The old Chevrolet, which had bumbled along the flat country, jostling and jolting its passengers from one pot-hole to the next, began to splutter as the gradient increased and the excessive load began to tell. To the splutter was added a hiss, and just as the engine expired, the boy on the front wing jumped off and put a chock under the wheel because the brakes were quite incapable of holding the vehicle. And this he did time and time again before we reached Kukong.

We all piled out and sat beside the road while the driver lifted the bonnet amid a cloud of steam. After a suitable interval the boy was despatched to find water with which to replenish the radiator. At length the engine was coaxed into life; everyone pushed until the brow of the hill was reached. Then we jumped aboard and careered headlong down the other side of the hill. The driver was bent on making the maximum use of any gradient in his favour.

The first of these hair-raising performances was thoroughly unnerving. God help us, we thought, should we meet anything coming in the opposite direction. God help us if we failed to negotiate a corner, since there was no escape from the back of the lorry except through the cab or possibly through a minute window.

160

God did help us! We did not meet anything in any awkward place. We did negotiate all the bends, and as the performance was repeated at intervals through the day, we gradually relaxed—as far as it was possible—between the bone-shaking jolts. We got used to this method of travel—there was no other except our own two feet, and they would not get us very far at this time.

About half past four in the afternoon the Chevrolet stopped in the little village of Lung Seung. Everyone crawled out to find a place to sleep. None was more thankful for the respite than the four of us. To our great relief we were guided to a Chinese inn which was clean and comfortable, and having dumped our few worldly belongings in a large room with four beds, John, Lynton and I went on a tour of inspection, leaving Duggie to rest. He was far from well as a result of malaria and had found the day very trying, although his stoicism would not allow him to admit it.

Lung Seung nestled under a hill. A swift-running stream of crystal-clear water, spanned by an imposing bridge, flowed between the houses. The bridge was very old and of great beauty. The pillars upon which the delicately curved arches stood were fashioned in the shape of a boat making its way upstream. We were intrigued by the thought of who might have been the architect and why so much care in design had been lavished upon it to serve so small a community. We remained on the bridge for a long time, now and then leaning over the parapet to watch the water ripple over the pebbles and then glide silently through the arches. Momentarily I was back in England, expecting a trout to rise, but there were no fish in that stream.

The village and country immediately around it were delightful and its air of tranquillity affected us all. It invited us to tarry a while and give up the overpowering urge to press on and rejoin the war-torn world. Reluctantly I turned away from the bridge. We all walked back to the inn to find Duggie taking to a well-educated Chinese. He was Robert Cheung of the Chinese Relief Association, and almost immediately he insisted that we should be his guests at the evening meal. He took us to a restaurant built on the side of the hill where the enterprising proprietor had erected a rickety verandah of bamboo, which swayed perceptibly when anyone walked on it. From here any of his customers who cared to could enjoy not only his excellent cooking but also a magnificent view.

The few hours spent at this attractive village were a real tonic, and after a bowl of rice gruel taken early the next morning with the kindly Robert Cheung, who had come to see us off, we took our leave in high spirits, especially when the driver announced that there was every chance of being in Kukong by the evening. It turned out that his optimism was totally unfounded.

We had a succession of punctures, four in all, so that it was not a matter of changing wheels but of actually mending the puncture there and then. There was a long stop due to carburettor trouble and innumerable shorter ones after the engine had boiled as it laboured up almost every hill. It seemed almost certain at one point that we would all spend the night beside the road but, in the end, we did reach a village. It was too late to get any food so everyone, hungry and discontented, lay down to sleep as best they could upon the floor of a disused attic.

No new predictions as to arrival time were sought the next day and none was offered. There was little doubt in our minds that there would be no change in the pattern of the previous day, and as the old Chev, amid many stops, was coaxed to the top of each succeeding range of hills, the road could be seen winding its way into the distance, an unending yellow ribbon loosely laid upon a patchwork quilt of varying shades of green and brown.

Since the beginning of the Sino–Japanese war, cities, towns, villages, waterways and roads had all been subjected to bombing and strafing. Small wonder that the Chinese lived in mortal fear of every *fei gei* (aeroplane), for they had no defence against them. However, over the years, a remarkably effective warning system had been devised whereby any place likely to be attacked from the air was alerted ten minutes or more before the raid. This gave almost all the inhabitants a chance to evacuate their towns and villages and disperse in the countryside. It was more difficult to give adequate warning against low-flying aircraft, especially those bent on strafing the lines of communication and the villages beside them, but many spotter posts had been set up which were permanently manned and from which gongs sounded the alarm the moment that there was any suspicion an aircraft might be in the vicinity. The closer we approached Kukong, the more frequent were the posts, the more frequent were the alarms and the slower became our progress.

The first came in a hamlet where we had stopped for food while running repairs were made to the engine. We were in the middle of negotiating the purchase of some honey when suddenly a gong sounded, followed by shouts of '*fei gei*'. Everyone dropped everything. They seemed to run in all directions to get away from the road and the buildings. No one ran further or faster than our driver, who

162

we were fascinated to see disappearing over the skyline of the nearest hill, while we remained standing in the now totally deserted hamlet before deciding ourselves that even in China discretion was still the better part of valour.

Just beyond the houses we found a convenient ditch running at right angles to the road, which would have afforded almost everyone excellent protection against anything but a direct hit by a bomb. We sat on the edge of it and waited.

Nothing happened. No *fei gei* was seen or heard. Very gradually people began to trickle back, and we were able to complete our purchase of the rich honey, ingeniously packed in large bamboo stems cut into sections just below each knot which made splendid unbreakable containers. But there was still no sign of the driver.

When at last he did reappear and we started once again on our way, we discovered that his fear of *fei gei* amounted to panic because he had been buried in a house during a raid and had been rescued only after hours of digging.

Scriven told us before we had left Waichow that there was an interesting Buddhist monastery which should be visited if it were possible to persuade the lorry-driver to stop. We had no need to prevail on our driver because rather less than a mile short of the monastery a puncture, the eighth since leaving Lo Lung, brought us to the all too familiar abrupt stop. For once we were not irritated. We marched off to the monastery, having asked to be picked up in the village when the tyre had been mended.

At that time I had never seen a Buddhist monastery, nor did I know anything about Buddhism. It was a pity, I felt, that there was no one to explain the significance of the innumerable different effigies. Many had recently been renovated, which rather spoilt the effect when we knew that the monastery itself, laid out in a series of terraces, had been in existence for rather more than a thousand years. At the entrance gates two gigantic figures frowned hideously upon all who entered. Having braved their ferocity, we found ourselves in a courtyard. On either side of the approach to the first temple there grew fruit trees interspersed with ornamental specimens. Beyond it were a series of terraced courtyards, one above the other, each with its centrally placed temple, each with its own effigies increasing in grandeur as one progressed until, finally, we stood at the foot of an ancient pagoda in front of which was a particularly fine old bell.

Douglas Scriven had been right: a visit to the monastery had been most worthwhile. Within its precincts there was a calm; the reality

163

of the outside world did not exist and probably had not existed for a thousand years.

The lorry was waiting in front of a small stall selling tea and sweet cakes. It would take no more than an hour to reach the outskirts of Kukong, we were assured, and as if to prove it, the driver set off at breakneck speed. We braced ourselves among the sacks of salt to stop being flung from side to side. Even the boy on the front mudguard had difficulty in maintaining what was, at the best of times, a precarious perch. Having accelerated furiously down the first part of a long incline, the driver put the gear into neutral, a trick they all had to save petrol. Driven by the sheer weight of the cargo, the lorry continued to gather speed. We endured a petrifying five minutes, far worse than anything experienced before, until at last the road levelled out, the speed began to reduce and the juddering felt less as though the whole lorry would disintegrate. It was still travelling a great deal too fast on a road surface where an axle could easily be broken if the driver failed to avoid some of the deeper pot-holes. However, we had relaxed slightly when suddenly the near-side front wheel hit one of these pot-holes. The tyre burst with a loud bang, the lorry veered violently to the right and headed for a rice field. The driver, whether by luck or skill, corrected it just in time. Then it veered the other way. He corrected it again and yet again until, finally, the lorry stopped on the right-hand verge.

By this time we passengers in the back were all on top of each other. But as twenty-three thoroughly shaken folk disentangled themselves and emerged onto the road, no one had suffered more than a few bruises.

The tyre was in shreds, the wheel buckled. Gone was another prediction because, on past form, it was likely to take an hour or more to repair the damage, presupposing that another tyre and an inner tube could be made serviceable to carry the lorry the last few miles to Kukong.

This was the ninth blow-out since the start of the journey, and the remaining selection of outer covers and tubes presented a sorry sight. There was no tread on any cover, two were down to the canvas, the third had an ugly patch on the side wall, while each of the inner tubes had been patched many times.

After much deliberation the cover with the ugly patch was selected, and while the threadbare tyre already on the spare wheel was being removed, we had a look at the patch. Believe it or not, it had been repaired in the same way that we had dealt with our lilo. The split in the wall of the tyre had been taped both inside and out, and to give added strength, thin metal plates had been placed over the tape and bolted together through the tyre itself. It worked but for how long we were never to know, for the lorry pulled up at the Customs gate on the outskirts of the city without further incident. At this point we abandoned this ageing monarch of the road, having no stomach for still more delays while the cargo was checked.

And thus it was that four bedraggled, unshaven and filthy individuals, preceded by their worldly possessions carried by one coolie woman upon a bamboo pole across her shoulders, arrived in the centre of Kwangtung's war-time capital, to complete the second phase of a frustrating, arduous but infinitely rewarding journey.

Chapter 19

Kukong proved a milestone of real significance. It was a city, sufficiently sophisticated to make us feel we were back in civilization. I doubt whether any of us had given much thought as to what we might expect when we arrived there. We did not expect a fanfare of trumpets or welcoming shouts but, on the other hand, we did not expect to be thrown out of a Chinese hotel. Douglas Scriven had told us to go to a certain hotel to make contact with Lieutenant-Colonel L. T. Ride. He was a well-known Hong Kong character who had been in command of the Volunteer Field Ambulance Unit. He now ran a British Intelligence operation of which Scriven was part. We found the hotel not without difficulty. The coolie woman dumped her load in a heap on the floor just inside the entrance, and we were still in the process of paying her off when a little man descended on us in a state of considerable agitation but obviously intent on throwing us out.

We understood little of the torrent of Cantonese which flowed from him, proprietor or receptionist, whatever he was, but his gesticulations made it abundantly clear that he wanted us and the rubbish on the floor in the street without more ado.

Indignant at this outburst, we stood firm while John did his best to explain what we wanted. It was a ridiculous incident, and one we were to laugh at later, but at the time we were in no mood for such a charade. In the end we managed to find out that Ride was at the British Methodist Mission, and there we were given beds for the night. Next to a hot bath, the biggest joy of the evening was being able to listen to a news broadcast from London, something we had not done for many months. Next morning we moved to one of the houseboats on the river, where we were made comfortable for the whole of our stay in Kukong.

Lieutenant-Colonel Lindsay Ride was known to all his friends as 'Doc'. He had been Professor of Physiology at Hong Kong University. Duggie, John and I knew him quite well, in spite of a considerable age gap, since Doc was a keen cricketer and we had often played together during the past three years.

Having listened to our story, he told us of his own experiences, how he had made his way to Chungking and how Brigadier Grimsdale, the British Military Attaché, had sent him back to Kukong with the object of setting up an organization to help anyone coming out of Hong Kong and, if possible, encourage further escapes.

Since March he had been in the process of building up what was about to be known as the British Army Aid Group, but in the field he and other British elements operating in South China were faced with a huge problem. There was little or no unity among the Chinese commanders, whose main preoccupation was to vie with each other in self-interest. Thus, any effort to seriously oppose the Japanese or to help the Chinese was continuously dispersed like water off a duck's back. Ride, whose special operations needed care, secrecy, discretion and co-operation, found these essential elements almost totally lacking. Doc went on to tell us that Grimsdale, accompanied by John Keswick, was on a tour of inspection and was expected in Kukong within the next two or three days, when it was hoped that discussions with the local dignitaries might induce some co-operation. He thought that the latest information, which we were able to give, would be most useful, but from our own point of view, Grimsdale's arrival could not be better timed since he would, no doubt, give us our future orders. In the meantime, Doc suggested that we should relax and enjoy ourselves as best we could. We were delighted to follow his advice and did little more than eat and sleep for the next two days.

I had met John Keswick on only two or three occasions. The last was when he and his elder brother, 'Tony', stopped in Hong Kong for a few days *en route* to London. It was shortly after 'Tony', as chairman of the governing body of the International Settlement in Shanghai, had been wounded by a Japanese bullet during a public meeting. (Both he and John were knighted after the war.)

For three generations the Keswick family had played a leading role in the affairs of Jardine Matheson, and these, in turn, had continued to be inextricably bound up in almost every aspect of Britain's relationship with China since 1832, when the firm was founded. Indeed, it had not been without influence in Japan, for it is said that John's grandfather had been one of those who helped smuggle a young prince of the imperial family to Europe. That young prince, soon after his return, became, with the aid of his Western experience, one of the architects of modern Japan.

John had been posted to Chungking to serve in the British Embassy, especially as he had already become—in his early thirties—an influential figure in China, steeped as he was in the great Jardine tradition.

When he and Gordon Grimsdale arrived and we had given a résumé of our experiences, Grimsdale saw each of us separately. When it came to my turn, he said almost immediately, 'I have told the others what I want them to do. Since they are serving Gunner officers, they now come under my command and I have given them their orders, but I am not at all sure what we should do with you. You are in a rather different position.'

Although he said this in a kindly way, my immediate reaction was that he must be referring to my humble rank as an NCO, so I said, 'I quite realize, sir, that I am only a sergeant but . . .' and I was about to explain why I had not taken a commission at the same time as John Pearce when he cut me short.

'You don't have to worry about that,' he said with a smile. 'Your position is different because I don't believe that you are any longer a serving soldier and consequently I can't give you orders.'

How ridiculous I thought, but I said nothing and waited for him to continue.

'As a member of the Volunteer Defence Force, you were only pledged to serve in Hong Kong. Clearly, you are not in Hong Kong now,' and he smiled again as he said it. 'So, as far as I can see, you are an entirely free agent.'

'How wonderful! But what am I? A refugee or a Jardine representative on tour in South China?'

He laughed, and so did John Keswick who had been listening to all that had taken place.

'What do you want to do, David?' John asked.

Without a second's hesitation I replied, 'I want to go home and be commissioned in England.'

For a moment there was dead silence. 'H'm, that's not so easy, is it, Gordon?'

Grimsdale nodded and my heart sank a little.

John Keswick went on, 'I would like you to come back with me to Chungking. There is a lot you could do. Come and have supper with me this evening and we can talk about it.'

'Thank you very much. I would love to.' I hesitated. 'Of course, if there is no chance of getting home, I am very ready to do whatever you suggest.'

I went back to the houseboat to compare notes with the others. Duggie was to remain with Doc and return to Waichow; John was to go to India, and Lynton was to accompany Grimsdale to Chungking before flying to India himself.

The parting of the ways had come earlier than any of us had expected, and as I left the others to meet John Keswick for supper, I wondered what Grimsdale would have done with me had John Keswick not been there to take me under his wing. I wondered also whether it had been John Keswick who had suggested the line which Gordon Grimsdale had taken because there really was a job for me to do in Chungking. Whatever the truth may have been, I counted myself extremely lucky that John Keswick had been there.

During the course of the evening I learnt that their trip to the south had been planned to take place rather later in the year, and it had been my telegram sent from Waichow which had prompted them to bring it forward.

John told me that there were a number of ways in which I could help him, but my first task would be to work with a section of the Embassy in which a register was being compiled of all British subjects thought to have been in Hong Kong at the time of the Japanese attack and of what had happened to them.

'There have been innumerable enquiries from relatives in Britain, Australia and Canada, and it has been impossible to give any positive reply to many of them. I am sure you will be able to help greatly.'

'I will try,' I said.

As we left the restaurant, John told me that he was giving dinner to Generals Chu and Wong the next evening and lunch to General Yu Han Mow the following day.

'David, I would like you to come to both.'

'Thank you so much, that will be most interesting,' I replied.

I was fascinated by the idea of meeting the army commander of the Chinese forces in Kwantung because in the early days of the fighting in Hong Kong he had become a legendary figure who it was thought would attack the Japanese in the rear and relieve the British in Hong Kong. Lieutenant-Colonel Harry Owen Hughes, it was said, had flown out in the last plane to leave Hong Kong with the express purpose of persuading General Yu Han Mow to make such an attack. If this were true, and if our own intelligence had been any good, it must have been recognized as a forlorn hope. There was never any question that Yu Han Mow or any other Kuomintang commander would commit his forces against the Japanese if he could possibly do otherwise. The annihilation or capture of the British forces was of no consequence. Japan might be China's enemy, but the Chinese were prepared to do no more than make encouraging noises to bring about their defeat. The Kuomintang officials knew that, when their defeat did come, their own real fight would start, the fight against Communism under Mao Tse Tung. It was for this fight that they were determined to keep their powder dry, no matter at what cost to their Western allies.

Instead of celebrating our last evening together by going to some restaurant, we had dinner quietly on the houseboat, listening to the wireless, which was still something of a novelty, and speculating when and where we all might meet again.

Just as we were about to go to bed, John asked, 'When do you and Lynton leave tomorrow?'

'In the evening. The trains travel at night to avoid being shot up by the Nip aircraft. We get to Hengyang before it's light.'

'What do you do after Hengyang?'

'Take another train to Kweilin, the next evening. Grimsdale and Keswick are going to visit some school for guerilla tactics which has been set up near Hengyang. I shall be interested to see Kweilin. It's supposed to be a very beautiful walled Chinese city despite the attention it has received from Jap bombers.' I paused. 'You'll have to go there, won't you, John?'

'I'm not sure. That's the reason why I'm interested in your movements.'

'You'll have to fly the Hump. You can only fly to India from Kunming. You'll be going over the Himalayas, but how the hell you get from Kweilin to Kunming I've no idea. Our party will go north-east from Kweilin to the railhead,' I said. 'And, in my case, from there we drive to Kweiyang, which, I gather, is on the "Burma Road" between Kunming and Chungking but nearer Chungking. Apparently we have a military mission in Kweiyang.'

'Well,' said John, 'it doesn't sound as if you are going to do any more travelling in an overloaded salt lorry. Neither should I, with any luck. Poor old Duggie is the one who faces that. He's gone to bed because he's still feeling lousy.'

'I agree. It's a bit hard to be sent back to Waichow. He needs a break rather more than any of us, with malaria still in him.'

'Do you feel you've got a break yourself, David?'

'Good God, yes. It's been a real bonus that Keswick should have appeared at this moment.'

'That may be, but aren't you afraid of getting stuck in Chungking? I thought you had set your sights on England.'

'I have and both Keswick and Grimsdale know that I want to get a commission in England not India.'

170

(At that time little did any of us know that it was the prerogative of every prisoner of war who made good his escape to claim repatriation, and furthermore, he was under no obligation to return to active service in the same theatre of war. Also, little did I know that I had eight months to serve in China, and a remarkable journey lasting six months which would take me half way round the world before I was to set foot in England.)

'I wish you luck,' John said.

'Thank you, John, and I wish you the same.'

'Now before we go to bed you must give me the telephone number of that girl of yours as I will see her long before you.'

'For God's sake, don't go on calling her "that girl of yours"—you've known her name for years.

'All right, all right, Hazel; what's her number?'

'Capel 2239, but you won't find her at home.'

'God! that's a big dangerous,' said Lynton who appeared in the middle of our conversation.

'No, it isn't,' I replied. 'John already knows her address. In any case, to make doubly certain, somehow or other I will send a special message to warn her against this man Pearce!'

'So you concede defeat,' said John.

'Not a bit of it,' I replied.

'You can be as cautious as you like, say what you like, but I will be taking Hazel to dinner in London while you are still ten thousand miles away.'

He was right. He did.

Chapter 20

It was almost dark as Lynton and I gathered together our worldly belongings, which all too easily fitted into our army packs, and set off to the station accompanied by Duggie and John. The rain had stopped but it was hot and the air was saturated. The humidity was probably a hundred per cent. Throughout the week in Kukong, rain had thundered down. From the comfort of our houseboat it was bearable and fascinating to watch on the water.

I was glad to be on the move again, especially as the next phase of our travels would be in comparative comfort, and I spared a thought for Duggie, who would be returning to Waichow, presumably by the same route and by the same method as we had used to get here.

At the station, John Keswick and Gordon Grimsdale were surrounded by a small knot of people who had come to say goodbye. We boarded the train, and it was soon puffing slowly out of the dimly lit station into the darkness of the night.

We were travelling on a section of the Canton–Hankow railway, both terminal points of which were under the control of the Japanese. Our destination was Hengyang, a town south-west of the city of Changsha which had suffered harshly at the hands of the enemy, but the Chinese had managed to keep a limited service going on the central section of the line.

It was four o'clock in the morning when we arrived at Hengyang, having travelled some 250 miles. The chill of the morning bit into our bones through our scant clothing. It was not really cold but the sudden drop of twenty degrees from the hot and humid Kukong made us shiver, and it was a great relief to be ushered into a car which had been sent by the Bank of Canton for the distinguished gentlemen with whom we were travelling. Lynton and I did not accompany them on their tour of the training centre. We were taken to a palatial mansion where Mr Ho, head of the Bank, gave us a most courteous welcome and suggested that we should rest and join him for lunch.

We were taken to a sparsely furnished room done in the usual way of Chinese houses and totally without heat of any sort. Fortunately, the room had two hard beds, and on each was a duvet in which we rolled ourselves to keep warm.

On the way to lunch we discovered that Mr Ho, apart from holding an important position in the bank, was also the Mayor of Hengyang and had arranged a special lunch to celebrate our safe arrival in his city. We found it difficult to believe it was for us and felt sure that it had been prepared for John Keswick and Gordon Grimsdale. They were from the British Embassy in Chungking and merited such attention, but, of course, they were still on their inspection. Anyway, we were given what may justly be described as a banquet, for which we were most improperly dressed in shorts and shirt with an army sweater rather the worse for wear—no one seemed to mind and it was exceedingly nice to be treated as special guests. That evening we were all four taken back to the station to catch the train for Kweilin, where we arrived early the following morning.

From what I had been told about this legendary walled city and its surrounding countryside, I was eager to see it. The name itself, pronounced 'Gway-lin', so attractive to my ear, seemed to have a fairy-tale ring about it, a touch of magic. Would it live up to the picture which I had conjured up in my mind, despite knowing that it had been damaged during the war and that its ancient walls were no longer intact? It fully lived up to my expectations.

No sooner had we arrived at the hotel than the air-raid warning sounded. This was the signal for a general exodus. Shops were shuttered, men, women and children poured from every building and streamed out of the city to take refuge in caves nearby. We were just about to have breakfast but the alarm forced us to join the exodus. Even if we had not, there would have been no one to serve us. The fear of air raids was very strong, so much so that Kweilin became a ghost city each time the alarm sounded.

The broad, clean thoroughfares in its centre, some of which were tree-lined, were totally deserted. There were side roads which led to the old wall, parts of which still existed, and here people passed out of the city through massive archways, each with picture-book Chinese houses built on top of it.

Beyond stretched what must be an almost unique countryside. One studded with rocky pinnacles on which grew gnarled and stunted coniferous trees. They were like giant fingers and thumbs. In many there were caves, and it was into these natural limestone air-raid shelters that the population so frequently disappeared.

For me, one of the great joys of seeing this strange land-formation was gaining some small understanding of a part of

Chinese art. Many scrolls depict hills and knolls as if they and the little figures upon them are floating on an ethereal mist, thereby giving an appearance of total unreality. Around Kweilin they become a reality because often a light mist clings to the ground covering the base of the pinnacles. As the sun begins to penetrate the mist, it is as if man and nature were floating upon a gentle wispy cloud, and it is easy to see what has inspired the Chinese artist.

We spent three days in Kweilin. Keswick and Grimsdale had to work. Lynton and I had nothing to do. Time might have hung heavily on our hands but for the marching back and forth between the city and the caves. We tried, when the shops were open, to replenish our wardrobe but were horrified by prices which, as far as we could recall, put those in Savile Row to shame, and so we walked around in what we had.

On the evening of the third day, before setting out for the station to take the night train to the railhead, John Keswick gave a memorable party, memorable if for no other reason than that it was the first time I had eaten suckling pig *à la Chinoise*. At any time such a dish is delicious; at that time, when I was still permanently hungry, it was something never to be forgotten.

The excellence of the sleeper in which we had travelled from Hengyang to Kweilin was not to be equalled from Kweilin to the railhead. I had enjoyed the suckling pig. Bed-bugs now enjoyed me. The carriage was infested with them. Their constant attack made sleep impossible.

When the sun came up, the bugs disappeared, fat with our blood, and left us trying hard not to scratch their bites. The Brigadier had brought a pack of cards so we played bridge to take our minds off the irritation. The cards also took our minds off the fact we could get nothing to eat on the train.

By the time we arrived at the railhead and had collected the car—a comparatively modern Chevrolet, there remained no more than four hours of daylight and John Keswick said, 'I have no intention of driving after dark. We'll make only a short run to a place called Ho Chi where Gordon and I stayed on the outward journey.'

It was a wise decision, for much of the road was pitted with pot-holes, some deep enough to break an axle if taken at any speed, littered with loose rocks, some large enough to crack the sump, while on many of the frequent corners loose stones caused wheel-spin and skidding. I have always enjoyed the challenge of driving under such conditions, driving to minimize strain on the engine and the chassis and yet to give as great a degree of comfort as possible. John was like-minded and handled the car with great skill. The same could not be said of the other two. John politely did his best to curtail the time they spent behind the wheel. He told me this when he and I got up at dawn to check the car before leaving Ho Chi, and I was thankful to hear it, especially when he explained that a full two days of driving lay ahead of us before we could arrive at our next objective, the British Military Mission at Kweiyang.

That morning is as vivid nearly forty years later as it was at the time. It would be hard to say why. I can only put it down to seemingly small things. Perhaps it was that John talked of the job to be done in Chungking. I remember he asked whether I wished to return to China after the war, which gave me an opportunity to vent my enthusiasm to do so. Perhaps it was simply the pleasure I derived from doing something useful again in checking the car and the anticipation of driving it over tortuous roads. Perhaps it was no more than the beginning of my recovery from starvation. Although there were to be lapses, not surprisingly, I was conscious for the first time of feeling well, conscious of my great good fortune in travelling through this remote part of central southern China and conscious that there were still fascinating experiences to come.

I'm certain of one thing. I was intoxicated by the fresh morning air which lay so still among the hills of southern China on that twenty-third day of May 1942. I had been free for six weeks. It was good to be alive, which, but for the grace of God, I would not have been. And in this happy state I found most exhilarating the sound of the Chinese national anthem sung as a local unit raised the Nationalist flag at dawn.

Soon after leaving Ho Chi, we began to leave the limestone formations behind us and entered more rugged country where the road wound its way through imposing gorges and over mountain rivers spanned by beautifully constructed bridges such as we had seen on our way to Kukong.

On arrival in Kweiyang, the car was handed over to a mechanic in the British Military Mission in order to prepare it for the final stage of the journey, some four hundred miles to Chungking.

We stayed at the Mission and there was a good deal of coming and going, but one mountain of a man seemed to be a fixture. He was a Swede, George Soderbohm. For reasons I cannot recall, he had spent years in Outer Mongolia. He regaled us with many stories, seeming to conjure up the camels which frequented his stories to such an extent that I could almost smell the dung and the unwashed tribesmen who tended the beasts.

The scheduled stop-over in Kweiyang was just two nights. On the morning of the one full day, I went to investigate at least a part of this large walled city, the provincial capital of Kweichow, and in my wanderings found yet another superb bridge with a house built upon it, but I can remember little else because my notes for that day were taken up by recording a sudden change of plan.

Returning to the Mission compound, John Keswick called me and said, 'We have a report that the Japanese may be planning to move up the Haiphong–Kunming railway from French Indo-China. In case this happens, we must provide transport to evacuate the British Consulate, and I want you to take one of our five-ton trucks to the Consulate in Kunming. It will give you a chance to make contact with Sandy Urquhart. I have sent him a signal to say that you will be leaving here the day after tomorrow, which will give you time to prepare the truck and to learn a few words of Mandarin.'

Like hell it will, I thought, knowing my propensity for languages, but I said, 'OK, John, out of the frying-pan into the fire. Bosanquet doesn't seem to have much option.'

'No, he doesn't! In any case, you should enjoy the drive and then fly to Chungking after a few days with Urquhart.'

I left him to think over for myself this new development. The thought of driving a truck some seven hundred miles down the famous Burma Road gave me quite a thrill.

The truck was in excellent condition, and apart from my almost total lack of knowledge of the language, I drove out of the Mission compound without any apprehension of the long drive before me. I had a co-driver, a Chinese. The fact that I could converse with my co-driver only by signs didn't worry me at all.

The only time language presented any problem was within Kweiyang itself, where for some reason we were held up at the transportation centre. I suppose it had something to do with the movement of trucks on the Burma Road, but the authorities eventually let me go when they found that they could make me understand nothing, and to whatever they said I repeated in Chinese over and over again, 'I go British Consulate Kunming.' I was glad to have learnt the phrase the previous evening!

Once on the road I handed over to my co-driver, and for the rest of the morning we bumbled along from one pot-hole to another across flat and uninteresting country. I was not impressed by the way my companion handled the vehicle on a comparatively easy stretch of road, and so, after a midday meal in An Shan, I took the

176

wheel myself because I could see mountains ahead. Indeed, we soon began to climb, twisting and turning up the sides of the mountains. Rounding one corner with a sheer wall face of rock on one side and a drop of hundreds of feet on the other, we met an abandoned lorry head-on almost in the middle of the road. The rear axle had a jack under it, and one wheel was missing. No doubt this was the reason why it had been abandoned but, of all places on such a treacherous road, it was beyond comprehension that its driver had made not the slightest attempt to draw in to the side. Could we get by? I thought it was just possible, but not so my Chinese driver, who was all for turning back.

Sitting in the passenger seat and looking over the edge, there was reason for his anxiety but we could lose a day if we turned back. There had been almost no traffic on the road, so perhaps we would even lose two days before anyone returned to move it.

We both got out and examined the situation with great care. I checked that the verge was firm and considered there was just room to get past, providing the initial angle of approach was made correctly. I inched forward with the door of the cab off the latch in case I made a mistake; I was glad to be on the inside; my companion watched the outside wheels and beckoned me forward. When I was safely past, he walked back behind the truck, pointed to the tyre marks on the verge, smiled and, as he jumped into the cab, said just one word, '*Hao*'—Good. I knew I had gained face.

As we continued to climb, I soon began to hear the gentle roar of a waterfall growing louder and louder. From the road I could just see the water as it plummeted over the ledge of the fall, but as there did not appear to be any great weight of water, I did not get out and take a closer look, partly because I'd seen many others and also I was keen to push on to the next sizeable village to spend the night. It was a great mistake. I was told afterwards that the main fall was out of sight of the road and, although it was quite narrow, it was thought to be higher than Niagara.

After the falls, the road began to wind its way down into a magnificent gorge which was spanned at the bottom by a fine suspension bridge. It seemed remarkable to find such a bridge miles from anywhere until one stopped to think that this road had become China's life-line after the capture of Canton and the Japanese occupation of Haiphong.

From the bottom of the gorge, the climb out of it seemed unending. The gradient of the road was remarkably good but on many of the hairpins, even in an unladen truck with a powerful Ford engine, I had to come down two gears. It was hard work, and at the end of a long day I was glad when at last we ran into An Nan, high up in the mountains.

While we checked and refuelled the lorry from the fifty-gallon drum which was carried in the back, a small crowd of interested spectators gathered. This made me realize that I could not possibly leave it unattended, since the lorry was open and there was nothing to prevent anyone from helping himself to my precious petrol. So I decided to try by signs to make my co-driver understand that I was hungry and to bring me some food from a nearby restaurant before he found a bed for the night. I intended to sleep with the petrol drum, come hell or high water.

It was heavy going. The more I gesticulated, the more it amused those who stood around. They too began to wave their arms making the same gestures. Soon everyone was roaring with laughter. This added to the crowd.

Eventually a young man who, quite obviously, had come to join the fun, stepped forward and announced that he spoke English, adding, as an afterthought, American too!

'Are you an American?' he asked.

'No, I'm English.'

He nodded his head, saying very seriously, as if the fate of the world depended upon it, 'You do not speak Chinese?'

Trying to keep a straight face, since it was painfully obvious I did not, I replied, 'You are quite right. I do not speak Chinese.'

I then explained what I was trying to tell the driver, and the young man told me that it would be quite unnecessary for me to eat in the lorry. He would take me to a restaurant where it could be parked immediately outside the entrance, and we could sit at a table just inside so as to keep an eye on it. We moved slowly down the village, together with the younger element of the crowd hugging the sides of the lorry, sitting on the front mudguards, anywhere for a ride. At the restaurant I invited the young man to have supper.

During the course of the meal I discovered that he was older than I and yet still a student. He was very derogatory about the Japanese and assured me that the day would come when they would be driven out of China, but when I asked whether he intended to join the army and help to achieve their expulsion, he seemed genuinely surprised at such a suggestion and made it abundantly clear that it was far more important for him to complete his studies. The army was beneath his dignity. Fighting was the task of coolies.

I was already aware that such an attitude existed but this was the

178

first time I had been confronted by it. It had been a self-enlightening evening, I thought, as I climbed into the back of the lorry among a few gunny sacks with my pack once again as my pillow. An army of coolies and an intelligentsia who would not deign to fight would never drive out the enemy. It would be British and American forces alone who would force them to leave.

Myriads of stars sparkled in a clear sky. The sounds of the village died away and, untroubled by mosquitoes at this altitude, I slept soundly until the chill of early morning forced me to wake. I was pleased to be wide awake and ready to leave as the first streaks of dawn began to appear because I knew we had a long day ahead of us and I was determined to reach Kunming before dark.

The owner of the restaurant opened his door and not long after produced some tea, followed by a steaming bowl of rice over which I cracked two raw eggs. We were on our way by six o'clock, and I was the passenger.

Barely a mile from An Nan, another enormous gorge lay before us, far bigger than the one which we had negotiated on our approach from An Shan. At first I could not see the bottom but I could see the road winding away on the far side. The scene was breathtaking and I gazed at it transfixed until, out of the corner of my eye, I saw my driver throw the gear lever into neutral and switch off the ignition just as we approached the first hairpin bend. I seized the hand-brake and shouted, 'Stop!' The little man trod on the foot brake and we slid to a stop.

On our journey from the East River to Kukong I had experienced the free-wheeling tactics of the Chinese in an effort to save fuel, and that had been bad enough on a road far less tortuous and steep. I signalled for him to get out of the driver's seat, still holding the hand-brake, and as he jumped to the ground, slipped into it myself.

As we started again and I changed from second to third on the short straight and back to second for the next hairpin, I tried to demonstrate why I had acted so fiercely. I could not tell if he understood but since I had no intention of allowing him to drive again, it was of little consequence. I could see by his face he thought me a stupid, wasteful foreign devil.

Down and down we went. I counted no less than twenty-three true hairpin bends. Many graphic signs were well placed to warn drivers of dangers ahead. All corners where there was a sheer drop into the gorge without a vestige of protection were appropriately marked by a skull and crossbones. I found the climb out of the gorge more exciting than the descent. I revelled in the need to use the gears correctly. Many corners required a double change from third, through second, into first gear, and it was the latter which was difficult to judge. Fortunately, the road was dry and, providing care was taken not to spin the rear wheels on the loose stony surface, there was no danger of going over the edge.

Even when we were out of the gorge and the country became more open, the road continued to climb and I felt I was driving to the top of the world, which was true because the western land-mass of China leads into the eastern ranges of the Himalayas, and much of the province of Yunnan is over six thousand feet above sea-level.

The colour of the soil changed to a glorious red, and in the brilliant sunshine the light and shade upon the hills gave a striking variation to their colouring, especially in the early stages of the journey where grey limestone rocky outcrops dotted some of the hills, giving them the appearance of gigantic cemeteries. These hills gave way to those with gentler slopes, many of which were terraced and cultivated. Gradually we ran onto a vast plateau, and it was then that I was able to push along my trusty steed, for until that moment I had almost given up hope of reaching our destination that evening. In the end I drove into Kunming just after six o'clock and had covered over three hundred miles in twelve hours.

When at last I found the Consulate, it was only to be told that Sandy Urquhart lived a further ten miles beyond the city. I set off alone, leaving my erstwhile companion, who had been called upon to do so little and yet whose presence I had been glad to have, to find lodgings in town. By this time I was very tired and I prayed that the instructions I had been given would be easy to follow. They were. And with a feeling of relief I hammered on the doors of the compound wall which surrounded the house. It was quite an appreciable time before a panel opened and a torch shone in my face.

'Master have got?' I asked and in answer the panel slammed shut. I waited for the doors to open but they did not. I hammered again and when this brought no immediate result I manœuvred the lorry so that the headlights shone directly at the doors, pressed the horn and let long blasts shatter the silence of the still evening. It did the trick. Sandy and a Chinese appeared.

'Good God,' he said, 'I was expecting you tomorrow evening. Did you leave a day early?'

'No. I came today from An Nan. Had a damn good run.'

'I should bloody well think so. Anyway come in!' he said.

Inside he apologized for the reception, adding that his watchman

180

had returned to the house in quite a state of agitation. Although I had spoken English, he did not understand and had quite genuinely been frightened by my appearance, suggesting that, if I took a look at myself, I would see why.

I was filthy. Of course, I had not washed since leaving Kweiyang. Superimposed upon a layer of grey dust from the first half of the journey was another layer of fine red particles from the good red earth of Yunnan. My hair was red, so was my bearded face—a beard which had not been trimmed since the end of January. I looked a very ugly customer in every sense of the word.

A drink, a bath, supper and bed where sweet oblivion was immediate. I did not stir until the sun began to pour into the funny little room which had been built against the compound wall as a spare bedroom because there was no room in the main bungalow. Sandy had turned two of them into offices when a transmitting-station was set up within his compound.

The bungalow, at the foot of the western hills, looked out over a large lake, and mountains rising in the background. The air was pure and exhilarating at six thousand feet. I felt it would be no hardship to relax for a while in such attractive surroundings. Indeed, the first two or three days were bliss, until, without warning, I collapsed. Whether it was some bug which attacked my tummy or whether it was reaction to earlier physical and mental strain, I never knew. At one moment Urquhart thought that I should be flown out to Calcutta for treatment. Undoubtedly, it would have allowed me to arrive in Chungking refreshed instead of being plunged into its rigours as a sick man.

As it was, I remained in Kunming for two weeks and was briefed by Sandy Urquhart as to the role he played. He also taught me the code so that I would be able to receive and send messages through the Embassy in Chungking if and when necessary.

Of course, there was no business activity and no real need to go to Jardine's offices but they were in such splendid surroundings that it was fun to do so.

They were approached from the street through a magnificent pair of heavy wooden doors of some antiquity and interestingly carved. As these doors were swung open by the attendant watchman, an attractive courtyard was revealed through the archway, in which a variety of flowering trees and shrubs were growing. Around the courtyard were a series of balconies, all with painted frescoes. A pungent, musty smell, a smell of stale Chinese tobacco, pervaded the air. Once through the archway with the heavy doors closed behind us, shutting out the noise of modern traffic, I felt translated into another world. It was no longer 1942 but 1882 or even 1842. That courtyard had not changed. The Chinese who moved within it still wore gowns and the traditional black slippers.

It was as if I were being taken to call upon a great mandarin whose support, or at least not active opposition, had to be secured before any trading venture stood a chance of success. And, as if to bring home the reality of my dream, a venerable old gentleman in a beautiful shantung silk gown came forward to greet us as we entered one of the rooms. Formal introductions over, we sat round a small table while green tea was served in handleless cups with lids from which we sipped the tea by pushing back the lid a fraction but never removing it.

The old gentleman spoke no English, but Sandy explained that Jardine's had shipped to him huge quantities of blankets and piece-goods from our mills in Shanghai. Never had a written contract been exchanged. Never had our friend failed to meet any payment on due date. I am not suggesting for one moment that it was commonplace to conduct business in such a way. It was not, but being told of it added greatly to the romanticism of my first visit to that most attractive establishment. No other place, before or since, anywhere else in China, gave me such a vivid sense of what previous generations may have seen and experienced in their time.

Not until the moment came to book a flight to Chungking did I give any thought to the fact that I had no passport, and since no ticket could be issued without it, I called again upon the Consul, to whom I had already delivered the lorry. Of course, there was no problem in the issue of a new passport but he did suggest, rather charmingly I thought, that I should decide whether or not I intended to keep my beard before having the necessary photograph taken. I had it removed but as a compromise kept my moustache for a few more months, and the next day I was a proud possessor of a new passport, one which I considered extra special and which I kept even when it could no longer be further extended. The reason was this. The old name for Kunming was Yunnanfu. Not only has the word itself a music to it but, for me at least, it conjured up every kind of colourful picture of the past glories of China, whereas the name Kunming did nothing to my soul. Also, to most people, Kunming could be anywhere on that vast continent. To have a passport which stated 'Place of issue—Yunnanfu' gave me great pleasure, a sense of oneupmanship perhaps, but I like to think it excusable.

Chapter 21

There was little of interest about the flight to Chungking except the arrival. There were two landing-strips, one some way out of the city along the road to Chengtu, the other on an island in the middle of the great Yangtse Kiang. For a good part of the year the island airstrip was under anything from sixty to one hundred feet of fiercely swirling water rushing headlong at ten to twelve knots to the China Sea fifteen hundred miles away. The river was nearly a mile wide, and at low water the current still ran so fast that if anyone fell into it he was usually swept away or battered to death. Come the melting of the snow, the river could rise to sixty or seventy feet overnight and sweep away anything or anybody who remained on the banks below the high-water mark. Each year in Chungking the river claimed many lives. I suspect it still does.

In the middle of June, snow on the Himalayas had still not begun to melt sufficiently to raise the water level at Chungking so the DC3 was deposited safely upon the island airstrip. The pilot was skilled enough to come over the top of the huge electric cable which stretched directly across the flight path from one bank to the other—at a height of some two hundred feet. I can think of nowhere else where such a hazard would have been allowed to remain. Typically, the Chinese government never thought to remove it.

From the water's edge to the road and waiting transport was a walk up a flight of some three or four hundred steps. It was hot and humid. Many were the pauses before I reached the top in a lather of sweat.

Here a car was waiting. I was taken to a house near the Embassy where various members of the staff lived *en famille* and where there was room for me. The house had been badly damaged during the air-raids, and one end wall which had almost entirely collapsed was shored up by timber covered with the then equivalent of polythene in a vain attempt to keep out the weather. On hot, humid summer days it mattered little but in winter, when it could be as cold and damp as in England, the prospects didn't thrill me. The bug I had attracted in Kunming was still in me. I felt ill, and but for the warmth of my reception, what I saw that day of China's war-time capital gave me little pleasure.

Chungking had risen to the dizzy heights of being China's capital when Nanking had been overrun by the Japanese earlier in the Sino–Japanese war. The Japanese had been tightening their grip on the Chinese coastal ports and cities since 1937 with the object of bringing China to her knees. And, in spite of the huge population of over 400 million at the time, China had been totally ill-equipped to defend herself against the modern might of Japan. General vied with general. Chinese general even fought Chinese general— particularly so if he were thought to be a Mao Tse Tung supporter. Often in the years between 1937 and 1942 whole Chinese armies of 200,000 men were deserted by their leaders, who left them in the field and retired to their own town or village in the countryside to protect their own wealth. Small wonder that many rallied to the cause of Mao Tse Tung, where at least they were helped to obtain the bare necessities of life.

There was very little real sense of unity, except among the guerillas such as we had met. The soldier had always been low on the Chinese list of careers. It's all very well to have a tradition of five thousand years of written history as did China, in which the scholar and the poet are honoured and the soldier despised, but the brutality, ignorance and cruelty of the Japanese were something which should have bound them together to fight if they had had leadership and better equipment.

It didn't. Nor did the fact that they were continually ill-led, ill-fed and ill-treated by their own leaders. The seeds of the Communist revolution fed on these facts, and the ever-patient Chinese people simply ran from their bombed, burning homes and returned to devastation when it was over.

Chungking had been a provincial capital and essentially remained that with the greed, bribery and corruption of the Nationalist government superimposed on it.

The results of Japanese bombing lay about untouched, and there were constant power cuts. It was a drab city in 1942 and we made our own entertainment in our own houses.

The first few weeks were mainly spent poring over lists of names, writing letters and reports about people from Hong Kong, especially any about whom I had first-hand knowledge, either during the fighting or in camp. In many cases, the information I was able to give was the first to be received by relatives in many parts of the world.

At the same time, John Keswick took me with him whenever he

had occasion to visit Chinese bankers or those officials in charge of selling raw silk and bristles which he, on behalf of the Ministry of Supply in London, was buying for ourselves, the Americans and Russians. The silk was required for parachutes, the bristles for paint-brushes, and each consignment that was bought had to be flown over 'the Hump' into India at vast expense.

It was, perhaps, just as well that John took so much trouble in those first few weeks to take me about with him, because shortly afterwards he was posted to Washington and I took over the buying of silk whenever they had any to sell. It was not arduous but it was at times frustrating. It took me some time to discover the ploy which the Chinese adopted to extract higher and higher prices for their produce. They would make an offer to sell a quantity of silk at a given price subject to a reply from London within seven days. Almost without exception, acceptance was received late and the Chinese, knowing this, would then counter-offer at an enhanced price to take account, so they maintained, of 'inflation'. After this had happened two or three times and the Ministry continued to disregard the signals sent through the Embassy telling them of the Chinese tactics, I took the matter into my own hands. While I was not permitted to make a purchase without authority from London, I bargained hard with the Chinese for their initial offer. Then I quoted London fifteen per cent above the offer in hand. When the reply arrived late, as it always did, I could still bargain without further contact with London. When I went back to the Chinese, they as usual raised the price five per cent, expecting me to be forced once again to refer to London, which would give them another chance to obtain ten per cent above the initial figure. But this time I was able to clinch the deal on the spot.

When I first did it, they were so taken aback that I had some difficulty in keeping a straight face at their loss of composure. The following year when I reported to the Ministry of Supply in person and gave them chapter and verse of the savings effected, the whole affair was treated with a total lack of interest. Typical of bureaucrats anywhere in the world!

One of the more interesting aspects of this business was that it brought me into contact with the USSR Trade Representation, an off-shoot of the Russian Embassy. I was required to advise them of all purchases made, and my contact was a young Second Secretary about my own age, Nicholas Kuzminsky. During my stay in Chungking, we met frequently.

At first it was always I who had to call at his office, but as the ice

185

began to thaw, he came often to visit me. I enjoyed his company but he was very apt to overstay his welcome. He would come perhaps in the middle of the morning, and stay for lunch and throughout the afternoon. I liked him and I liked the way he freely discussed political topics, but I was always left with the feeling that his friendship was countenanced because it afforded Nicholas a wonderful opportunity to improve his English.

He returned my hospitality by inviting me to the October celebrations at the Russian Embassy, where real vodka flowed like water and tables groaned under mountains of caviar, but it was not so much the food and drink which has remained imprinted on my memory but rather the guards on duty at the gates. All other embassies were content to accept Chinese soldiers; but not so the Russians. These guards were certainly not Chinese. Nor did they resemble any of our hosts or other guests at the party. Indeed, they were unlike any other human species which I had yet encountered, being solid and short of stature with unduly long arms and a hairline starting almost immediately above the eyebrows. I was not alone in wondering where these obvious sons-of-toil were bred in Mother Russia.

A few days before I left Chungking, we persuaded Nicholas to bring his attractive and accomplished wife to dine with us. It was a delightful evening, and at the end of it he presented me with an English translation of Russian fairytales suitably inscribed by himself. I was touched and have remembered both Nicholas and his wife to this day.

Chapter 22

Colonel Jimmy McHugh of the United States Marine Corps was the US Naval Attaché, and he had a large house, by Chungking standards a nice one, number 17 Kuo Fu Lu. He was a wonderfully open-hearted man, a lover of China and knowledgeable of its affairs. Since any kind of accommodation was scarce, he ran the house as a mess, of which John Keswick and Gordon Grimsdale were members. The others at that time were two Americans, the eminent columnist Joe Alsop and Whitey Willauer, who was General Chennault's right-hand man. The General commanded the famous Flying Tigers who flew their aircraft out of Kunming. Besides these two were Erik Watts and a colourful character called Petro, a White Russian who had married Jimmy McHugh's sister. Erik, in December 1941, had been the senior executive of the Kailan Mining Administration in Shanghai, and as a fluent Chinese speaker he wasted no time in walking out of Shanghai with his servant. On arrival in Chungking he was appointed Press Attaché in the British Embassy. Last, but by no means least, there was Hugh Richardson, an Indian civil servant of considerable distinction who had already spent a part of his career in Lhasa and was an authority on Tibet. He was in Chungking as secretary to the Indian Agent General, the dynamic Sir Zaffrulla Khan. Shortly before John was due to leave for Washington, he told me that I would be invited to take his place in Kuo Fu Lu. It came at a time when I was still unwell, far from happy and craving to get away, with no immediate prospects of doing so. It also came as a great surprise for I was years younger than any of the others besides being no more than a very humble appendage to the Embassy. It was an act of great kindness and saved me from becoming quite unbalanced during the rest of my stay in Chungking. My problem was that I did not have enough to do once the Hong Kong lists had been completed and, but for the evenings, found I was very much on my own.

'You'd better come to the little farewell drinks party I'm giving,' said John, sensing my enthusiasm. 'It will give you another chance to meet them all again before you move in.' Characteristically John produced something special, something rarer than gold-dust in

Chungking at that time—real Scotch whisky. How we all appreciated it! But perhaps I more than anyone else. Not because I had had very little to drink for many months but because the next morning I woke feeling well for the first time in weeks. Apparently I had successfully drowned the tummy bug which had attacked me in Kunming. From that day onwards I had no recurrence of the trouble.

The same evening I was delighted to meet again a friend of long standing, Edmund Teesdale. Eddie and I had been at Lancing together and we had continued to meet after leaving school, albeit infrequently, for he had won an Exhibition to Oxford where he obtained a blue as a miler and became President of the Oxford Athletics Association.

On coming down from the 'Varsity, he joined the Colonial Service and arrived in Hong Kong just one month ahead of me. As the war clouds gathered, he was one of those sent to Singapore to train in guerilla tactics and since, as was the case with all Government Cadets, he had spent the first eighteen months to two years learning Chinese, he spoke Cantonese dialect fluently.

When war came, he and a small band operated behind the Japanese lines as they advanced on Hong Kong Island and consequently was able to walk into China after the capitulation. It was good to see him and exchange experiences.

After the war, he and I were in Hong Kong again when, in early 1946, before I was posted to Shanghai, he walked parts of the New Territories with me to make contact with people who had helped us.

When we revisited the village of Chung Mei on the shores of Plover Cove, he asked the villagers whether any escaping English had passed their way and was told that there had been four. None of the little party to whom Eddie spoke could remember much about the four until one of them volunteered the information that one of them had been an old man with a beard. There was much amusement when I, through Eddie, was able to introduce myself as the old man with a beard! And our visit ended on a particularly happy note for, when we asked whether there was any improvement to the village which might contribute to the lot of all of them, we were told that a solid permanent bridge across the stream just above the village would help greatly in the daily task of collecting drinking-water from some way up the valley, and in taking their produce to market. Government almost immediately authorized the expenditure, and a fine concrete bridge was built in recognition of the help which the village had given us.

Number 17 Kuo Fu Lu was some distance from the Embassy and further still from the down-town office which Jardine's retained. I had no transport and, unless I got a lift with the others early in the morning, I walked everywhere and quickly learned the short cuts through the back alleys and what may best be described as 'rat runs'. It would be hard to find any city anywhere which could boast of a greater rat population.

In the days before the war, much of the produce from Szechwan was handled by foreign companies operating river steamers between Ichang, immediately below the famous Yangtse gorges, and Chungking, and those earlier merchant adventurers had sensibly built their godowns and houses on the rather attractive South Bank opposite the city. Jardine's had long since disposed of their property and employed agents; consequently, it was seldom necessary to go there, although it was a pleasant change to do so.

To cross to the South Bank from the city, it was necessary to walk down flight upon flight of steps—I counted 365—to the pontoon from which to board the ferry. On either side of the steps, literally thousands of the inhabitants lived in the most appalling squalor; their squatter huts were knocked together from scraps of wood or tin to give them some crude shelter. Each year, as the river rose, many were swept away and those in them if they left their move too late.

Even by day there was no pleasure in negotiating those steps of the Wong Li Mun, as they were called, but one afternoon I stayed later on the South Bank than intended and was forced to climb them in the dark—a mistake I never made again. The steps were alive with rats scavenging among the filth which had been dropped. Each step I took, it was as if the next moved in front of me as the seething grey bodies scurried out of my path only to close in behind me the moment I had passed. My horror of rats had returned; I was terrified that I might slip and was convinced that if I fell they would attack me, there were so many of them. I did not fall, but the climb remained a nightmare long after I was safely back in the house on Kuo Fu Lu.

'Doc' Ride arrived the next day and stayed with us for two or three nights. I had not seen him since leaving Kukong. He had come to report to Gordon Grimsdale and, no doubt, discuss his continuing problems in building up the British Army Aid Group and making it effective.

It was during his stay that I discovered positively that the guerillas, who had done so much for us, were firmly labelled as

Communists and were considered the principal enemy by the Central Government in Chungking and also by the various warlords vying with each other for supremacy in South China. The fact that the Communists were actively operating against the Japanese was of no consequence. It was they who had to be exterminated. The Japanese menace was entirely secondary.

Such an attitude is hard to believe but it was so. It accounted in a large measure for Doc's many problems. As a British officer operating in an allied country, he came under the control of the British Military Attaché who, in turn, was bound to seek agreement from the Chinese General Staff for any move he wished to make.

General Tai Lee was Chief of Chiang Kai-Shek's Secret Service who, some months before the Japanese attack, had visited Hong Kong, where he attempted to set up an utterly abhorrent private 'Kempeitai' organization. When this was discovered, he was promptly asked to leave. As a result he became violently anti-British and left no stone unturned to be obstructive. Doc Ride's efforts took the full brunt of his resentful attitude. A lesser man than Doc would have given up the unequal contest, not of the enemy's making but of those supposed allies. He did not give up, but won at least a degree of confidence with the Communists, 'our guerillas', who, between Japanese strong-points, controlled the coastal belt around Hong Kong. BAAG (British Army Aid Group) agents established contact with the POW camps, and although the desperate lack of escape-mindedness persisted, these contacts did help to improve morale. He turned his attention in these directions. Men forced to work for the Japanese outside the camps were smuggled out. During the course of the war more than thirty American airmen shot down over South China were spirited away before the enemy could get to them and were brought to safety through 'the rat runs' which BAAG had established.

Of course, none of this would have been possible without the support of the ordinary Chinese people themselves, but it was they too whom Doc was helping. He provided medical aid where the Chinese Army had none. He even provided food in time of famine. Indeed, his untiring efforts, despite seemingly insuperable obstacles, did more than anything to re-establish British prestige throughout South China. Yet they received scant, if any, recognition in either Chungking or London.

It was not until many years after the end of the war that he received a richly deserved knighthood as Vice-Chancellor of Hong Kong University.

190

In the autumn of 1942 Doc was not looking for accolades. He had come to Chungking to put his case, hoping for support in his dedicated mission to help both the Chinese people themselves and the Allied cause.

In November I received the news I had been praying for. Gordon Grimsdale, who had by then been promoted to Major General, returned from a conference in Delhi and told me he had arranged a pass which would permit me to land in and to leave India without being called up. This was great news because until that moment I was liable for military service upon arrival. However, the problem of how to get home from India remained, and in any case I first had to obtain permission from Matheson's in London to leave.

When everyone had gathered that evening for a cocktail before dinner, the possibility of getting a passage for me was raised. This cocktail hour before dinner was always a good time for me. But this evening was special. Normal spirits were unobtainable, but the local concoction known as 'Chungking gin', providing its taste was disguised by orange juice, made a palatable drink. However, the alcoholic content of each bottle could vary to such an extent that the effect on any of us after no more than two could be remarkable. Equally, four from another bottle could have no effect at all. Anyway, it was Joe Alsop who suggested that I might well get a passage in one of the American liberty ships bringing China Aid to India for onward carriage by air and that he would help me to do so if need be. A letter was on its way to London by the very next King's Messenger who carried the diplomatic bag.

My plea was sympathetically received but there was to be no quick release. For some reason which I've never fully understood, the firm thought it necessary to have a Jardine representative in Chungking and said that I must remain until someone could be found. Unfortunately, this took two months to achieve.

By selling two hulks moored on the South Bank of the Yangtse, Jardine's had amassed a considerable sum of Chinese currency. At the time it had been possible to negotiate the purchase of Chinese government bonds repayable in American dollars at the end of the war, but only a proportion of our funds could be committed in this way, hoping against hope that the Chinese would be in a position to redeem them on due date. The country's economy was woefully weak, and for the man in the street foreign currency of any kind was at a premium. A flourishing black market had developed. Each month, sometimes weekly, the value of the Chinese National dollar depreciated in terms of sterling, US dollars and the Indian rupee. It was easy to see that the firm's local currency balances would become almost worthless unless some prompt action were taken. So I entered the black market, purchasing travellers' cheques in varying currencies, drafts on New York by which many of the American personnel were paid and any cash on which I could lay my hands. I can't say I was without apprehension about what my directors in the City might think, but it was to prove worth the risk. By the time I was due to leave Chungking, I had reduced our local currency balance to reasonable proportions but I had still to get 'my loot' safely to India, where it could be encashed.

At last the day came; the 21st January 1943. I was delighted to find that Erik Watts was travelling on the same plane as far as Kunming, where he intended to stay a night and follow on to Calcutta the next day. I was to continue in the aircraft from Chungking.

I had little luggage, for no one leaving Chungking took any clothes which might be useful to anyone remaining or anyone who, like myself, might arrive in rags. In fact, I had been clothed in suits left by a 'great' Dane. He must have been excessively tall but spare. None the less, a Chinese tailor had no great difficulty in making the suits fit quite well after removing six or seven inches off the trouser legs and three inches or more off the jacket sleeves! I still had my pack, and that, together with a small, cheap Chinese suitcase, was quite sufficient for all my worldly belongings.

The aircraft climbed quickly through the cold grey cloud which hung over the city, into a clear blue sky, and it was good to have Erik with whom to share something of the exhilaration of that moment of release. Chungking still filled me with gloom; I was incapable of arousing any enthusiasm within myself for it. I am sure in retrospect that it was an excellent experience for a young man of my age because I was immensely lucky to have moved into number 17 Kuo Fu Lu, where everyone had been kind and helpful. I had been comfortable and well fed, and I was able to participate in the entertaining of all interesting and important visitors, for so many came to Kuo Fu Lu, either to drink our 'Chungking gin' or to dine. Wendel Wilkie, when Vice-President of the United States, dined there and I remember vividly an evening when the American journalist Ed White was taken to task for an article he had written while Madam Chiang, with her charm, was beguiling the American people into sending ever more aid to the beleaguered people of China in their 'gallant' fight against the Japanese, whereas the

Generalissimo and his entourage had not the slightest intention, as his wife well knew, of using any such aid for any purpose other than the coming struggle against Mao Tse Tung after the war.

Even looking back, I know my disenchantment had to be attributed mainly to my single-minded determination to return to England. Erik, whether or not he truly understood this obsession, had always been sympathetic, and his wise counsel throughout my stay was greatly appreciated.

There was a stop-over at Kunming of about forty minutes while the plane was refuelled for the next leg of the journey over the south-eastern end of the Himalayas into Assam. The Hump was the route for all aircraft because any plane showing itself on a more southerly route was an easy target for Japanese fighters operating in Burma. Many aircraft had been lost in this way. On its own, this section of the flight in a twin-engined DC3 was hazardous enough without any attention from the Japanese. The DC3s could climb to twenty thousand feet but actually had a normal ceiling of ten thousand. Yet the powerful and rugged little aircraft made thousands of flights over the Himalayas into Assam.

The aircraft was fitted with war-time netting seats along the fuselage to achieve maximum payload. On this particular occasion the payload included about twenty Chinese soldiers and their equipment. We taxied out onto the grass runway and were soon airborne.

Unbeknown to me, at that moment, Erik, having made contact with his friends, discovered that the weather over the mountains had closed in. However, it was not just concern for my safety which prompted Erik to try to get me off the plane but rather that I would miss the chance of a lifetime and not see the grandeur of that spectacular part of the world. Alas, he was moments too late.

For the first hour the flight was much like any other, and I was beginning to wonder how soon I would catch a glimpse of the mountains ahead, when we began to fly into cloud and lost sight of what lay below us. I was bitterly disappointed because I could not conceive of ever making the flight over the Hump again. As we flew on, it became colder and colder in the unpressurized cabin. I put on everything I had with me but it seemed to make no difference. It was too cold to read, I could not concentrate, and, of course, it was far too cold to go to sleep.

The poor Chinese soldiery were suffering tortures from the cold in their tropical uniforms and could do no more than huddle together on the floor under groundsheets. I was only slightly better off hunched up in my netting seat. There was not a vestige of heat in the main body of the aircraft. It was none too easy to breathe. My head began to ache. Normally oxygen masks were worn in DC3s above ten thousand feet. I do not know how long we endured the intense cold and lack of oxygen but it must have been three hours.

At last the plane started its descent. But our troubles were far from over. Whether it was the process of thawing out or whether it was normal altitude sickness, all in the cabin were in agony. I have never experienced such a blinding headache. And when the door of the aircraft was opened and the hot, humid air of Assam wafted into the plane, it was almost unbearable. We staggered out, clutching our heads; some of the Chinese rolled on the ground. I went to do a pee but gave up five minutes later when nothing happened although I badly wanted to do one. Besides the change in altitude, the change of temperature from minus goodness-knows-what to one hundred degrees within so short a time was almost too much for the human frame to stand. Returning to the plane, I begged the pilot to speed the refuelling, take us up again as quickly as possible and let us down gently before landing finally at Dum Dum Airport outside Calcutta.

There was some relief when we took to the air, and by the time we reached Calcutta the piercing pain in my head had subsided to some extent and I had managed to do my much-needed pee, but it was a further forty-eight hours before I fully recovered. When I met Erik two days later and told him of the hideous experience, he confessed that his American friends who, incidentally, had flown him out to India in clear weather, had expressed some concern that the scheduled flight on which I had travelled was permitted to leave Kunming.

It did not take me long to gather my meagre luggage and make my way to Immigration and Customs. I hoped that the examination would be cursory, since I had so little, and that no one would discover the not inconsiderable quantity of rupee notes which bulged in more than one of my pockets or the demand drafts and rupee travellers' cheques which nestled at the bottom of my pack. I did not fear for one moment that the authorities would object to my wealth of US dollars and sterling in any form. I was concerned about the rupees.

As I stood in line awaiting my turn to present my passport, I felt a tap on my shoulder. Looking round, I found a Sikh policeman standing beside me.

'Please follow me, Sahib,' he said, turning on his heels, and I obediently picked up my pack and suitcase. As I followed him into what appeared to be a waiting-room, I thought it strange that he had not asked my name. It was obvious that I had come from China but he knew nothing else. No one could possibly know what I was carrying, so why had I been singled out?

'Who wants to see me?' I asked.

'Please wait, Sahib. I am taking you to my Commanding Officer.' Without giving me a chance to say more, he disappeared through a door only to reappear a moment later. He held the door open to allow me to pass, and a tall figure walked round from behind his desk. It was Lieutenant Colonel Harry Owen-Hughes, lately second-in-command of the Hong Kong Volunteer Defence Force, the officer flown out of Hong Kong to make contact with General Yu Han Mow in a vain attempt to persuade the Chinese commander to attack the Japanese in the rear and so relieve the pressure on the beleaguered garrison.

'Harry!' I exclaimed in astonishment with perhaps a touch of relief, and I dropped my bags on the floor to shake him by the hand.

'Very good to see you, David, and many congratulations on your escape. Sit down,' he said in his quiet voice.

He told me that he had been given this job at Dum Dum because no one seemed to know what to do with a senior Volunteer officer from Hong Kong, to which I replied that the same could be said of extraneous sergeants of the same ilk. He went on, 'All passenger lists pass across my desk, and the moment I saw your name I thought it would be fun to plan a little surprise for you.' I thought to myself, 'Little do you know, Harry, the apprehension your little surprise caused me until I saw you.'

I had to cut short my meeting with Harry because Hector Tod, Jardine's Shipping Manager in Calcutta, was to meet me and would be wondering why I was taking so long to appear. Harry came with me to find him and escorted me through the Customs hall. All formalities were waived.

Hector drove me to the Great Eastern Hotel where we had a drink together, and since I still had a cracking headache, he left me to have an early supper and retire to bed. It felt good to be in India and I went to sleep with the thought that the first big step towards England had been accomplished.

Chapter 23

The next morning, as I walked into the large dining-room at the Great Eastern Hotel, with dozens of fans hanging from the high ceiling gently disturbing the warm air, many of the tables were already occupied by Sahibs, Mem-Sahibs and Burra-Sahibs having breakfast. Some were in uniform, some were not, and as I was ushered to a table by one of the many bearers, immaculately attired, I suddenly became conscious, self-conscious perhaps, of my cheap cotton shirt and shorts, bare legs still showing the marks of ulcers, ankle socks and shoes adequate enough for tramping the streets and 'rat runs' of Chungking but altogether out of place in the halls of the British Raj. My best pair of shoes, despite the harsh treatment they had received, were still those which had been thrown over the wire to Victor Nunes' kindly wife.

I enjoyed my breakfast, bare legs hidden under the tablecloth, savouring the thought of an immediate visit to the best Indian tailor that Calcutta could provide. I hoped he would match the excellence of Ah Man Hing Cheong, who had made all my clothes in Hong Kong. This important sartorial business took much of the morning.

It was almost midday before I walked into Hector Tod's office. In general, our affairs were then looked after by Jardine Skinner—there was no direct financial link between the two companies—but since Calcutta in peace-time had been a terminal port for our shipping line, a member of our own staff was always stationed there. Hector was that man and had been in Calcutta some time before the Pacific war started. I hardly knew him. Our paths had barely crossed before, and when I disgorged the contents of my pack upon his desk, his first reaction gave me the firm impression that he wished they had not crossed then! However, I managed to persuade him to deal with the rupee element of 'my loot' and accepted, since he wanted nothing to do with the other currencies, that I should take them on to Bombay myself but that they were to remain in his safe until I left.

On my way back to the hotel, my spirits were raised still further when I found that the tailor had finished two smart silk shirts, and I returned to my room relishing the thought that I would be able to appear at dinner reasonably well dressed for the first time in more than a year. At that time I wore shirts with cuffs and separate collars. These new shirts had been made that way. I had a leisurely bath, took one of the shirts and only when I had put it on did I remember that they needed studs and cufflinks. I had none. Disconsolately I had to take the shirt off, dress once again in my old clothes and go in search of some. They were easily found but somehow, as I put on the shirt for the second time, much of the pleasure had been lost. It was a ridiculous incident and I only tell it to illustrate that it takes time to re-adjust from a period in the wilderness.

I was keen to continue my journey to Bombay, from where all shipping left for the Cape and thence home. And the best way to Bombay was via Delhi, some thousand miles north-west. From there the rest of the journey would be a further thousand miles in a train. I also came to realize that, although Bombay was the shipping terminal at that time for all passages west, the ships were infrequent, always overloaded and with a passenger waiting-list months long.

Chris Sewell, an American friend I'd known in Hong Kong, most kindly met me at dawn and gave me a room. Later he took me to see the sights and fascinated me with his intimate knowledge of the history of the Indian capital. Finally, he arranged for both of us to travel to Bombay in his air-conditioned compartment. I still remember his kindness vividly.

There was a small Jardine's office in Bombay, dealing almost exclusively with the few remaining ships in our once compact fleet. I knew every one of them, and they immediately set about trying to get me a passage to England, even if it meant my signing on as an extraneous member of the crew. But any kind of berth seemed an impossibility because there were so many ahead of me on the waiting-list. Then I thought of Chungking and of Alsop's offer to help. I sent a message to him via the American Embassy begging help. While I waited for a reply, it was suggested I go to Karachi, stand on the airfield and thumb a lift in one of the US transports returning to the United States. At the time it sounded an absurdly outrageous suggestion but had I taken the advice the chances are that I would have made the journey to New York in days instead of the long, arduous months that it eventually took me.

For a time Bombay was a wonderful break but days turned into weeks, and weeks into eternity, and no prospect of my next move came. Even the beauty of Juhu beach with all its luxuries began to

197

lose its appeal.

One day everything suddenly changed as a result of Joe Alsop's intervention. Authorization was received in Bombay for me to travel in any liberty ship returning to the United States which might have spare officer accommodation since there was no passenger provision in any of them. I would have to sign on as crew but pay for the passage. In the first week of March the office was told that a ship would be sailing for the States which was short of its full officer complement, and if I was prepared to leave in forty-eight hours, I could occupy the cabin normally reserved for the Third Engineer. Forty-eight hours! That was more than ample notice. I could have walked on board in forty-eight minutes.

Once again though, there was a snag. Had I known that I was walking into one of the longest and most exhausting situations I'd yet had to face, I might have changed my mind and made for Karachi and a kite to the US after all.

The good ship *Archbishop Lamy*, a liberty ship flying the US flag, set sail from Bombay in the early afternoon of a cloudless day at the beginning of March. As I climbed the gangplank at Pier 4 outside the 'Gateway to India' memorial at Bombay docks, I had a feeling I was entering a totally different world. I was shown to my cabin, small but adequate. I left my luggage in it and leant on the ship's rail watching the activity on deck, as the port itself and the coast of India began to fade into the distance. My last look at the East for a long time. No one took the least notice of me. I was pleased to be left alone with my thoughts. So many things surged through my brain. I was leaving the East for the first time in over four years, in which it was hard to believe so much had happened. I thought of those in Shamshuipo more directly than I had for months. How many more years of that existence did they face? But for the recurring nightmare when I dreamed that I was back again in the camp, Shamshuipo seemed in the distant past, and yet I had been free less than a year. Kweilin, with its pinnacles, the Burma Road, 'Stingking' as many of us called Chungking, the Hump (that had been hell), India and now this voyage; what unknown adventures did *it* hold? Whatever they might be, I was committed—equally committed to being the only passenger and the only 'Limey' aboard. I went back to my cabin to unpack.

I had just finished when a member of the crew put his head round the half-open door to say that Captain Arnesen would be pleased to see me in his cabin. The Captain gave me a thoroughly friendly welcome, invited me to sit down and have a drink, explaining that the ship was dry but that he always maintained a supply of whisky, and hoped that I would join him before supper as that was the only time he took a drink. I looked at my watch: it was ten to five! A bit early for a drink before supper, I thought, but he explained that supper was at 5.30. Anyone hungry before they turned in at night raided the fridge on the mess deck. I accepted the drink, and almost each evening throughout the treacherous voyage he and I sat in his cabin, drank one whisky and talked together for about forty minutes before joining the other officers at supper.

I got to know him very well. He was a dear old man. He was sixty-seven and had sailed before the mast. He was Norwegian, a first-generation American, of which he was immensely proud. But he was no less proud of his American accent. To my ear he had scarcely a trace of one but I never let on and always raised my glass to it.

The Old Man took me in to supper. It made the initial introductions a great deal easier than if I had appeared on the mess deck by myself; I sat quietly through that first meal listening to the chatter, fascinated by the many different accents. I could hardly take my eyes off the Chief Engineer. He was the spitting image of Wallace Beery. The Steward sat at the opposite end of the table to the Captain, which was just as well, I thought, since he was a mountain of a man, bigger than the Chief. Had these two sat on the same side of the table, there would have been little room for anyone else. The Chief was tough and hard, the Steward fat and flabby. Flabby he may have been but he was a kindly, sympathetic man with a wide range of interests. Of all the ship's officers, I enjoyed his company the most. He became a good friend. The Purser was young, little older than myself, born of Basque parents who had emigrated to America when he was a small child. The Second Engineer hailed from New Mexico. He was tall, with jet black hair, flashing eyes and so swarthy that his origin could only have been south of the border. He kept very much to himself and said little. The one remaining ship's officer was the Mate, short, a quiet, unassuming man, good at his job, no doubt, but lacking the personality to take command. He was a Dane, a first-generation American.

Liberty ships had gun emplacements on the stern and carried a Navy guncrew commanded by a junior officer. In our case, the young man was an ensign from the heart of Texas. I delighted in listening to his southern drawl, although I have to admit that the content of what he had to say left the impression that his world started and finished with one small part of Texas.

Now I, the Limey, was closeted in the closest possible quarters with so many different elements that make up America, and it never ceased to amaze me that so small a company of officers in one ship should have been so diverse in parentage and early background and yet were all part of the same whole. It was a remarkable experience for any young man, and while it dragged on too long, it was one from which I benefited greatly.

The next evening I asked the Captain what our plans might be. He told me that he did not know beyond the first port of call, Cape Town, which, if all went well, it would take us eighteen or nineteen days to reach. Sensing my utter amazement that it should take so long, he explained that his orders forbade him to take the shortest route, and were I to visit the bridge, which I was most welcome to do at any time, I would notice changes in course at varying intervals and to varying degrees throughout each twenty-four hours. I should also remember that our maximum speed was eleven knots.

Eighteen days! It was an eternity. There was nothing I could do about it.

I took out my notebooks and with the aid of an old typewriter started to write down everything from the beginning again. Names I thought I'd forgotten came back. I saw other things in perspective. I became absorbed as the story fell into place and the ship chugged along on one of the glassiest of Indian Oceans ever imagined. Of course, I had already spent many hours in dull Chungking writing.

So for eighteen days we steamed ahead, sideways, north, south, almost it seemed in any way but west. We saw nothing but a few flying fish until the nineteenth day when we entered Cape Town's harbour. At the time we gave no thought to our good fortune in having arrived at all. We knew nothing of the penalizing shipping losses suffered by the Allies in the Indian Ocean at the end of 1942 and the beginning of 1943. In the first week of March, while SS *Archbishop Lamy* was discharging in Bombay, twelve vessels were sunk. The reason behind these U-boat successes has only recently come to light through James Lessor's fascinating story *Boarding Party*.

A German ship together with three other Axis vessels had taken refuge in the small neutral enclave of Portuguese Goa on the west coast of India. It was not suspected, until the disastrous sinkings persisted, that the German ship had a secret radio transmitter and that a master spy was transmitting precise movements of Allied shipping to U-boats operating in the Indian Ocean.

Although Goa was neutral territory, a handful of courageous members of the Calcutta Light Horse—a Volunteer unit made up of British businessmen—sailed round the coast in an innocuous-looking old 'tub', assaulted the German ship and destroyed the transmitter.

This happened at almost the same moment the *Archbishop Lamy* left Bombay and, as like as not, was the principal reason why we saw nothing but a few flying fish during our passage to Cape Town. Providence had intervened yet again.

I had had to tell the Captain of my escape when I came aboard in Bombay, because he wanted to know why I had been allowed to join the ship. Just before reaching Cape Town, I told him that I hoped we might celebrate the first anniversary, as by that time the news had got around the ship almost as quickly as news spread in the prison camp. He agreed to have a celebration, providing everyone was strictly rationed to not more than two drinks per head and that anything I bought was left in his cabin. I bought a whole case of South African brandy and got it aboard, suitably disguised, without anyone knowing its contents. The Old Man had laboured the point, rather excessively I thought at that stage, although I was to change my mind later. The crew were a rough lot, and with a few drinks inside them they were likely to become almost uncontrollable.

However, the precious liquid was safely secreted in his cabin while everyone but he and I was none the wiser.

We sailed that night for a bay about a hundred miles north on the Atlantic coast. There had been considerable submarine activity in the vicinity of the Cape during the previous two weeks, and the Captain had instructions to remain at anchor there until it was possible to form a convoy.

At dawn, when we were just south of the entrance to the bay, a ship could be seen stranded on the rocky coast. I was on the bridge with the Mate. It was obviously a recent stranding, and as we approached I was finally able to read her name through binoculars: *City of Hong Kong,*. At least, I thought, she was capable of salvage, just as we would salvage Hong Kong one of these days. We passed through a narrow entrance to the bay and dropped anchor. There was not a sign of life nor a building of any description on the low hills around as they sloped down to the water's edge.

No one was allowed off the ship. We remained there for seven frustrating days during which the monotony was broken only by the arrival of other merchantmen. When at last the orders were given to weigh anchor, the escort vessels awaiting us at sea instilled little confidence. There were three of what appeared to be no more than glorified tugs, and what they might be able to do against a submarine attack remained a mystery. Worse still, because one of the convoy was so encrusted with barnacles, the speed of us all was reduced to seven knots. For four days and nights we 'tugged' along apprehensively, and we were only too relieved when the convoy was finally ordered to scatter—we to our next destination, Bahia in Brazil, another fifteen days across the South Atlantic.

Chapter 24

Everyone hoped the ship would call at Rio de Janeiro, but since our stay was to be no more than a few hours, a port with only limited temptations was better. I didn't care, only for God's sake let's get on with it! By this time we had been fifty-five days out of Bombay, and the crew had had but a brief time ashore at Cape Town. The pressures of being cooped up for so long were beginning to tell. To have allowed his men no more than a brief glimpse of the bright lights and no doubt the red-light district of Rio would have faced the Captain with insuperable problems to maintain his schedule and yet sail with the necessary complement. As it was, the ship was late leaving Bahia!

The Steward, Purser and I went ashore together but did little more than go to a restaurant already well patronized by Americans off other ships in the harbour. We sat down and were drinking a glass of wine while contemplating what to eat when one of them came over to the table and stood staring at me. The others gave him some sort of greeting but he continued to stare, swaying slightly, as if I was some sort of freak. Then, ignoring me entirely, he turned to the Steward.

'God dammit, you've got a Limey with you.'

The Steward nodded.

'Where did you pick him up?' He did not wait for the answer but moved off slowly, saying repeatedly in a loud voice, 'Those guys have got a bloody Limey with them.'

A few looked up and then looked in our direction, but most were too busy eating and drinking to be distracted.

'Sorry if you have been embarrassed,' said the Steward.

'Good Lord, it doesn't worry me. I'm just surprised that the Limey in me should stand out quite so much as a sore thumb even when I don't open my mouth. I hadn't thought about it before.'

'It sure does,' the Steward said with a broad smile.

Once more at sea, my routine began to get a rhythm again. I continued to write, to walk up and down the limited deck space and to re-read what little in the way of books was on board. I longed to do a manual job, but any work had been taboo from the outset.

Union rules forbade it. I was told emphatically that there would be hell to pay if I so much as lifted a little finger. The fact that we were at war made no difference. My manual idleness continued as we slowly ploughed our way round the great land-mass of Brazil bound for Dutch Guiana, there to take on a cargo of bauxite since the ship, having delivered its outward cargo, had returned, so far, in ballast.

It had taken us nearly three weeks to cross the South Atlantic, and until the Captain made me study a map, I found it difficult to believe that our sailing time to Paramaribo would be only one, possibly two days less than three weeks. I had thought that, were we to scuttle along the coast, no more than half that time would be needed. The Old Man was much amused by my lack of appreciation of distances. He brought this home to me by saying that it would take all of twenty-four hours to cross the mouth of the Amazon. It did. In any case it was not considered advisable to scuttle round the bulge of Brazil, because, as off the Cape of Good Hope, recent U-boat activity had been deadly.

The bauxite loading-point was some sixty miles up river from Paramaribo, and moving both up and down that sluggish waterway, lined for the most part by thick, marshy tropical vegetation, we joined a veritable queue of ships. The depth of water was such as to restrict the load to four thousand tons, so each ship, having received its quota, sailed for Port of Spain, Trinidad, to complete loading. On the way downstream we stopped again at Paramaribo for a matter of two, perhaps three, hours. I did not go ashore, for the town appeared to consist of nothing but most uninspiring tin-roofed shacks, although one of the crew, as I learnt that evening over the daily drink before supper, found something of interest in it for he missed the ship.

By the time we arrived in Port of Spain, there were already many ships in the large open bay, and the mooring allotted to us was a long way from the waterfront; consequently, launches running between ship and shore were none too frequent.

The Captain went off the next morning to report the missing sailor to the American Consulate and to seek, no doubt, advice on what action he should take should the man re-appear. I returned just in time to have a drink before supper, and on my way up to the Old Man's cabin I was told that he had been beaten up while ashore.

I knocked softly on the door.

'Glad to see you,' he said immediately. 'I hoped you'd be back this evening.' He was sitting in his armchair with a large plaster along one eyebrow, another down the side of his other eye, an ugly bruise on his cheekbone; his mouth had been cut and he was not wearing his false teeth.

'My God, Captain. What the hell's happened to you?'

'Pour me a drink and I'll tell you,' he replied.

'I'd say you need one. Can you manage or would you like me to get a straw from the Steward?' I asked, handing him a glass.

He shook his head and took a sip before saying, 'That goddam son of a bitch.' The way he said it reminded me of the old Chinese salt in whose house we had rested the morning after crossing Mirs Bay. 'That goddam son of a bitch attacked me outside the Consulate.'

He went on to tell that he had done no more than register the fact of his absent seaman with the Consul and was walking away from the Consulate when the missing man, who had jumped aboard some ship which immediately followed the *Archbishop Lamy* and had arrived in Port of Spain at first light, set on him. Both his glasses and his false teeth had been broken, and tough as this old man might have been, he was thoroughly shaken.

'Where! is the seaman now?' I asked.

'On board,' he replied.

'What!' I exploded. 'You have allowed him to rejoin your ship?'

He nodded.

'Captain, it is none of my business. I'm not an American and I know nothing of your regulations but . . .' I hesitated.

'Go ahead,' he said.

'In war, surely no man has any excuse to miss his ship? To do that is bad enough but later to assault an officer in the execution of his duty compounds the original crime into one of most serious dimensions. I beg of you to return to the Consul tomorrow and demand the man's arrest and transport back to the States in another vessel. If that man remains aboard this ship, your authority will be undermined with the rest of the crew throughout the remainder of this voyage!'

He seemed appreciative of my vehement outburst and took no umbrage that it came from someone less than half his age. Later that night I was able to speak to the Steward alone. He was the only one in whom I felt I could confide, and while he agreed with me, he said it was not his place to interfere. I hammered on at the Old Man until he visited the American Consulate again. But the offender remained a member of the ship's company, and he persuaded me to believe that, until the ship eventually docked in the States, the incident was closed.

For the next three days I took myself ashore and stayed in a cheap seamen's hostel in the port area of Port of Spain. The bed was clean if nothing else—but the weather was damp and humid. The town seemed drab and dowdy. Apart from the exercise, I derived little pleasure in wandering about by myself, and I returned to the ship ahead of time, hoping against hope that loading was continuing quickly and that we would soon sail on the last leg of our journey.

Luckily, we had no more than two days to wait, during which there was a good deal of coming and going for the last shore leave. No one knew the ship's destination, but the evening before we sailed, the Steward and I were sitting together, having raided the fridge, when he told me that he guessed we would head for New Orleans. And, if we did, he had every intention of leaving the ship there, whatever happened. If I cared to do the same, he would take me to his home in Arkansas, where we could stay for a few days. Then he would drive me to New York. It was a wonderful offer. What better way of seeing something of the States, I told him, and if we were to dock at New Orleans, I would be right with him!

While we continued to talk, we heard a commotion on the deck above, near the entrance to our cabins. We went up to see what was going on. The Second Engineer, in a wild, drunken fury, was attacking the Mate's cabin door with a heavy sheath-knife, and as others tried to dissuade him, he turned upon them, knife in hand. They wisely retreated and he immediately attacked the door again. Within the cabin the Mate was shouting that if the door broke he would shoot. It was an ugly scene which went on for some half an hour until the Second Engineer lunged a bit too hard at one of the Mate's rescuers, lost his balance and was overwhelmed before he could regain it. I did not enquire what was done to the man when the others got him into his cabin, but the Mate was persuaded to emerge, revolver in hand. Apparently the fracas had developed from some trivial remark, and according to him he had been lucky to reach his cabin unscathed. Although all was quiet, I took the precaution of locking my cabin door and, as I did so, thought to myself that we could not get to a home port soon enough.

The ship was underway the next morning at first light. We, and ten or more other vessels, were to join a convoy bound not for New Orleans but for New York. I was glad in one way but sorry to miss the overland trip which the Steward had proposed.

We took station about midday. There were many tankers among the liberty ships, all fully loaded and low in the water, as indeed was our *Archbishop*. However, there was one exception, a 25,000-ton liner in ballast, centrally stationed immediately astern of us, which towered over the remaining forty-odd ships in the convoy. She was a captured German vessel being taken back to the yards at Brooklyn for repair. Only one turbine was functional, and she was capable of no more than nine knots.

Preceded by a destroyer zigzagging ahead of the convoy and two other escort vessels on either flank, a course was set to take the ships and their precious cargo right out in the Atlantic, thereby substantially reducing the chance of a U-boat attack.

A large convoy is a fine sight under any circumstances, but it was still more impressive to watch an intricate manœuvre such as the one our convoy was called upon to perform with the prize vessel in its very heart. For the prize vessel suddenly began to swing out of control, her one remaining turbine stopped. To maintain radio silence the Commodore's orders were run up the mast of his vessel by flags, and each ship with guardsman-like precision altered course, leaving a clear channel for the liner to drop astern without fear of collision. Immediately she was clear, the convoy closed ranks and proceeded on its way, albeit at a reduced speed in the hope that the engines might be restarted without too much trouble and the stricken vessel might catch the convoy again later. While all this was taking place, the destroyer dashed to the aid of the liner and was still standing by as we disappeared over the horizon, feeling rather naked without our principal escort vessel. However, she was back on station the following morning, although it was another twenty-four hours before the superstructure of the ex-German liner was again sighted far astern of the convoy. She never did regain her station but managed safely to reach some port on the eastern seaboard of the United States.

Not long after this incident the weather began to deteriorate and for the first time on that long voyage mountainous waves were crashing upon the decks. At night it was so rough it was almost impossible to sleep. I joined the Captain on the bridge while it was still dark. The ship groaned each time that she was lifted perhaps a hundred feet or more by one wave only to be thrown into the trough of the next. Gradually, as it became light, it was just possible to see the ships to port and starboard appear and disappear as each was tossed about like a cork, testing man's seamanship.

Then suddenly a gigantic wave smashed into the ship's superstructure, wrenching one lifeboat away from its davits so that it hung and then crashed into the upper deck as the ship rolled to starboard. Every available man, me included, was rushed to secure it before too much damage was done. But all our combined efforts were too puny against the storm. The Second Mate came forward and cut the lifeboat free, allowing it to fall into the sea.

One joker among the crew, seeing me standing by, soaked to the skin, turned and grinned at me. Then I heard someone else shout, 'There you are, Limey! If you want to get back to England so bloody much, that'll be there before we will ever get to port.'

'No thanks,' I said. 'I would not pass up the opportunity of setting foot in America for the first time!' Then another wave half submerged the ship, completely flooding the galley, with the result that there was no hot meal for many hours.

By evening the storm began to abate and the Old Man, who had been on the bridge throughout the day and most of the previous night, was prepared to relax for his drink before supper. He told me that the lifeboat which had been lost was the only one with an engine in it.

'You don't have to worry,' he said, thinking that I might be alarmed. 'You'll be quite safe in my boat if needs be.'

'Thank you, Captain, I'm sure I will.' Then I paused, smiling. 'If the boat includes the Second Engineer and that idiot who beat you up, you must promise one thing.'

'What's that?' he said.

'To sit in the bow with a loaded revolver and to shoot the first man who disobeys an order,' I replied.

He changed the subject quickly, for he knew there was an element of truth in my remarks. In fact, I had made a joke of it, but underneath I was in deadly earnest.

We had no need to take to the boats. Five days later we arrived off New York on a June morning which promised to be clear but was hazy. I had been told by almost everyone for days that I must not miss the magnificent spectacle of New York Harbour. It had no equal in the world. I had no reason to doubt this but I had been overfed immodestly the fact that America possessed the largest, the longest, the tallest, the most expensive, of very nearly everything.

My first glimpse of New York's mighty skyscrapers was through the light haze. Only the upper storeys were clear of it but, if anything, that seemed to accentuate the magnificence of the skyline and held me in animated suspense waiting to see the whole as the mist was slowly dispersed by the sun and while the ship, equally slowly, made its approach towards the Statue of Liberty, yet unseen.

Those of the crew not immediately engaged in some task were on deck, among them one of the stokers with whom I had spoken occasionally when my period of exercise on deck happened to coincide with his appearance from the bowels of the ship. He once told me he was at sea because he didn't want to join the army.

'We've made it,' I said, joining him beside the rail. 'It's been a long haul.'

'Yeah,' he replied, 'I can't wait to get off this old tub.' Needless to say, I felt the same, although for rather different reasons.

'Will you go to sea again or join the army?' I asked.

'Dunno. Don't like the sea, don't like the army,' he said with a laugh.

We continued to talk and while he pointed out some of the more important buildings, we suddenly noticed a gigantic ship bearing down towards us from the Hudson River, and other members of the crew came to watch.

'Now that is a ship,' he said. 'I didn't know we had any that big.' I was amused by this typical reaction which I had almost grown to expect during the last three months.

'You haven't, as far as I know. I think you will find she flies the red ensign,' I replied, perhaps a little smugly. A few minutes later the name on her bow was visible for all to read.

'*Queen Elizabeth*,' said someone. 'Quite a ship.' And casting all modesty to the wind I added, 'Quite a ship, the largest afloat.'

It was a great moment for me. The sheer majesty of her size and beauty of line could be impressive anywhere at any time. Against the backdrop of the skyscrapers of Manhattan, with their tens of thousands of windows glistening and sparkling like diamonds as the sun played upon them, that majesty was enhanced twofold. Indeed, that great ship, slipping silently out to sea, herself enhanced the magnificence of Manhattan, the one a complement to the other, as if saying, 'We are the greatest each in our own way.'

Chapter 25

We tied up and waited for Customs and Immigration. My only New York contact was Henry Lennox, who had been a senior executive of Jardine's in Shanghai. He and his wife had been in the US on leave and were due to return the very day the Japanese attacked Pearl Harbor. They stayed in New York where his friend, C. V. Starr, had offered him a job for the duration of the war. He was no longer of military age and had done his service in the first war.

I had sent him a telegram from Trinidad. Perhaps he thought after two months' silence that I'd been lost at sea. I was able to make a ship to shore phone call. Greatly to my relief, I was soon speaking to him. He had a booming voice and very abrupt manner. But behind his apparently iron exterior, he was the most kindly of men. I had just put down the phone when the Purser said, 'There's a guy here to see you, David.'

I turned to see a tall man in a grey fedora standing by the door, his hands in his jacket pockets.

'I'm from the FBI,' he said, showing me his badge. 'And I'd like to talk to you, Mr Bosanquet—in private.'

I gulped. What had I been up to now? Once alone I was soon to find out that it was about the attack on the Captain in Port of Spain. He asked me all sorts of questions about the ship's discipline and took a statement from me. Later in Washington the FBI took another statement from me.

As soon as the interview was over, I went ashore and met 'Len', as Lennox was always called. He immediately took me home to lunch with his wife, Doreen.

'There's a bed for you here, David, while you are in New York, if you don't object to the small spare room,' she said.

'Object! Nothing could be better as long as it doesn't put you out.' I stayed with them until I left for England.

Among Len and Doreen's many friends was General Telford-Smollett, whom they had known in Shanghai before the war. The General dropped in for a drink the next day.

He had a high-level job in New York at that time. He was interested in my exploits and strongly suggested a number of people whom he would like me to meet.

'You know,' he said, 'if the Press got hold of this story, they could make your life a plague.' He paused meaningfully. 'On the other hand, it will be good for British prestige if it receives some exposure.' He paused again. 'Are you game?'

'Yes, of course I'm game. I'm certainly not looking for any wild notoriety, General, but I have no inhibitions about the Press. In fact, I firmly believe that all first-hand information on conditions in the Japanese POW camps should be exposed whenever possible.'

'If that is the case,' he said, 'I will have a word with the Duchess of Leinster, who has a radio spot. She's a sweetie, you'll like her. I think she calls it "News Behind the Real News", which could hardly be more appropriate. But first I want you to meet someone else.' He then asked Len and Doreen to bring me to a cocktail party which had been arranged for Admiral Sir Percy Noble, who would be coming up from Washington for a brief visit.

I was being launched into New York life and what proved to be one of the most fascinating three weeks of my life. After prison camp, deprivations, the frustrations of Chungking and the long voyage, the contrast of New York, and the US nation still living the measured and mellow life of peacetime, was very exciting to me. Yet I still had to find a ship! In the meantime, New York was heaven.

The Duchess of Leinster was on the telephone the next day. Someone who had escaped from a Japanese prison camp was more than a strange novelty—indeed unique in 1943. Later the Duchess came to the flat, where we could talk undisturbed. The General was right, she was an absolute 'sweetie'. We talked for hours, and at lunchtime on the 6th of June 1943 Mrs Edward Fitzgerald, as she called herself, told a section of the Great American Public something of my experience in both North Point and Shamshuipo, under a pseudonym.

Next I went with Doreen and Len to the cocktail party for the Admiral, who had been C-in-C Far East in 1941. The General found us soon after we had arrived.

'Come and join the queue to meet the Admiral,' he said. 'I'll introduce you.' It took some time before he shook hands and had a few words with Doreen and Len about Shanghai and how fortunate they were to have been away when war broke out.

As they moved on, the General said, 'Sir, I would like to introduce to you a young man who escaped from the POW camp in Hong Kong last year.' The Admiral looked at me and, instead of shaking me by the hand, as I had expected, raised his left hand in front of the General's face and said, 'Don't tell me his name.' Turning to me he asked, 'Do you play rugger?'

'Yes, sir,' I replied.

'Did you play for the Club in Hong Kong?'

'Yes, sir.'

'Did you play for them in the seven-a-side competition in the spring of 41?'

'Yes, sir.'

By this time everyone was agog at these questions and answers. The General obviously could not understand what was going on. Doreen and Len stood the other side of him, no less surprised.

'It was a filthy wet day, wasn't it?'

'Yes, sir, it was.'

'You beat the Navy in the final.'

'Yes, we did.'

'Were you the only player to wear gloves?'

When he asked that question, I thought I knew what might follow.

'Yes, I think so. My job was to run. String gloves, when the ball is wet and greasy, make it a lot easier to cling on to a pass.'

'Um,' he said with a broad smile. 'Just one more question. When you ran on to the field, putting on your gloves to the shouts of "pansy" from the stand, did you turn round and bow to the crowd?'

'Guilty,' I confessed.

'I thought so,' he said. 'Your name is Bosanquet,' and he added, 'Well done. If you can come to Washington, make sure you see me. I should like to hear something of your story.'

I thanked him and moved on.

'Well, well, you certainly made a deep impression on the Admiral, whatever you were up to. You'd better tell us the story, David,' said Len.

I told them. It had been a filthy day and any team in the final of the seven-a-side competition performed three times during the course of the afternoon. I had asked my Chinese *amah* (servant) to pack two changes of rugger clothes so that, when we won the first-round match, there was no need to sit around in wet jersey and shorts while the other matches were played. It never crossed my mind that there might be cat-calls when I alone appeared immaculate for the second game. But for the gloves, perhaps my change might have gone unnoticed; the combination of the two was too much, especially as I began putting them on while running on to the ground. As shouts of 'pansy' rang out from one section of the stand, I felt certain that they came from some of my friends who were wont to give voice on the slightest pretext, so what better way, I thought, than to acknowledge their derisory acclaim, friendly as I knew it to be, by giving a deep bow before putting on the second glove. What I had quite overlooked was the presence of the Governor, the Admiral and the General, who were all sitting in the stand. I was told some time later by the Governor's ADC, Tim Fortescue, who was a friend of mine, that it had caused some amusement among that distinguished party, and it had been he, when asked, who had told them my name.

I said, 'It's incredible how the Admiral remembered that nonsense.'

'He's a splendid person, and that was no idle invitation to visit him in Washington. He wants to see you. You must go,' said the General, turning to introduce me to other people.

It was then that I met Odette Higgins, a real Irish charmer, light brown eyes surrounded by a white, freckled face and a lot of auburn hair. To me, she sparkled. It had been a long time since I had had any female company. I was starved for it. But Odette would have been charming under almost any circumstances. We were soon laughing and getting to know each other very quickly. The vibration between us did not go unobserved by Doreen, who invited her to have supper with us after the party, and that night I danced—for the first time since that fateful night at the Gripps in Hong Kong. That had heralded the beginning of my 'war'; would this herald the beginning of a new era in my life? I saw a lot of Odette in New York.

I soon found that obtaining a passage to England was almost impossible for a private individual. The General's office and others were doing what they could to help. There was no hope from the people I approached every day. Apparently half of the US was trying to get there, plus whole troopships of soldiers, British, Canadian and newly trained RAF pilots. Nurses, doctors and medical help were volunteering. It began to look as if I might have to wait months.

In any case, plans were being made for me to go to Washington to make a further report about the incident on the *Archbishop Lamy* and, of course, to visit the Admiral.

A few days after the cocktail party, the General said to me, 'I was visiting Mrs Vanderbilt yesterday and mentioned your story. She asked me to bring you to tea next Thursday, and that, let me tell you, is an invitation which no one refuses.'

I began to smile. 'But General, I wouldn't think of refusing anything you suggest. If I smile at the thought of a tea party, it is because it reminds me of a very dear but imperious aunt with whom I used to stay as a boy. It would have been as much as my life was worth not to have attended her tea parties.'

'You will find Mrs Vanderbilt imperious too but, if she likes you, golden hearted. By the way, you don't *have* to drink tea.'

Mrs Vanderbilt, then in her seventies, lived in one of the remaining mansions on lower Fifth Avenue. The General and I walked up the steps to the front door, which was immediately opened by the butler who led us across a beautiful marble floor to one of the sitting-rooms, where our famous hostess greeted the General with all the grace and charm for which she was renowned.

She then turned to me, gripped my arm and propelled me from one group of her guests to the next, explaining to each group that I had escaped from the Japanese. There were no more than twenty people in the room so it was a very intimate affair, and Mrs Vanderbilt was embarrassingly effervescent about my exploits. When we came to say goodbye, she told me there was to be another little gathering the next afternoon to which she would like me to come and meet more people.

As she said this, I saw the General look at me as if to say, 'Refuse if you dare.'

'Thank you, Mrs Vanderbilt, I would love to come.' I meant it, somewhat perhaps to the General's surprise, and told him as we walked down Fifth Avenue that I had enjoyed the tea party. It had not been the stuffy affair that I had expected. Everyone had been very friendly, and I looked upon a repeat performance the next day as no hardship at all.

I went the next day. The pattern was the same but when it came to my turn to take my leave, she said, 'No, not you, young man. Wait, I want a word with you.' Dutifully I waited until everyone had left.

'Now,' she said, 'we can talk. Come and sit down.' Surprisingly, she asked no more than a few questions about my exploits and was more concerned as to where I was staying in New York, whether I was being looked after, whether I was meeting the right people and, above all, enjoying myself. Of course, I told her that I was being overwhelmed by kindness, not least of which was her own. In the midst of all this she said, 'I will call you David.'

'Oh, but of course, Mrs Vanderbilt, please do.'

I must have stayed for almost an hour after everyone else had left, by which time I had been shown the remarkable collection of her signed photographs. Many of the crowned heads of Europe since the turn of the century were there, and in front of each little group she stopped to tell me the circumstances under which the photographs had been given to her. When she came to a photograph of Lord Louis Mountbatten, she said, 'You must know Lord Louis! Such a fine young man and he is doing so many gallant things. Now, David, he is the man you should go and see as soon as you get back to England.' Fortunately I did not have to answer, as she had already moved on to the next subject and I was able quietly to smile to myself at the unreality of her entirely sincere suggestion.

Two days later, when arrangements were complete for me to visit Washington the following day, I received a message from the General's office to say that the Duke and Duchess of Windsor were visiting Mrs Vanderbilt later in the week and that Mrs V. had informed the General, who was to be presented to them, that she wished me to be at the gathering. This was indeed a royal command.

Again there were not more than two dozen people to meet His Royal Highness and the Duchess, all of whom were American except the General and myself. I had been presented to the Duke once before, while I was still at school. Waiting at the end of the receiving line, I was struck by how small the Duchess was, very chic but minute. When Mrs V. was introducing HRH to the General, I never gave a thought to her eclectic personality.

But when HRH was opposite me, Mrs V. said, 'I want to present a young countryman of yours.' She hesitated. 'Let me introduce one David to another.'

I nearly died. If I could have disappeared through the magnificent marble floor on which we stood, I would have gladly done so. Plainly HRH was embarrassed and took a moment or two before he shook hands.

'And it's a jolly good name, too,' he said.

Who else, I wondered, has ever been presented in such sophisticated surroundings, to their own royalty, in such a manner? At the time I felt I could well have done without the distinction!

I left for Washington the next day but not before receiving firm instructions from Mrs V. that I must report as soon as I got back.

In Washington the Admiral gave me far more of his time than I expected. He took a surprisingly detailed interest in my story and, having served in the Far East himself, asked questions to draw me out. He also asked what plans I had for getting home. Naturally I told him of the difficulties. He picked up the phone and said, 'When does the next big 'un sail? Is she full?'

The voice at the other end spoke for some time. 'I see, and the next one?' he asked. 'I have a young man with me at the moment. I want to get him back to England as soon as possible.' There was more talk. 'You may book him as civilian or military personnel. It doesn't matter as long as he gets a berth.' He rang off. 'There,' he said, 'we will get you home in one of the big 'uns. Can't give you an exact date but you must be ready to leave at short notice any time after the end of next week.'

I thanked him profusely.

'You might have to put up your sergeant's stripes but I don't s'pose that will bother you if it saves you three weeks at sea in a slow convoy,' he said with a broad smile.

'Not a bit, sir. I'll paint them on my arm if necessary! And thank you again.'

'Good,' he replied, 'You deserve it.'

Having given his secretary all the information she needed, I walked out of the Pentagon Building as though my feet were on springs. Even the heat and humidity did nothing to dampen my spirits. It did dampen my body, for a summer's day in Washington is hot and it was a long walk to the hotel.

In a bath I had ample time to reflect upon my good fortune. Never in my wildest dreams could I have expected my ability to play rugger to pay such dividends, but perhaps I owed it as much to the weather on that rainy February day in Hong Kong for without that need to wear gloves there would have been no bow to the crowd, and undoubtedly it had been that spontaneous act and not my plethora of tries which had made its mark upon the Admiral.

On my return to New York, Odette and I had dinner together. We had seen a good deal of each other by now without either of us realizing just how much it had meant. She had helped me to shop and turned a chore almost into a pleasure. She had taken me to see some of the sights of New York and I much enjoyed her cheerful company, but my heart was in England, where I had left it almost five years earlier; and I quite failed to see what was happening until that evening.

Odette was unusually quiet as I, bubbling over with the result of my visit to Washington, told her that I had a passage home in one of the next sailings on the 'Queens'.

As I burbled on, she put her hand on mine.

'Oh, David. You mean you are leaving?' She paused. 'This war, it's so . . . so horrible, it takes everyone away. My brother has just joined the Canadian Black Watch. He'll be going to Europe quite

soon. The thought of it has depressed my parents. It rubs off on me.'
I now realized how unhappy she was. I was upset.

'This is the first time I have seen you anything but cheerful,' I said.

'I've been depressed underneath for some time.'

'If you have, you've hidden it wonderfully well.'

'I've been so happy doing things with you, David, and now you are going away.'

'Yes, but not for a week or so. There are still lots of things I hope we can do together. Please, please continue to be my attractive, cheerful and very charming guide.' She smiled. I squeezed her hand. 'Let's dance.'

The next morning I received warning to be ready to leave at any time after 9 a.m. on the following Wednesday. Full details of where to report would be given to me not less than twenty-four hours in advance of the actual sailing time. This gave me five more days in which to make the most of New York. Suddenly there seemed many things to be crammed into them; indeed, they proved very full and most rewarding. There were a good many people to be thanked for their generous hospitality, not least among them, of course, Mrs V., but since I was going to 'tea' yet again that afternoon, to thank her presented no problem, or so I thought.

When I arrived, as I expected, she wanted to know what I had done and whom I had seen in Washington, and as soon as I mentioned the Admiral, she asked, 'And is he going to help you get to England?' I told her that he had. 'When do you leave?'

'It is not absolutely certain yet but I have been warned to be ready at short notice any day next week.'

'Ridiculous,' she said. 'You must know.'

'I don't know for certain, I promise you, Mrs Vanderbilt.'

'Well, if you won't tell me, you must come to breakfast, lunch or dinner on Monday, Tuesday or Wednesday.'

'Really, Mrs Vanderbilt, you are very kind, but I can't manage Monday because I've a date to climb the Statue of Liberty and I couldn't possibly let down my very charming escort. I think Tuesday should still be safe and I would love to come to say goodbye then if I may.'

She thought for a moment. 'Then you had better come to lunch; a number of interesting people are coming.'

'Thank you so much. That will be marvellous. All your guests are always interesting.'

'Not all,' she said.

217

That night Odette and I dined at the Plaza with Len and Doreen and, if for no other reason, I remember it so well because it was the first time that I had been to such a sophisticated establishment where two bands provided non-stop music. As one section of the stage sank beneath the dance floor with one band, the other section rose with the second band playing them out. In fact, the evening was a great success. Both Len and Doreen were in splendid form, and Len was in particularly good voice, which no doubt was the reason why I overheard him say to Doreen, 'It strikes me that David will be leaving at least one broken heart in New York when he goes.' Of course, I knew he was referring to Odette. I would love to have heard Doreen's reply!

Odette and I set out on Monday morning on 'operation tripper'. We took the subway to the Battery, then the furthest station downtown on Manhattan Island. The weather was kind, a hot June day which made the boat journey out to the Statue of Liberty all the more refreshing. I told her of the quite magnificent sight which I had been lucky to see as the *Archbishop Lamy* entered New York Harbour and how that long, long voyage of almost nightmare proportions had already begun to fade into the past due entirely to all the wonderful people I had met in New York. It was a happy day, munching a hamburger and eating ice cream, goggling at the sights from the top of the 'Lady' and allowing ourselves to be windswept and spray-covered as we returned to the jetty.

Back at the apartment Odette produced a long, cool drink, and for a few moments we stood together looking out of the window upon the hustle and bustle in the street below, each engrossed in our own thoughts.

'Do you know when you are leaving? Are you sure it will be this week?' she asked.

'It is certain to be this week; I expect actual confirmation tomorrow morning unless someone in the General's office has been in touch with Len or Doreen while we've been out.'

'Why, oh, why must you go?'

This was the moment I had been dreading. I knew where this question was bound to lead. I knew that she was the one who was going to be hurt, whatever I might do or say, and I hated myself.

'You know I have to go. You know I'm longing to get to England after so long and to see everyone I love.'

'Couldn't you love me?'

'I could very easily.'

'Then why can't you?'

218

'Because I'm here today and gone tomorrow.'

'Can't you see what's happened to me? Can't you feel how much I love you?'

'Yes, of course I can. I both see and feel. That's just the trouble. It would have been so easy to make love to you and, at the end of it, simply walk out of your life.'

'Don't walk out of my life. Oh darling, let's get married.'

'Dear, dear Odette, you have touched my heart. You don't know this man who's suddenly popped into your life and is about to pop out again. If you did, you would realize that he could be passionately, madly, head over heels in love and would still be too stupidly practical to marry when things are so uncertain.'

I smiled, hoping to break the tension.

'I know you think I am silly, but, David darling, please don't laugh at me.'

'I'm not laughing at you. I've never felt less like laughing.' I paused and looked at her. She smiled wanly and looked down. I said, 'I'm just trying to bring everything down to earth.'

Had I not known that within the next two weeks, God and U-boats willing, I would be seeing, hugging and kissing the one girl who had been in my heart through almost five years of separation, the girl who had waited, the girl who had still waited when I had been posted as missing believed killed, our relationship might have been different. Perhaps I should have told Odette, rather than hinted at where my heart lay, but 'Let's get married' had never entered my calculations.

Among Mrs V's guests next day at lunch was an eminent Romanian who had resigned from his country's diplomatic service in protest against Romania's entry into the war on the side of Germany and who, after many vicissitudes, had arrived in New York.

Rather naturally the conversation had centred on him and his views of the period after the fall of France. This delighted me not only because he was so entertaining but also because it saved me from being questioned about my exploits, which had so often been the case on previous occasions; it was a pleasant change to be able to sit and listen. Perhaps I was doing so too intently, for he stopped and, fixing his penetrating gaze upon me across the table, said, 'If I were an Englishman, I would be very proud.' Everyone stopped talking and, although rather embarrassed, as any young man would have been in that company, I felt I had to respond, so I said, 'You are looking at a proud Englishman,' and added, 'but I have always been under the impression that it is just this trait which so many nations dislike about us.'

There was a murmur round the table but the Romanian just smiled, 'Have no fear. One day the peoples of the world, both great and small alike, will realize the debt they owe to the British.'

Although the same thought has been expressed by others at different times, to have heard it oneself, spoken, as it was, with deep conviction, gave me a sense of rare privilege. It could not have been said for effect unless to impress the sentiment upon everyone around the table, because none, other than I, was English. For me, it was just one more memory to treasure of my visits to that unique house and its equally unique mistress.

As the front door closed behind me, I could not help wondering whether I had expressed my thanks adequately. I felt a twinge of regret as I thought of Mrs V's last but now familiar comment, 'If you are here tomorrow, I shall expect you.' I knew that I would not be in New York at lunchtime tomorrow but aboard the *Queen Mary*, sailing away.

I wandered slowly down Fifth Avenue and then across to Lexington, savouring the fantastic three weeks Len and Doreen had made possible by their very presence in New York and a great deal more besides. Thinking, had I not been befriended by those in 17 Kuo Fu Lu, far away in Chungking, the idea of getting part-way home in a returning 'China Aid' ship would never have materialized. There would have been no New York. I might still have been in China, but I wasn't, I was on the way back to the Lennoxes' apartment to pack for the final leg of a remarkable journey, and how I blessed them, and how well I remember Len's farewell the following morning, 'Keep your head down, David. We need you after the war.'

Chapter 26

The *Queen Mary* lay at her berth in the Hudson River, and the moment I went aboard it was like entering a different world. In just a few paces I had stepped from the gay, apparently normal and peaceful world of New York to the austere reality of the world at war. Men were everywhere. They littered the decks, they filled the holds, they jammed the companion-ways. Every inch of space appeared to be occupied. In fact, there were some thirteen thousand troops aboard, a few hundred folk like myself and, of course, the crew.

The legend of the number of Atlantic crossings made by the two 'Queens' and the number of troops and other personnel who were safely transported by them, has passed into history.

Perhaps there were some, like me, who were surprised that the two remaining great ships did not steal out of New York at the dead of night but instead, just as I had seen the *Q.E.* leaving in broad daylight, the *Q.M.* made her departure in the morning for anyone to watch from any number of windows in many buildings. And, casting all security to the wind, the two blasts from the ship's siren—'I'm going astern'—seemed almost more poignantly to draw attention to her sailing. I watched the very last of that famous skyline while indulging myself in the memory of all the kindness which had been so generously lavished upon me.

I had been allotted a berth in the dressing-room to one of the state rooms on the sun deck. On the whole, this was lucky. In it two tiers of bunks had been erected, leaving no more than two feet six clear space between the bunks and the stateroom wall. Within these restricted confines eight of us, with some luggage, had to exist. It was only possible for one, or at the most two, to be out of their bunks at the same time. A great advantage, however, was that the dressing-room had its own basin and we were able to wash in our own minute surroundings.

Because of the numbers, no more than two meals a day were served—four sittings in the morning and four again during the course of the evening—and this in itself meant something in the order of 27,000 meals daily, which could only have been a catering nightmare. The crowd was such that it could take anything up to an hour to reach the dining-saloons from our cabin on the sun deck, and while there was a canteen where biscuits and chocolate could be bought to stave off the pangs of hunger between one meal and the next, seldom did any of us attempt to use it because the queues were intolerable.

As dawn began to break on the first day of July, we were approaching the coast of Northern Ireland and I was on deck, determined to see the first landfall and our entry into the Clyde. However, it was not land which first caught the eye but an immense convoy heavily escorted by naval vessels, an umbrella of aircraft above it and bound for the Mediterranean, we were told. The *Q.M.*, well to seaward of the convoy, did not slacken speed but continued to race for the Firth of Clyde and in no time at all, so it seemed, majestically was brought alongside at Greenock.

A train bound for Glasgow carried us there, and I could see no point in kicking my heels in Glasgow so I caught the next train to London. It was a long, slow journey of which I did not tire since I was happy to spend much of the time gazing out of the window. Inevitably the train was late into King's Cross. It was now night and there was no alternative but to stay in London. An acquaintance with me was meeting his family at the Dorchester Hotel, so we shared a taxi. It was as good a point as any from which to find a room if none was available at that hotel. There was no room.

While a most helpful man on the desk undertook to telephone a variety of hotels, I took the opportunity to make a call myself to a very special ATS officer who had sent me the telephone number where she was billeted in Sussex, forty miles away. I gave the number to the operator, hoping against hope that Hazel would not be on duty that night. The number rang and rang, before at last a female voice answered, but it was not the female voice I had longed to hear.

'Could I possibly speak to Hazel Richardson?' I asked.

'I'm afraid not. She is out,' came the reply.

'I realize it is already rather late, but is there any chance of her being in if I ring a little later?'

'No, she has gone to a dance in the officers' mess but I could give her a message in the morning if you like. Who is speaking?'

I did not answer. I said, 'Oh, I see,' trying to sound not too disappointed while collecting my thoughts as to whether I should or should not leave a message. I had wanted so much to tell her myself that I was home.

'Who's speaking?' repeated the voice at the other end of the line.

'I'm sorry to keep you,' I said, 'but I think I will leave it and try again tomorrow. When would be the best time to catch her?'

There was a pause and then rather hesitantly came the question, 'Are you David by any chance?'

'Yes, I am.'

'Oh, I am Peggy. Hazel and I have worked together for some time. I know all about you. She will be so thrilled that you are back at last. You must let me tell her. She has been expecting you for such a long time.'

'Yes,' I said rather reluctantly. 'I know she has. It is nearly six months since I left Chungking and I could hardly expect her to know my arrival time.'

'Where arc you?' insisted Peggy.

'In the Dorchester.'

'She'll ring you there, then.'

'She can't. They have no room, and neither does any other hotel, so it seems. I look like spending my first night at home on the Embankment!'

Peggy laughed. 'Don't be silly. Phone again when you've found somewhere.'

I didn't phone again. It was 2 a.m. before I had a bed.

By the time I was able to ring the next morning, Hazel had gone to ground—quite literally.

Soon after the fall of France, when a German invasion of England looked almost certain, Hazel had joined a small, highly secret unit and after a short period of training was commissioned. All the girls specially selected for this unit were then strategically housed in twos or threes on their own in different parts of the country where they were called upon to man underground communication centres, the existence of which was known only to the High Command. The object of these sophisticated concrete 'dugouts', equipped with the latest wireless transmitting and receiving sets and superbly camouflaged, was to have a communication link behind the enemy lines were an enemy landing to succeed, the totally mistaken premise being that, if they were discovered and found to be manned by women, the Germans would respect them as such and not treat them as ordinary troops or civilians, actively operating behind their lines. It speaks volumes for the integrity of these girls that only a handful of people ever knew anything of the unglamorous and tedious role which they fulfilled voluntarily.

When I rang her billet for the third time, the voice I'd longed to hear for almost five years answered.

'Darling,' she exploded. 'It's really you!'

'Yes, it's really me,' I answered rather tamely.

'Peggy told me.'

'I was afraid she would. I so wanted to tell you first myself. When can you get away?'

'Peggy will stand in for me. But still I can hardly believe you are really home.'

'Then come to London, darling, and I'll prove it to you as best I know how.'

She did.